The New Americans?

The New Americans?

Immigration, Protest, and
the Politics of Latino Identity

Heather Silber Mohamed

University Press of Kansas

Published by the University Press of Kansas (Lawrence, Kansas 66045), which was organized by the Kansas Board of Regents and is operated and funded by Emporia State University, Fort Hays State University, Kansas State University, Pittsburg State University, the University of Kansas, and Wichita State University.

Library of Congress Cataloging-in-Publication Data

Names: Mohamed, Heather Silber, author.
Title: The new Americans? : immigration, protest, and the politics of Latino identity / Heather Silber Mohamed.
Description: Lawrence, Kansas : University Press of Kansas, 2017. | Includes bibliographical references and index.
Identifiers: LCCN 2016055780| ISBN 9780700623853 (cloth : alk. paper) | ISBN 9780700623860 (pbk. : alk. paper) | ISBN 9780700623877 (ebook)
Subjects: LCSH: Hispanic Americans—Politics and government. | Hispanic Americans—Ethnic identity. | United States—Emigration and immigration—Government policy. | Hispanic Americans—Social conditions.
Classification: LCC E184.S75 M616 2017 | DDC 305.868/073—dc23
LC record available at https://lccn.loc.gov/2016055780.

British Library Cataloguing-in-Publication Data is available.

Printed in the United States of America

10 9 8 7 6 5 4 3 2 1

The paper used in this publication is recycled and contains 30 percent postconsumer waste. It is acid free and meets the minimum requirements of the American National Standard for Permanence of Paper for Printed Library Materials Z39.48-1992.

For Nick, Miriam, and Lilah, with love and gratitude

Contents

List of Figures and Tables

TABLES

Preface and Acknowledgments

On some level, I have always been fascinated by the ways in which context, and becoming the "other," can change one's own identity and perspective. My maternal ancestors hail from Poland and Macedonia, whereas my father's side of the family is Cuban-Jewish, a community that challenges generalizations about either group. More than half a century after my relatives fled Cuba, for many family members, this experience continues to color their perspective on politics and life in the United States. This enduring influence has helped to shape my own ideas about the diversity underlying the "Latino" experience and has also guided my search for a better understanding of the dynamic relationship between politics and identity.

In particular, my paternal grandmother, who passed away in 2009, defied stereotypes in ways that continue to inspire me both professionally and intellectually. At an age when most grandparents retire, she became the first author in our family, publishing a book about sewing in both Spanish and English. Although we regularly talked politics, the most emphatic I ever heard her was in 1999, when protests erupted surrounding the case of five-year-old Elián González, whose mother drowned at sea while bringing him from Cuba to the United States. Miami's Cuban community mobilized in support of Elián's Florida relatives, who sought to keep him in the United States, while his father fought to bring him back to Cuba. Nearly four decades after leaving the island, my grandmother insisted that were she younger and healthier, she would have stopped traffic alongside the protesters to keep Elián from being sent back to Cuba—marking the first and only time I ever heard her threaten civil disobedience. This exchange was one of many reminders of the fascinating ways in which premigration experiences can shape an individual's political views far into the future.

As with many first books, this project began as my doctoral dissertation at Brown University, though it has morphed into something far beyond that. Over the many years during which this book has been a work in progress, I have benefitted from the support of many people who have contributed to my scholarly development. Most importantly, I owe a tremendous intellectual debt to my two mentors. My dissertation chair, Marion Orr, remains an advisor, friend, and ongoing source of advice, inspiration, and insightful feedback. My former advisor, the late Alan S. Zuckerman, was instrumental in encouraging me to undertake this project and in shaping my early theoretical ideas. During my dissertation research, we lost Alan prematurely to pancreatic cancer. I am one of many who were fortunate to learn from Alan's keen intellect. Both Alan and Marion spent countless hours reading my work and helping me to develop my ideas. I have benefitted immeasurably from their wisdom and guidance as well as their kindness and patience.

Other faculty at Brown provided essential feedback and motivation throughout this process. Wendy Schiller always pushed me forward, giving me critical direction, strategic insight, and all-important deadlines. Jim Morone enthusiastically shared his visionary perspective and incredible knack for big picture ideas. Both Wendy and Jim offered comments, advice, and intellectual support invaluable to the development of my work. Marty West provided crucial methods training and helped me to test some of my early ideas. I was also fortunate to receive intellectual support and generous feedback from other faculty members at Brown, including Melani Cammett, Pauline Jones-Luong, Richard Snyder, Susan Moffitt, Rebecca Weitz-Shapiro, and Jack Combs. Brown's Graduate School and the Department of Political Science provided essential institutional and financial support for much of my dissertation research. I was also privileged to work as a dissertation fellow at Brown's Center for the Study of Race and Ethnicity in America, and I am grateful to the center and to Evelyn Hu-DeHart for providing that opportunity.

I finished the manuscript while an assistant professor at Clark University, where I received tremendous support from my colleagues, particularly Valerie Sperling, Ora Szekely, Johanna Vollhardt, Mark Miller, Rob Boatright, Odile Ferly, Kristen Williams, and Janette Greenwood. The university also provided essential financial support through faculty startup funds as well as the Elmer Plischke Annual Faculty Research Award.

Beyond Clark, I benefitted enormously from the excellent feedback I received through the Gender and Political Psychology Writing Group. I am especially grateful to Mirya Holman for inviting me to join the group, for her constant advice and encouragement, for sharing her many insights on the mysteries of publishing, and for helpful comments on a number of chapters. Emily Farris has provided both friendship and scholarly advice since the earliest days of graduate school. Other group members gave extensive feedback on various chapters, including Jennie Sweet-Cushman, Tiffany Barnes, Julie Wronski, Ray Block, Nichole Bauer, Angie Bos, and Anna Mahoney. I am also thankful for the constructive suggestions provided at various stages by Melissa Michelson, Nicholas Valentino, and Ezra Zuckerman. Additionally, I am indebted to the anonymous reviewers for their insightful and detailed feedback, which helped me to significantly improve this project.

Much of this book analyzes data from the Latino National Survey (LNS), the largest survey of the Latino electorate in history. I am deeply grateful to the survey's principal investigators, Luis Fraga, John García, Gary Segura, Rodney Hero, Michael Jones Correa, and Valerie Martinez-Ebers, for what they have produced, for quickly working to make their groundbreaking dataset available to scholars, and for their consistent willingness to respond to questions large and small about their data.

I owe a tremendous debt of gratitude to many other dear friends, new and old, who have been an essential source of support and motivation through the ups and downs of writing a book. Sònia Muñoz has consistently shared her wisdom and expertise, helping me to navigate all aspects of the PhD and beyond. My dear friend and study partner, Eli Feiman, provided critical support throughout this process, particularly in the early years. I am grateful to many others for their encouragement, advice, friendship, and laughter, which sustained me throughout this process. Although I could not possibly mention them all, some deserve special recognition, including Jenn Lucas, Shanna Pearson-Merkowitz, Maria Angelica Bautista, Mila Dragojevic, Angelica Duran Martinez, Trisha Nakano, Julianne Fisher Breitbeil, Katie Callahan Durcan, Kathryn Dunkelman, Kate Marin, and Jennifer Prewitt-Freilino. I am also thankful to Mercedes Weekes, who provided so much care and assistance to our family during the book revisions.

I am especially grateful to Chuck Myers, former director at the University Press of Kansas, for his patience, expert advice, constant professionalism, and ongoing encouragement, and to Kelly Chrisman Jacques and the editorial team at UPK for their help throughout the production process. I am also thankful to Nathan Cruz for his research assistance, particularly toward the end of this project, and to Tess Reichart for her prompt and precise proofreading skills. Some portions of Chapter 5 appeared as "The Boundaries of American-ness: Perceived Barriers among Latino Subgroups" in *Latino Politics en Ciencia Política: The Search for*

Latino Identity and Racial Consciousness, edited by Tony Affigne, Marion Orr, and Evelyn Hu-DeHart, 132–157. Sections of Chapter 6 were published previously as "*Americana or Latina?* Gender and Identity Acquisition among Hispanics in the United States," *Politics, Groups, and Identities* 3, no. 1 (2015): 40–58, and parts of Chapter 7 appeared in earlier form as "Can Protests Make Latinos 'American'? Identity, Immigration Politics, and the 2006 Marches," *American Politics Research* 41, no. 2 (2013): 298–326.

My family has been a constant source of love and encouragement throughout this process. My mom, Esther Negrin, instilled in me a love of learning and worked to ensure that the best educational opportunities were always available to me. I am also deeply grateful to Rachel Silber Anderson; Darrell Anderson; and Seema, Wali, and Shabana Mohamed.

Most importantly, I am thankful every day for my husband, Nick, whose endless support, advice, wisdom, patience, and love have made this entire endeavor possible. Nick has helped me work through the challenges and celebrate the joys of this process, always providing critical perspective and encouragement along the way. He has read and reread my work and has provided indispensable assistance, particularly in the final stages of this project. I could not ask for a better partner. I dedicate this book to him and to our daughters, Miriam and Lilah. Both girls quite literally grew with this project. Miriam, six, was born during the dissertation-writing stage, and Lilah, three, was born while I was in the midst of the book revisions. Their love and laughter brighten my day, and their enthusiasm and curiosity bring me new perspective on the world. Their arrival in our multiracial, interfaith family has further deepened both my scholarly and personal interests in questions of identity and belonging, as I wonder how they will see and describe themselves someday. I look forward to the day when they are able to read and understand my work.

The New Americans?

1 | "We Are America"

In December 2005, the US House of Representatives passed far-reaching legislation for immigration reform. H.R. 4437 (US House of Representatives 2005), also known as the Sensenbrenner Bill, contained a range of proposals that opponents viewed as highly punitive, including increased penalties for illegal immigration, expanded construction of a nearly 700-mile fence along the US-Mexico border, and classification of unauthorized immigrants and anyone helping them enter or stay in the United States as felons.[1] As the Senate moved to consider its own immigration proposal, between 3.5 and 5.1 million people, mainly of Latino descent, protested across the country in an unprecedented demonstration of "Latino pride and power" (Félix, González, and Ramirez 2008; Janiot 2006; Oz 2006).

Yet, the language used at these events emphasized Latino pride in a unique way—by affirming that Latinos are part of America. At these protests, which are often seen as the start of the contemporary immigrants' rights movement, participants advanced claims of belonging and citizenship in the United States (Rosman 2013). US flags were widely distributed and displayed, along with other patriotic songs and symbols. Protesters carried signs proclaiming "We Are America" and "Today We March, Tomorrow We Vote" (Fraga, Garcia, Hero et al. 2010; Oboler 2014; Pallares and Flores-Gonzalez 2010).

With their emphasis on inclusion and patriotism, these events contrasted starkly with earlier decades of Latino organizing, which typically highlighted differences with the Anglo majority. In 1994, for instance, California voters considered Proposition 187, a popular referendum that sought to deny undocumented immigrants access to social services. Across the state, the Latino community took to the streets to protest the referendum in mobilizations dominated by foreign flags and images and the Mexican flag in particular. After California voters passed the referendum, critics argued that these foreign images fostered a sense of ethnic threat among white voters, leading many who had been undecided to support the proposal (Martin 1995).[2]

A decade later, following a media backlash in which memories of the Proposition 187 vote were invoked, Latino organizers took a different approach to protesting H.R. 4437 (Chavez 2006; Pineda and Sowards 2007; "The Power of Symbols" 2006). Rather than emphasizing a distinct culture or community, the spring 2006 protests highlighted the commitment of Latinos to the United States as well as their claims of belonging in this country.

What led to this change in symbolic imagery? What effects did the protests, and their patriotic frame, have on Latino attitudes and self-perception? Also, what did this new identity mean? As Citrin and Sears (2014, 38) explain, "The choice of identities is often regulated by politics." I build upon that idea by demonstrating how the debate over immigration policy, the protests that emerged in response, and their patriotic frame, or story line, reshaped Latinos' identities as Americans. This book was written prior to the 2016 presidential election, in which Republican nominee Donald J. Trump brought questions of immigration policy and what it means to be American back into the forefront of US politics. The increased prominence and polarization of these discussions underscore the timeliness of the arguments made throughout this book.

The discussion over who counts as American, and whether "new" Americans should be created, defines the United States as a country as well as the boundaries for who is included in US society. At the most basic level, the federal government defines the categories of "us" and "them" through laws about citizenship and immigration. These regulations provide an objective definition of an American identity (Conover 1984; Huddy 2001). Yet, identities are also frequently subject to contestation, or debate, over their content and meaning (Abdelal, Herrera, Johnston et al. 2009). Thus, like other identities, an American identity can also be more subjective (Citrin, Reingold, and Green 1990; Citrin, Wong, and Duff 2001; Huddy 2001).

As in previous eras of US history, the immigration policy debate in the twenty-first century has created changing categories of "us" versus "them." In earlier debates, questions of membership and inclusion have targeted a range of groups, including immigrants from Europe and Asia. In the contemporary debate, Latinos have become the new "them," with questions of immigration and references to immigrants often seen as synonymous with Latinos in general and Mexicans in particular (Chavez 2008; Hero and Preuhs 2007; Newton 2008; Rim 2009).

In recent years, however, Latino leaders have worked hard to frame themselves as the new "us." This book studies the effects of those efforts, evaluating the ways in which the immigration debate and responses around a particular frame can affect the broader process of Latino inclusion and political incorporation within US society. A range of existing research assumes the existence of an identity-to-politics link in which self-identification drives policy attitudes (Lee 2008). I view this relationship as more iterative. My theory develops the idea of a politics-to-identity link in which political debate and protest can influence self-identification in multiple ways, focusing specifically on the 2005–2006 congressional debate over immigration reform and the unprecedented wave of Latino protests that followed. My analysis offers a new view of the effects of the immigration debate on Latino self-identification. In so doing, I advance our understanding of the ways in which political debate and protest can influence public opinion and subjective perceptions of identity categories.

Accordingly, my book responds to recent calls for more research to better understand "the role of context in increasing the salience of national identity" (Huddy 2016, 14; see also Schildkraut 2014). To date, much of this research focuses on the influence of political context on the extent to which members of the *majority group* embrace a national identity. For instance, during times of increased threat—whether related to national security, racialized contexts, or tension over immigration—national identities become more prominent and more influential in shaping political attitudes (Davies, Steele, and Markus 2008; Falomir-Pichastor, Gabarrot, and Mugny 2009; Kam and Ramos 2008; Transue 2007).

With respect to minority groups, similar circumstances are thought to result in a reactive ethnicity in which individuals embrace an alternative "ethnic" identity rather than identifying with the majority group (Aleinikoff and Rumbaut 1998; Bean, Stevens, and Wierzbicki 2003; Massey and Sánchez R. 2010; Neckerman, Carter, and Lee 1999; Rumbaut and Portes 2001; Schildkraut 2005b). In contrast to existing explanations, this book explores the *varied* ways in which a context of political threat and social movement mobilization can shape Latino attitudes and self-perception. I ask whether, under certain circumstances, contentious policy debate and a hostile political context can lead a marginalized group to have increased feelings of *inclusion* rather than increased distance from the majority group. I address this question by examining Latino attitudes about immigration policy and self-identification before and after the 2006 protests.

My research also highlights an important paradox: Latinos have long indicated that they prioritize other policy issues, such as the economy and education, over immigration. Yet, the immigration debate is uniquely poised to mobilize a majority of the Latino population and to influence its political incorporation into the United States. I develop this idea while also studying the variation that underlies this paradox. Because the debate over immigration reform does not affect all Latinos equally, my analysis emphasizes intragroup differences within this population. For instance, Puerto Ricans are born US citizens regardless of birthplace, and Cubans have received preferential immigration status in the United States for decades, making immigration policy less salient for members of these national origin groups. The immigration debate is also less central to more established Latinos, such as those who are more acculturated or have been here for many generations (García Bedolla 2005). I find that distinct subgroups within the Latino population respond differently to the immigration debate and the 2006 protests, with the politics-to-identity link contingent upon issue salience.

Why Latinos?

The US Census defines a person as Latino or Hispanic if that individual is of Cuban, Mexican, Puerto Rican, South or Central American, or other Spanish culture or origin, regardless of race (Ennis, Rios-Vargas, and Albert 2011). As this definition suggests, Latino is commonly thought to refer to an individual's ethnicity, considered separate and distinct from one's racial category. Although race traditionally refers to skin color, ethnicity suggests a shared culture or experience and may include individuals of any race. For the Latino population, language and religion are two commonly cited indicators of this shared culture.

In 2003, Latinos officially overtook African Americans as the country's largest minority group (Segura and Rodrigues 2006). At the time of the 2010 US Census, an estimated 50.5 million Latinos lived in the United States, constituting approximately 16 percent of the overall population. This figure represents a sharp increase from the 35.3 million Latinos counted in 2000; indeed, more than half of the *total* population growth in the United States during that ten-year period reflected growth in the Latino population (Ennis, Rios-Vargas, and Albert 2011).

As the Latino population grows, so too has this group's potential to influence electoral outcomes. Between 1998 and 2008, the Latino share of the national electorate doubled, from 3.6 percent to 7.4 percent (Barreto and Segura 2014). In 2012, for the first time, Latinos constituted an estimated 10 percent of the national electorate (Lopez and Taylor 2012). High concentrations of Latino voters in key swing states such as Nevada, Florida, and Colorado have left this population poised to play a decisive role in the nation's presidential election process. The Latino electorate was instrumental in contributing to President Barack Obama's 2012 victory, with the candidates' distinct positions on immigration policy significantly influencing Latino voting choices (Barreto and Collingwood 2015). Although this book was written prior to the 2016 presidential election, both the Latino electorate and the immigration debate remained central to that contest. Group members have also had a growing influence in local and state politics across the United States (Farris 2013) and in key US Senate and House races (Rodriguez 2012).

Yet, the extent to which the Latino population embodies a set of similar experiences, attitudes, and preferences in US society is less clear. Latinos in the United States hail from more than twenty different countries, representing vastly different historical and political backgrounds. Some arrived seeking economic opportunity, and others came as refugees from a bloody civil war, military takeover, or regime of single-party rule. Some have roots in prosperous democracies, whereas others have no experience with democracy and no understanding of the basic underpinnings of the US political system. Still others have ancestors who became Americans by conquest; for instance, through the acquisition of Puerto Rico in 1898 and territory originally belonging to Mexico in 1848. As will be discussed throughout this book, this diversity shapes the perspective through which individuals view US political life as well as attitudes about their identity as Americans and sense of belonging in the United States.

As the Latino population expands, it is also becoming ever more diverse. Table 1.1 illustrates the growth of the Latino population since 2000, focusing specifically on the five largest national origin subgroups. As this table demonstrates, Mexicans constitute almost two-thirds of the Latino community in the United States today and represent much of the overall growth within this population. However, other national origin groups are growing fast.

Between 2000 and 2010, the Salvadoran population in the United States increased by more than 150 percent, making this community among the fastest-growing national origin groups (Ennis, Rio-Vargas,

Table 1.1   Change in Latino Population by Five Largest Subgroups, 2000–2010

National Origin	2000		2010		Change, 2000–2010	
	Number	% of Total	Number	% of Total	Number	% of Total
TOTAL	35,305,818	100.00	50,477,594	100.00	15,171,776	43.00
Mexican	20,640,711	58.50	31,798,258	63.00	11,157,547	54.10
Puerto Rican	3,406,178	9.60	4,623,716	9.20	1,217,538	35.70
Cuban	1,241,685	3.50	1,785,547	3.50	543,862	43.80
Dominican	764,945	2.20	1,414,703	2.80	649,758	84.90
Salvadoran	655,165	1.90	1,648,968	3.30	993,803	151.70

Source: US Census Bureau (Ennis 2011)

and Albert 2011). Indeed, estimates from the 2011 American Community Survey suggest that Salvadorans may have surpassed Cubans as the third-largest national origin group in the United States, with populations of 1.95 million and 1.89 million, respectively. The Dominican population is not far behind, with an estimated 1.4 million living in the United States as of 2010 (Lopez and Gonzalez-Barrera 2013).[3]

For immigrant groups, experiences before coming to the United States significantly influence political attitudes and behavior upon arrival (Wals 2011). To the extent that existing research on Latino politics in the United States explores variation by national origin, much of this literature focuses on distinctions in attitudes and political behavior between the three historically large subgroups: Mexicans, Puerto Ricans, and Cubans (Abrajano and Alvarez 2010; DeSipio 1996a; Oboler 1995). The rapid growth of other national origin groups underscores the need to better understand Latino diversity beyond traditional populations, and particularly how group members' varied experiences influence their identification as American and their political participation.

In addition to national origin, a growing body of research highlights intragroup differences based on factors such as language proficiency (Abrajano 2010; García Bedolla 2003), immigrant generation (García Bedolla 2005), and gender (Bejarano 2014; García Bedolla, Lavariega Monforti, and Pantoja 2007; Hardy-Fanta 1993; Jaramillo 2010; Jones-Correa 1998a). Immigrants have also moved into "new settlement areas," adding additional geographical variation to this already heterogeneous population (Marrow 2005; Massey 2008).[4] Demonstrating this rapid growth, between 2000 and 2010, the Latino population increased by more than 50 percent in the majority of states and by more than 100 percent in nine states, from South Carolina to South Dakota (Ennis, Rios-Vargas, and Albert 2011). Thus, questions relating to Latinos' sense of identity as "new" Americans, their political participation via protests, and their incorporation into US society are increasingly national ones. With the contentious debate over immigration policy once again at the forefront of US politics, the distinct ways in which group members' experiences interact with the heated rhetoric of the immigration debate hold important implications for the country's political system and polity.

Outline of the Book

My politics-to-identity theory explores varying Latino responses to the 2006 immigration debate as well as the distinct ways in which this debate and ensuing protests influenced Latino political incorporation into the United States. Drawing on a range of primary and secondary accounts, the first part of this book presents important theoretical and historical background to support later arguments.

Specifically, Chapter 2 develops my politics-to-identity theory, incorporating scholarship on policy feedback, social movements, and framing. I also explain key elements of the research design used in later chapters, which employ data from the Latino National Survey (LNS; Fraga, Garcia, Hero et al. 2006a). Interviews for this major national survey were conducted before, during, and after the spring 2006 protests.[5] Throughout the book, I take advantage of this rare natural experiment to study shifts in Latino attitudes about immigration policy and on questions related to social identities.

Chapter 3 places the 2006 immigration debate and ensuing protests in historical context. I begin by describing key developments in US immigration law over time. Then, I explore the varying ways in which Latino groups have framed identity over the last century. Whereas very early advocacy organizations advanced themes of assimilation and incorporation, by the 1960s, a rhetorical shift emerged. Groups began to emphasize differences with the majority, first in terms of national origin identity (for instance, the Chicano and Puerto Rican Nationalist movements), and subsequently around a pan-ethnic (Latino/Hispanic) identity. This chapter explores this evolution and the eventual shift to the "We Are America/ *Somos America*" message of 2006, which served as a rallying cry to unite a diverse community.

In later chapters, I argue that the immigration debate has varied salience to members of different Latino subgroups and that the effects of the immigration debate will be contingent upon these differences. As a precursor to these arguments, Chapter 3 closes with an overview of the five largest Latino subgroups in the United States and their varied immigration histories.

The second part of the book analyzes Latino attitudes about immigration policy, what it means to be American, and whether Latinos place themselves in this category. In addition to the LNS, these analyses use data from other major national surveys, including the General Social Survey (GSS) and the Pew Research Center's National Survey of Latinos (NSL).

Chapter 4 introduces the idea of the "immigration paradox": in national surveys conducted over many years, Latinos have consistently stated that immigration reform is not their top policy priority. Yet, this issue is uniquely poised to influence the attitudes and political behavior of some members of the Latino community. I examine Latino public opinion about immigration reform, establishing the varied salience of this policy debate. I then test the effects of the 2006 protests on Latino attitudes toward immigration policy. My analysis demonstrates that compared with similar respondents interviewed before these events, individuals interviewed afterward are more likely to express support for liberal immigration policies. Yet, even after the protests, significant variation persists in attitudes about immigration reform.

The fifth chapter turns to the question of what it means to be American. Although a growing body of research has begun to examine the varying ways in which members of minority groups define this term (Citrin and Sears 2014; Masuoka and Junn 2013; Schildkraut 2014; Silber Mohamed 2014), our understanding of differences both across and particularly *within* minority groups remains limited. Comparing Latinos with other racial/ethnic groups, I explore the extent to which Latinos understand American as a "closed" category, defined by ascriptive characteristics (for instance, skin color, birthplace, language, and religion). Importantly, placing greater emphasis on these characteristics suggests that the category is inaccessible to individuals who do not meet these criteria. I also evaluate intragroup variation in perceptions of what it means to be American. The final part of this chapter analyzes whether the 2006 protests—and their unique, patriotic frame—influenced Latino understandings of what it means to be American.

Chapter 6 explores variation in the extent to which Latinos identify as American. In particular, in this chapter, I am interested in understanding whether there are gendered differences in self-identification. Within the Latino population, men typically prefer continuity with their home country, whereas women prefer change (Jones-Correa 1998a, 1998b). Latinas are also more likely to participate politically in the United States (Bejarano 2014; Silber Mohamed 2015). Yet, across societies, women are commonly viewed as "carriers of culture," seeking to preserve traditional cultural values (Phinney, Horenczyk, Liebkind, and Vedder 2001; Warikoo 2006). I analyze the ways in which these competing tendencies influence Latino self-identification and attitudes about incorporating into the United States. I also explore variation in self-identification by national origin and language preference.

Chapter 7 returns its focus to the 2006 immigration debate and the ensuing protests. This chapter tests my politics-to-identity theory to see how the protests and their distinct frame influenced Latino self-identification. Consistent with the message of the protests, I show that respondents interviewed after these events are more likely to *see* themselves as American than those interviewed before and are more likely to say that Latinos should change to blend into the United States. My results counter the assumptions of existing literature, which assumes that in situations of adversity, an increased sense of discrimination will make all members of the Latino community more likely to identify in pan-ethnic terms.

My politics-to-identity theory also emphasizes the importance of issue salience, with the effects of the immigration debate likely to vary based on the relative importance of this policy to different Latino subgroups. Building on the findings of earlier chapters, I show that the shift in self-identification following the 2006 protests is concentrated among subgroups for whom the immigration debate is most salient, including Spanish-dominant respondents as well as Mexicans and Dominicans. This chapter demonstrates the power of political events and messages to shape individual self-perception and also underscores variation within the Latino community.

In the concluding chapter, I outline national-level developments with respect to immigration policy since 2006. Although this book was written prior to the 2016 presidential election, I also discuss the increasing politicization of this topic during the course of that campaign. Drawing on the theories advanced in this book, I speculate about the implications for Latino political incorporation, including the varying ways that different subsets of the Latino population might be influenced by this ongoing debate.

Conclusion

Although identity is frequently conceptualized as an independent variable associated with certain political attitudes or participatory behaviors, I demonstrate that politics and political debate can also influence identity in varied ways. As Chapter 2 outlines in greater detail, my politics-to-identity theory emphasizes that this process is contingent upon social movement mobilization, frames, and issue salience, arguing that political debates and protest can result in unexpected outcomes.

Throughout the book, I explore the ways in which Latino social movements respond to the politics of the day. Over time, these groups have repeatedly reframed their messages about identity, inclusion, and assimilation. As the United States continues to grapple with questions of immigration reform, and the Latino population continues to increase, my focus on this policy debate also holds important lessons for our understanding of the varied ways in which group members are incorporating into US political life.

In light of the growing political importance of Latinos in the United States, improving our knowledge of the malleable nature of social identity within this population, and the broader political incorporation process, is critical for our understanding of the nation's polity in the years ahead. Additionally, my analyses emphasize important areas of diversity within the Latino population, identifying variation by level of acculturation, national origin group, and gender. These differences are notable for both scholars and political actors seeking to better understand Latino responses to the immigration debate.

2 | Becoming American

The Politics-to-Identity Link

It is important to carry the American flag so that people see we respect this patriotic symbol.
—Eduardo "Piolín" Sotelo, host of the popular radio show
El Piolín por la Mañana (Piolín in the Morning)

As protests unfolded across the United States in opposition to H.R. 4437 in the spring of 2006, renowned Spanish-language deejay Eduardo "Piolín" Sotelo spoke in an interview with Univision about the importance of Latinos highlighting pro-American symbols and themes in their response (Fears 2006, translation by the author). Along with many other prominent Spanish-language journalists and Latino activists, Sotelo emphasized that Latinos should fight against this policy proposal by advancing a message of political incorporation. Consistent with these ideas, in addition to US flags, at events across the country, protesters carried signs proclaiming the themes "We Are America," and "Today We March, Tomorrow We Vote" (Fraga, Garcia, Hero et al. 2010; Oboler 2014; Pallares and Flores-Gonzalez 2010).

Some observers assert that anti-immigration proposals lead to a heightened sense of discrimination, causing Latinos to feel alienated from an American identity (Massey and Sánchez R. 2010). Others argue that ethnic organizing can threaten the cohesion of US politics and community life by highlighting identity-based differences with the general population (Huntington 2004b; Skerry 1993). What happens, however, when the response to these policies promotes messages of similarity and patriotism? Below, I present a theory of identity acquisition that emphasizes the influence of the immigration policy debate, and subsequent protests, on Latino attitudes and political incorporation. Focusing on the 2005–2006 congressional debate over immigration reform, and the protests that followed, I underscore the importance of social and political context in making certain identities more salient. Specifically, I examine popular mobilization in response to the immigration policy debate around a particular frame: *that Latinos are America and represent part of what it means to be American.* I demonstrate that this debate and the related frame influenced the attitudes and self-identification of some *members of the Latino community, contributing to their political incorporation in the United States.*

This chapter outlines the theoretical foundations for larger arguments made throughout this book. I draw on research related to policy feedback, which emphasizes the relationship between public policy and an individual's sense of belonging or citizenship. I also underscore the importance of social movements, protest, and framing. Although definitions of framing vary considerably, throughout this book I use the term to refer to "a central idea or story line that provides meaning to an unfolding strip of events" (Gamson and Modigliani 1987, 143; see also Gamson and Modigliani 1989, Shah et al. 2002), with frames helping individuals to understand and interpret the world around them (Benford and Snow 2000; Goffman 1974). Although existing literature commonly assumes an "identity-to-politics link" in which self-identification shapes political behavior (Lee 2008), here, I point to a "politics-to-identity link" in which public policy debate and a collective response around a particular frame can also influence self-perception. The chapter concludes with a description of the quasi-experimental research design used to evaluate the effects of the 2006 protests on Latino attitudes and political incorporation.

Political Incorporation and Identity

Throughout this book, I focus on "feeling American" as a step toward broader political incorporation into the United States. At its most fundamental, political incorporation can be thought of as the various avenues by which new social forces and groups enter the political system (Shefter 1986). Political incorporation is described as both a process that occurs over time and a specific outcome, such as naturalization, voting, or political representation (for a review of this literature, see Minnite 2009). Implicit (and to some degree, unexplored) in all of these definitions is a specific point at which members of excluded communities begin to see themselves as part of the dominant society through identification with the larger group.

A long tradition of research on immigrant incorporation emphasizes the significance of adopting an American identity. Classic works such as Milton Gordon's (1964) *Assimilation and American Life* underscore the acquisition of an American identity as a critical step in the process by which outsiders "become" American. Others emphasize the acquisition of American attitudes, values, and patriotism as potential measures of incorporation (see, for instance, de la Garza, Falcon, and Garcia 1996). As Zolberg and Woon (1999, 8–9) explain, incorporation entails "a reconstruction of a group's identity, whereby the line differentiating members from nonmembers is relocated," involving "the transformation of strangers into members, of the not us into part of us."

Adopting the identity of the national group is important for both theoretical and practical reasons, with an American identity associated with higher political participation as well as particular attitudes about a number of policy issues. Since de Tocqueville ([1848] 1969) first famously observed the United States in the early 1800s, scholars have viewed political participation as an essential part of the American experience. Yet, in order to participate, an individual must first feel a more general connection to society, with identity playing an important role in this process.

In contemporary scholarship, identity, such as race or ethnicity, is no longer thought to be static or "primordial" (Geertz 1973). Rather, research in the constructivist tradition emphasizes that identities can evolve and shift over time (Chandra 2009; Citrin and Sears 2014; Kastoryano 2002; Lee 2008; Varshney 2007). This body of research highlights the importance of social and political context (Chandra 2004; Citrin and Sears 2014; Posner 2004; Simon and Klandermans 2001), political messages (Holman, Schneider, and Pondel 2015), mobilization (Citrin and Sears 2014), and ethnic symbols and practices (Jiménez 2009) in activating political identities. My arguments connect to this research by exploring when identities become salient and studying the ways in which political debate, protest, and frames can shape self-perception.

In particular, I focus on the relational aspect of identities. Emerging from psychology research, social identity theory examines the ways in which an individual's sense of self is influenced by group memberships and relationships to others (Tajfel 1982; Tajfel and Turner 1979). A wide range of political science scholarship builds on this concept to establish a correlation between social identities and political attitudes and behaviors. Because social identity theory emphasizes relationships between *established* groups, it is most applicable in situations where identities are clearly delineated or assigned. In contrast, the theory's explanatory power is limited when identities are ambiguous or newly acquired (Huddy 2001), such as in the case of immigrants in a new society. My research contributes to our understanding of the role of social and political context in the acquisition of new identities—and in particular, an American identity by Latinos in the United States.

An individual may have multiple social identities, the salience of which may vary at different points in time (Abdelal, Herrera, Johnston et al. 2009; Nagel 1986). Like members of other immigrant groups, to some extent, Latinos have a choice as to how they identify (Waters 1990). Although an individual can adopt a range of identities, Latinos typically opt for at least one of three primary social identities: national origin, pan-ethnic identifier (Latino/Hispanic), and/or American.

Traditionally, Latinos in the United States have self-identified primarily based on national origin, referring to either a home country or place of ancestral origin (DeSipio 1996b; Fraga, Garcia, Hero et al. 2006b; García 2003). This preference for national origin identities reflects, to some extent, the varied experiences of Latino groups before coming to the United States; the term Latino refers to individuals from more than twenty countries embodying a wide range of political and economic circumstances. A history of geographical segregation by national origin subgroup within the United States as well as different conditions faced upon arrival further contribute to this emphasis on country of origin or ancestry. Despite widespread acceptance of the idea that individuals can identify in multiple ways, the preference for national origin identities has frequently been viewed as a roadblock toward establishing unity within the Latino population.

Yet, over time, a unifying identity has also emerged within the Latino population (Hero 1992; Jones-Correa and Leal 1996; Massey and Sánchez R. 2010). Scholarship on the acquisition of new identities by Latinos in the United States largely focuses on the conditions in which group members adopt a pan-ethnic identifier, or "generalization of solidarity among ethnic subgroups" (Espiritu 1992, 6). Notably, pan-ethnic identities such as Latino or Hispanic are a uniquely American concept; individuals do not arrive in the United States already thinking of themselves in these terms (Fraga, Garcia, Hero et al. 2010; Silber Mohamed 2015).

Existing research suggests three primary factors contributing to the emergence of a Latino/Hispanic identity. Reflecting the importance of policy feedback, the first of these factors is governmental categories. The term Hispanic first appeared on the 1970 US Census, and Congress passed legislation in 1976 (P.L. 94–311) requiring a question about Hispanic origin or descent on all future censuses and federal surveys (Rodríguez 2000).[1]

The government's grouping of individuals as Latino/Hispanic has given this category political meaning and imbued it with tangible consequences.[2] The government's role in the development of a pan-ethnic identity connects to a larger body of literature emphasizing the importance of state policy and institutions in defining how immigrants identify as well as the emergence of a politicized collective identity both within and beyond the Latino population. In this process, individuals come to see themselves as "(self)-conscious group members in a power struggle on behalf of their group" (Simon and Klandermans 2001). Importantly, identities emerging under these circumstances typically highlight *difference* from the majority group—for instance, Puerto Ricans in New York (Fuchs 1990), the emergence of a pan-ethnic identity among Latinos in the United States (Mora 2014), and identification with an ethnic or religious minority in France and Germany (Kastoryano 2002).

Another stream of research outlines the role played by Spanish-language media, advertisers, and advocacy organizations in constructing a Latino pan-ethnic identity. For instance, marketers sought to develop a cohesive "Hispanic audience" that businesses could more easily target (Davila 2001; Rodriguez 1999).

Finally, pan-ethnic identities are also thought to develop in response to situations of exclusion, particularly in circumstances where subgroup unity would be politically advantageous (Itzigsohn and Dore-Cabral 2000; Mora 2014; Padilla 1985). For example, Padilla (1985) describes the efforts of Mexicans and Puerto Ricans in Chicago to unite against poverty and discrimination, with a Latino identity emerging as a by-product of this collaboration. This line of research has led to the common assumption that in the face of discrimination or anti-immigrant sentiment, all Latinos will begin to *feel* more Latino (Barreto, Manzano, Ramirez et al. 2009; Benjamin-Alvarado, DeSipio, and Montoya 2009; Massey and Sánchez R. 2010; Portes and Rumbaut 2001). Here, I advance this line of research by exploring the varying ways in which contentious policy discussions, social movements, and frames can influence outsiders' sense of belonging such that this politicized identity becomes one of *similarity* with the national group rather than difference.

As for an American identity, scholars long assumed that assimilation in the United States would follow a "linear" pattern in which successive generations become increasingly integrated into society (Alba and Nee 1997; Park 1950; Warner and Strole 1945). Focusing in particular on European immigrants arriving in the early twentieth century, this model anticipates that immigrants would naturally acquire an American identity over time as the result of both structural and cultural assimilation, whereby all immigrants would learn to speak English, adopt "American" values, and join the same social and professional networks as other Americans (Gans 1973; Gordon 1964).

The assimilation model has been challenged extensively in recent years on a range of factors (for a review of this literature, see Massey and Sánchez R. 2010). In contemporary scholarship, the process of incorporation is no longer perceived as a straight line (Gans 1992). Instead, acculturation is viewed as a two-way process in which immigrants and the established group adapt to each other (Alba and Nee 2003; Fraga, Garcia, Hero et al. 2010; Hochschild and Mollenkopf 2009). Although length of time in the United States and immigrant generation continue to play a significant role in this process (Alba and Nee 1997; Waldinger 2007), many scholars agree that for contemporary immigrant groups, other factors are also influential. For instance, some argue that the path to assimilation is a "bumpy" line rather than a straight one (Gans 1992; Vasquez 2011a, 2011b). Others advance a theory of segmented assimilation, which contends that the interaction of certain characteristics, including English language skills, racial status, and socioeconomic background, result in varied outcomes for later immigrant generations (Portes and Rumbaut 2001, 2006; Portes and Zhou 1993; Zhou 1997).

By assuming that assimilation will occur automatically, the traditional model also neglects the range of forces working to incorporate earlier generations of immigrants economically, politically, and socially. Indeed, even for earlier immigrants, political elites and other actors played a key role in shaping their identities and overall political incorporation. Political parties, labor unions, churches, and other civic organizations worked extensively to transform immigrants into politically engaged citizens, promoting English, naturalization, and patriotism in the process (Connolly 1998; Erie 1988; Sterne 2001).

Some contemporary accounts of political incorporation have renewed this emphasis on the role of the state, underscoring the importance of institutions and governmental policies in the broader process of immigrant political incorporation (Gerstle and Mollenkopf 2001; Ramírez 2013). *I extend this research by focusing on the role of public policy debate, social movement mobilization, and framing as important parts of the political incorporation process.*

Why Does Identity Matter?

In the previous section, I describe efforts to understand when and why Latinos adopt new identities. Yet, why is it important to understand the conditions under which Latinos begin to see themselves as American? From a normative perspective, particularly in a "melting-pot" society, it is problematic to have large segments of the population who perceive themselves as separate and distinct from the national group. Illustrating this point, a range of political theorists highlight the importance of shared identity as a key factor for enduring democratic stability, both in the United States and in the abstract (Dahl 1998; Gutmann 2003; Kymlicka 1995; Walzer 1983). Likewise, recent survey data find that more than 90 percent of respondents think that feeling American or seeing oneself as American is very or somewhat important (Schildkraut 2011).

Whether an individual self-identifies as American can also have widespread consequences for a range of political attitudes and behaviors (Abdelal, Herrera, Johnston et al. 2009; Citrin, Wong, and Duff 2001; Huddy and Khatib 2007; Lien, Conway, and Wong 2004). Self-perception is associated with political participation in the general population as well as the Latino community in particular. For instance, García (1981) demonstrates that among Mexican immigrants, a group with low naturalization rates, an American identity is the most significant factor in determining whether an individual chooses to naturalize. Schildkraut (2005b) finds that depending on the circumstances, self-perception can work in competing directions for Latinos, increasing either political engagement or feelings of alienation. She argues that in the absence of discrimination, individuals who self-identify primarily as American are more likely to vote than those who self-identify in pan-ethnic or national origin terms. Elsewhere, I demonstrate that the relationship between an American identity and political participation is especially strong for

Latino men (Silber Mohamed 2015). Thinking about identity and one's sense of civic duty more generally, García Bedolla and Michelson (2012) find that brief conversations in which individuals are encouraged to vote are highly effective because they activate an individual's identity as a voter, demonstrating the power of identities to influence civic and political participation.

Along with Asian Americans, Latinos tend to participate in politics at lower rates than other ethnic groups in the United States (Leighley 2001; Ramakrishnan and Espenshade 2001). The rapid growth of both of these populations underscores the need for greater political involvement in order to achieve more representative electoral outcomes. Given the correlation between an American identity and Latino political participation in the United States, it is especially important to understand the varied circumstances under which this new identity is acquired in the first place.

In addition to changing political behaviors, self-identification can also influence policy attitudes and ideas (Barreto, Segura, and Woods 2004; Breton 2015; Hardy-Fanta 1993; Leighley 2001; Masuoka 2008; Pardo 1997; Sanchez 2006b; Stokes 2003; Uhlaner, Cain, and Kiewiet 1989). For instance, in the general population, identifying as American is associated with a greater willingness to make sacrifices for the collective good (Theiss-Morse 2009). Among Latinos, an American identity even shapes opinions about representation and the role of government (Schildkraut 2015). Positively identifying with a national group has additionally been connected to a range of other non-political attributes, including higher self-esteem under some circumstances (Spinner-Halev and Theiss-Morse 2003).

Importantly, whether Latinos adopt an American identity also affects the attitudes and behaviors of the general population toward this group. For instance, a significant portion of anti-immigrant sentiment can be explained by perceptions among the majority about whether immigrants want to become American, and whether they seek to blend into US society (Schildkraut 2005a). These findings are also consistent with the language used by anti-immigrant advocates and others who point to a "Latino threat" against US culture (Chavez 2008). Such arguments are frequently grounded in the concern that newcomers reject "traditional" American culture and characteristics (Huntington 2004a, 2004b).

In sum, self-identification has a range of practical implications, from formal political participation to influencing opinions on a range of public policy issues. Likewise, the outcomes associated with self-identification have both theoretical and practical repercussions for the nature of our democracy, including the question of whether individuals become active members of the polity. Moreover, the extent to which Latinos seek to become American affects the attitudes of *other* Americans both toward this group and toward immigration policy.

As the above discussion demonstrates, existing literature frequently treats an American identity as an independent variable correlated with some larger outcome of interest. In contrast, in this book, *I explore the emergence of an American identity as well as variation that exists within the Latino population. In particular, I focus on the ways in which political debate, social context, and framing can shape attitudes and self-perception.*

Policy Feedback and Identity Formation

Emphasizing that "policies produce politics" (Pierson 1993, 595), scholarship on policy feedback explores the ways in which specific policies influence subsequent political debates and popular mobilization (Heclo 1974; Lowi 1964; Schattscheider 1935) as well as political attitudes, behavior, and interests (Mettler and Soss 2004; Pierson 1993; Skocpol 1992). Focusing on objective identities, government policy determines who is eligible for legal membership in a society (Mettler and Sorelle 2014; Zolberg 2006) as well as the extent to which governments assist newcomers in the process of incorporation (Bloemraad 2006). Government policies and programs can also influence subjective perceptions of identity by significantly altering the relationship between individuals and the government, shaping their sense of citizenship and belonging (Campbell 2002, 2012; Pierson 1994; Schneider and Ingram 1993, 1997; Soss 1999, 2000; Soss and Schram 2007).

To date, research on policy feedback focuses primarily on social benefits or other policies that have already been enacted. In contrast, here, I examine a specific piece of legislation (H.R. 4437) passed by only one chamber of Congress and that ultimately never became law. Moreover, this proposal would have affected millions of undocumented immigrants, a group that currently receives no government benefits. Consequently, my research contributes to our understanding of the policy feedback process by demonstrating that even a contentious policy *proposal* aimed at a marginalized population might be sufficient to transform the attitudes and social identities of a much broader group of people.

As Pierson (1993, 620) explains, "Policies may generate 'focusing events' or cues that help social actors to interpret the world around them."[3] In particular, I explore the unprecedented wave of protests undertaken by the Latino community across the United States in response to H.R. 4437. These marches served as a focusing event in this policy debate. Increased levels of mobilization, heightened political participation (Campbell 2003; Mettler 2005), and social movements are also common characteristics of policy feedback.

Importantly, policy feedback can lead to a range of possible outcomes (Goss 2013; Omi and Winant 1994; Soss 1999; Soss, Fording, and Schram 2011). Some policies lead to a heightened sense of citizenship; for instance, Mettler (2005) explores the ways in which the G.I. Bill, which provided generous support to veterans after World War II, contributed to very high levels of civic involvement by the "greatest generation." In contrast, policy feedback can also result in increased alienation and mistrust (Soss 2000; Weaver and Lerman 2010). For example, encounters by African American men with the criminal justice system are associated with decreased feelings of citizenship and lower levels of political participation (Weaver and Lerman 2010). The possibility of varied outcomes suggests that the immigration policy debate could lead Latinos to feel *either* more alienated or more incorporated. Moreover, not all Latinos respond to this policy debate in the same way, underscoring even further variation within this heterogeneous pan-ethnic group (García Bedolla 2005; Silber Mohamed 2013).

Existing research suggests that individuals who feel they have experienced discrimination are less likely to adopt an American identity (Massey and Sánchez R. 2010; Schildkraut 2011). Rather, in such situations, individuals will "reactively reject" this identity (Aleinikoff and Rumbaut 1998; Bean, Stevens, and Wierzbicki 2003; Massey and Sánchez R. 2010; Neckerman, Carter, and Lee 1999; Rumbaut and Portes 2001; Schildkraut 2005b). Most recently, Massey and Sánchez (2010) draw on extensive interview data to better understand Latino identity choices, reiterating the finding that discrimination leads Latinos to reject an American identity. Noting that Latinos were more likely to report experiences of discrimination after the 2006 protests, they speculate that Latinos would be even less likely to see themselves as American after these events. Yet, they conducted their research before the debate over H.R. 4437 and the ensuing protests, and like much of this research, their focus is primarily on individual-level experiences with discrimination rather than a broader policy debate and collective response.

My theory departs from this approach by emphasizing the role of policy feedback and the collective mobilization that occurred around the "We Are America" frame in 2006. I differentiate between individual experiences with discrimination and collective responses to a large-scale policy debate, resulting in the emergence of a social movement around a particular frame. This distinction is critical in understanding the varying effects that experiences of discrimination might have on individual self-identification. Mechanisms underlying the policy feedback process, including social movements, framing, and policy salience, left the 2006 events positioned to influence Latino attitudes and self-identification in varied ways. Despite individual-level experiences with discrimination that might otherwise lead individuals to reactively reject an American identity, these mechanisms contributed to a greater sense of identity as American for some members of the Latino population.

Social Movements

Social movements represent important venues for the "struggle over the production of ideas and meanings" (Snow and Benford 1992, 136), making them uniquely poised to reshape an individual's self-perception (Gould 1995; McAdam, Tarrow, and Tilly 2001; Stryker 1968; Stryker, Owens, and White 2000). They are frequently thought of as "period[s] of rupture" during which ideas and identities are questioned and re-evaluated (Cornell 2000, 45). Similarly, existing research highlights the development of a "participation identity," referring to an individual's identification with social protest and the effect that this experience can have on social identification (Gould 1995; Snow and McAdam 2000; see also Stryker, Owens, and White 2000).[4] This line of research suggests that the mobilization in response to H.R. 4437 was poised to activate new identities among participants.

Examples of the ways in which social movements and protests influence identity abound in US history. For instance, the women's movement led women to reevaluate their ideas about their place in society and increased women's level of participation in public life (Carroll 1989;

Jenkins 2013). Likewise, the protests that occurred during the civil rights movement were a stepping-stone toward the broader political involvement of the African American community in the United States (Browning, Marshall, and Tabb 1984; Tate 1993; Verba, Schlozman, and Burns 2005). Although much of this research focuses on advances in participation at the group level, Verba, Schlozman, and Burns (2005) also find that social movements have significant effects on individual-level participation. Using data from the 1990 Citizen Participation Study, they demonstrate that nearly thirty years after the civil rights movement, African Americans who came of age at the height of the movement were still more likely to report participating politically. The 1992 riots in Los Angeles following the controversial acquittal of four white police officers for the beating of African American motorist Rodney King represent another example of protests influencing self-identification. Korean merchants, who believed they were experiencing racial victimization, took to the streets to defend their businesses. The unrest was a "turning point for Korean identity"; after these events, community members stopped thinking of themselves as just Koreans and began to think of themselves as Korean Americans (Bates 2012). Broadly speaking, this research illustrates the potential of protests and social movements to politically incorporate outsiders as well as the enduring effects of this mobilization.

In contrast to African American participation in the civil rights movement, many of the Latino protesters in 2006 were not legally US citizens, and some had language barriers and other significant obstacles to inclusion. Likewise, the scale, duration, and outcome of the civil rights movement are quite distinct from these more recent immigration-related events. Nevertheless, both of these movements featured a minority group mobilizing to assert claims of belonging, and they demonstrate the importance of social movements as a vehicle for political incorporation in response to policies of exclusion.

As with policy feedback, however, social movements may also lead to heightened feelings of exclusion and increased ethnic or pan-ethnic identification (Padilla 1985). For instance, Chapter 3 describes the identity-based movements of the 1960s, such as the Black Power and Chicano movements, both of which emphasized messages of difference rather than similarity. An important part of my argument throughout this book is that a movement's frame can help to explain these varying identity outcomes. Below, I discuss the importance of frames for refining our understanding of the link between politics, social movements, and self-identification.

Framing, Identity, and "We Are America"

Within social movements, collective action frames are thought to motivate individuals to support the goals and activities of social movement organizations. As Benford and Snow (2000, 631–632) explain, "Identity constructions are an inherent feature of the framing process." Collective action frames often incorporate messages related to identity frames, employing key cultural elements or symbols (Gamson and Modigliani 1989). For instance, the 2006 protests featured the widespread use of pro-American slogans, US flags, and other patriotic symbols. My theory underscores the importance of this frame of inclusion.

Consistent with our understanding of identities as socially constructed (Anderson 1983; Bates 1981; Chandra 2004; Posner 2004), I analyze the distinct frame of the 2006 protests in two ways. First, I examine the "We Are America" frame as a *dependent variable*, outlining the transformation that occurred between some of the early 2006 protests in which foreign flags were featured prominently, to later events at which pro-American messages, flags, and other patriotic symbols predominated. This shift is consistent with general research on the development of frames, which are thought to be the result of an interactive process between political elites, social movement organizations, and the media (Benford and Snow 2000; Gamson and Modigliani 1989; Klar, Robison, and Druckman 2013). Frames are also thought to emerge in response to changes in political opportunity structure, such as shifting political pressures or demographics (McAdam 1982; Tarrow 1998), and in response to counterframes, to which new frames respond (Benford and Snow 2000; Zuo and Benford 1995).

In contrast to research emphasizing frames created by the majority group (Massey and Sánchez R. 2010), I focus on efforts by Latino elites to advance a patriotic frame of inclusion in 2006 and the ways in which this message influenced the policy feedback process. After an issue or group has been framed in one way, the acceptance of a new frame is rare (Baumgartner, De Boef, and Boydstun 2008; Klar, Robison, and Druckman 2013), highlighting the importance of better understanding the widespread adoption of the "We Are America" frame in 2006. As described in the following chapter, Latino elites actively advanced this message, which developed in response to a backlash against earlier protests that prominently featured foreign flags. Among other strategies, movement leaders promoted this message through op-eds in English-language newspapers and through the distribution of patriotic messages and symbols at protest events. In these ways, Latino elites developed a specific social construction of Latinos by highlighting their inclusion in US society.

The emphasis on Latinos being American is similar to the development of other identity-based frames that have sought to preempt critics by underscoring patriotism and nationalism among social movement participants. For instance, Zuo and Benford (1995) detail the ways in which Chinese student protesters advanced collective action frames emphasizing patriotism and cultural narratives during the 1989 democracy protests in Tiananmen Square. Similarly, by advancing a patriotic frame in 2006, Latinos sought to influence the majority population's group construction of this group. Group constructions refer to the "target" population most affected by a policy as well as the characterizations, images, and symbols used in reference to this group. As Schneider and Ingram (1993, 342) explain, "Social constructions are manipulated and used by public officials, the media, and the groups themselves. New target groups are created, and images are developed for them; old groups are reconfigured or new images created." Social constructions can shape the social identities of members of target groups in certain ways (Canaday 2009; Mettler and Sorelle 2014; Schneider and Ingram 1993, 1997). Here, I emphasize a social construction of Latinos created not by the majority population but by group members themselves, examining their influence on Latino social identities.

Although the 2006 protests occurred in response to a public policy debate over immigration, their frame also transcended a specific policy debate, connecting to a larger discussion about the place of Latinos in American life. As one scholar describes, Latinos "joined together to collectively affirm their belonging to the nation" (Oboler 2014, xiii). As the quote by *el Piolín* at the start of this chapter suggests, the patriotic frame was also promoted extensively by prominent Spanish-language news personalities. The role of these individuals in building support for the 2006 protests is well documented; for example, one survey of protesters in Chicago found that about half of all respondents had learned of the protests from the media, primarily from Spanish-language sources (Flores-González, Pallares, Herring et al. 2006; see also Dionne, DeWitt, Stone et al. 2015; Fears 2006; Félix, González, and Ramirez 2008; Ramírez 2013; Sterngold and Hendricks 2006). Through their promotion and coverage of the protests, the Spanish-language media also helped to advance the frame of belonging that characterized these events. This unique frame, and the emphasis that ethnic media placed upon it, enabled the message of Latinos being part of America to reach an audience far beyond the actual protest participants.

In later chapters, I treat the protests—and their unique frame—as an *independent variable,* exploring shifts in Latino attitudes and perceptions after these events. To do this, I take advantage of a rare natural experiment that occurred during data collection for the Latino National Survey, or LNS (2006; Fraga, Garcia, Hero et al. 2006a). Interviewing for the survey occurred before, during, and after the 2006 protests, providing the opportunity to compare whether Latino attitudes and self-perception shift after these events. In this analysis, my focus is on framing effects, which occur when communications influence individual attitudes (Chong and Druckman 2007; Klar, Robison, and Druckman 2013). The existence of framing effects is established by a range of experimental research (Berinsky and Kinder 2006; Entman 1993; Iyengar 1991; Iyengar and Kinder 1987; Kahneman and Tversky 1984; Kinder 2003; Klar, Robison, and Druckman 2013; Nelson, Clawson, and Oxley 1997; Popkin 1994). This research focuses primarily on political attitudes and is typically confined to the laboratory setting. My research extends our understanding of frames to their impact on an individual's sense of belonging and self-identification, demonstrating the robustness of these effects. By taking advantage of the natural experiment described at the end of the chapter, I am also able to test whether framing effects occur in a real-world setting. Specifically, I hypothesize that the 2006 protests and their pro-American frame influenced both policy attitudes and individual self-perception among some members of the Latino population.

Importantly, the effects of frames are moderated by a range of factors, including preexisting beliefs (Slothuus 2010), the source of the frame (Druckman 2001), and the salience or relevance of the underlying issue to an individual (Chong and Druckman 2007). In particular, I argue that issue salience plays an important role in helping us to understand the effects of the 2006 events and their related frame. Indeed, as discussed in the next section, although immigration reform is an issue of significant importance to the Latino community, this policy debate does not affect all Latinos equally. Consequently, I anticipate that the policy feedback process, and the effects of the protest and their unique frame, will be uneven among group members.

Policy Salience, Intersectionality, and the Diverse Latino Population

A core argument of this book is that the debate over H.R. 4437 and the ensuing protests, as well as their pro-American frame, influenced Latino attitudes and self-perception. Yet, variation will exist within the diverse Latino community based on the salience of the immigration policy debate. To better understand the variation within this population, I draw on intersectionality research, which emphasizes the complicated ways in which "categories of difference" such as race/ethnicity and gender interact (Crenshaw 1994; Hancock 2007b; Hardy-Fanta 2006; hooks 1984; Strolovitch 2007). The concept of intersectionality emphasizes that these categories are "not separate and additive but rather interactive and multiplicative" (Carter, Sellers, and Squires 2002, 111), such that multiple disadvantages shape and reinforce each other. Thus, the common practice of focusing solely on the more privileged members of a disadvantaged group—for instance, assuming that Latino men are representative of all Latinos or white women are representative of all women—fails to capture the perspective of those with "multiple burdens" (Beltrán 2010; Cohen 1999; Crenshaw 1989, 1994). Importantly, this literature suggests that Latinas are likely to have different political attitudes as well as a distinct political incorporation experience compared to Latino men, a theme explored more extensively in Chapter 6.

More recent scholarship also emphasizes the importance of national origin in intersectional understandings of the Latino population (García Bedolla, Lavariega Monforti, and Pantoja 2007). In other words, intragroup variation is likely to exist by national origin subgroup as well as gender, underscoring the need to address variation along both of these lines to better understand the diversity within the Latino experience. Given the varied treatment of different Latino national origin groups under US citizenship law, country of origin is also likely to influence the salience of the immigration policy debate for group members. For instance, regardless of birthplace, all Puerto Ricans are US citizens, and Cubans have received preferential immigration status for decades. In contrast, members of other national origin groups have faced more adversity.

For immigrants, an individual's national or ancestral origin is thought to be an important source of political socialization (McClain, Carew, Walton et al. 2009; Portes and Zhou 1993), particularly because traditional socialization in which individuals "inherit" political views from their parents is often absent (Abrajano 2010). Moreover, premigration experiences influence Latino postmigration attitudes (Wals 2011), political behavior (Waldinger, Soehl, and Lim 2012), and sense of citizenship (Rocco 2014). In particular, Wals (2011) finds that newcomers bring with them political "suitcases" that influence subsequent civic and political engagement in the United States for immigrants as well as their descendants.

Research on national origin differences is frequently limited to comparisons between Mexicans and non-Mexicans or between Mexicans, Cubans, and Puerto Ricans, the three largest Latino national origin groups. This limitation is often because of the small sample size of other national origin groups in existing surveys. Yet, as the 2010 US Census reflects, other subgroups, including Dominicans and Salvadorans, are growing at a much faster rate than these traditional groups (Ennis, Rios-Vargas, and Albert 2011). As discussed below, the large and diverse sample size of the Latino National Survey (2006) is unmatched in other surveys of the Latino population and provides an unprecedented opportunity to better understand the diversity within this community. I hypothesize that national origin groups most affected by the immigration policy debate (Mexicans, Dominicans, and Salvadorans) will be more likely to demonstrate shifts in opinion and self-identification after the 2006 protests than Puerto Ricans and Cubans, for whom immigration reform is less salient.

In contrast to national origin, the effects of acculturation, including language proficiency (Abrajano 2010; García Bedolla 2003) and immigrant generation (García Bedolla 2005), on policy attitudes is well established (Branton 2007). For instance, later-generation immigrants, including individuals whose parents or grandparents were born in the United States, and English speakers are less likely to support liberal immigration policy options. Similarly, language usage is thought to significantly influence social incorporation (Fraga, Garcia, Hero et al. 2010), contributing to the distinct lens through which subsets of the Latino community understand US politics, and particularly the highly charged issue of immigration. Consistent with this literature, I anticipate that Latinos who are more acculturated (for instance, English speakers or later-generation immigrants) will be less likely to respond to the immigration policy debate and less likely to be influenced by the 2006 protests and their frame. Given that findings about acculturation are more established in existing literature, in some cases, I focus primarily on national origin, about which our understanding is more limited. Importantly, however, consistent with an intersectional framework, I anticipate that the effects of these demographic categories are likely to interact. In order to look for general trends across groups, I often begin by testing bivariate relationships. My analyses also include multivariate models as well as split samples, in which the sample is divided into subcategories such as national origin in order to better understand the factors that drive differences between subgroups (Burns, Schlozman, and Verba 2001; Masuoka and Junn 2013; Welch 1977).

By emphasizing variation within the Latino community based on gender, national origin, and level of acculturation, this book contributes to our understanding of the ways in which these variables interact with public policy discussions and influence the broader process of political incorporation. Moreover, most research on policy feedback focuses primarily on the target group, which consists of individuals most affected by a particular policy. The question of whether the feedback process also affects individuals not a part of the target group is largely neglected in existing scholarship (Campbell 2012; Mettler and Sorelle 2014; Oberlander 2003; Patashnik and Zelizer 2013; Soss and Schram 2007). Given the varied salience of immigration reform to the Latino population, my focus on intragroup differences contributes to our limited understanding of the ways in which policy feedback influences populations more broadly, beyond those with the most to gain or lose from the outcome.

The Latino National Survey and the Natural Experiment

Although a range of data is used throughout this book, much of the analysis in later chapters draws on the Latino National Survey (LNS 2006). Phase 1 of the LNS includes 8,634 respondents across fifteen states and the Washington, DC, metropolitan area. The survey includes at least 400 respondents from each of the five largest national origin groups (Cubans, Dominicans, Mexicans, Puerto Ricans, and Salvadorans), presenting the opportunity to analyze diversity within the burgeoning Latino population to a degree that was not possible with previous data. The survey contains approximately 165 distinct questions on a range of demographic, political, and social issues. Interviewing for the LNS was conducted by phone by Geoscape, a private marketing company, using spatially stratified random sampling, and respondents were given the option of completing the survey in both Spanish and English.

Interviewing for Phase 1 of the LNS was conducted between November 2005 and August 2006. Between February and May of 2006, a wave of protests unfolded across some 39 states and more than 140 cities as an estimated 3.5 million to 5 million people, mostly of Latino descent, took to the streets in an unprecedented mobilization of immigrants (Bloemraad and Trost 2008; Cordero-Guzman, Martin, Quiroz-Becerra et al. 2008; Pantoja, Menjívar, and Magaña 2008). Building on a tradition of research in psychology and economics, I take advantage of this rare natural experiment occurring between the protests and the LNS interviews (Campbell and Stanley 1963; Cook and Campbell 1986; Dunning 2008; Meyer 1995; Shadish, Cook, and Campbell 2001). Using a simple pre-post research design, I treat the protests and their pro-American frame as experimental stimuli in order to explore their effects. Consistent with this research design, I divide the LNS data into two groups: control (pre-protest) and treatment (post-protest), based on whether individuals were interviewed before or after the protests (Campbell and Stanley 1963; Cook and Campbell 1986; Dunning 2008; Meyer 1995; Shadish, Cook, and Campbell 2001). This research design provides the opportunity to evaluate claims about causal effects beyond simply using observational data (Campbell and Stanley 1963; Dunning 2008, 2012). I utilize this approach to study shifts in Latino attitudes toward immigration policy and on questions related to social identities.

In a true experiment, respondents would be randomly assigned into control and treatment groups. In contrast, in a quasi-experiment, the extent to which randomization occurred is simply a consequence of the order in which respondents were interviewed (Dunning 2012). The survey's design did not include any deliberate attempts to sort respondents into distinct, randomized groups, making the inclusion of control variables especially important in subsequent analyses. Adding control variables is necessary to ensure that any differences that appear between the treatment and control groups are not the result of sampling differences between the two groups. Given the high probability that the 2006 protests would also influence other political attitudes and behaviors such as political partisanship and interest in politics, control variables in the multivariate models are limited to fixed demographic characteristics that are unlikely to be changed by these events (e.g., age, income, birthplace, or gender).

In comparing the LNS control and treatment groups, some

differences exist in the demographic characteristics of the two groups (see Appendix B, Table B.1). For example, English speakers, as well as people with low income and lower levels of education, appear to be underrepresented in the control group.[5] In an attempt to mitigate these differences, throughout the book, I divide the full sample into multiple control-treatment pairs and run comparisons within each subsample. Most demographic differences disappear when the subsample is limited to Spanish speakers (see Appendix B, Tables B.2 and B.3). Likewise, when limited to Dominicans, Cubans, or Puerto Ricans, no statistically significant demographic differences persist between the treatment and control groups; among Salvadorans, Spanish speakers are overrepresented in the treatment group, but no other differences appear. Confining the analysis to specific subgroups thus serves the dual purpose of refining the theoretical argument and operating as a robustness check of the results.

Although a number of large immigration-related demonstrations took place in isolated states over several months in the spring of 2006, nationally, coordinated protests occurred between two key dates: April 10 and May 1. Moreover, although some large events occurred in late March, many of these protests were later criticized by Latino leaders for their preponderance of Mexican flags (Cable News Network 2006; Epstein and Sterngold 2006; Hendricks and Garofoli 2006; Martinez 2011). Across the country, newspaper opinion pages were filled with op-eds urging demonstrators to leave their foreign flags at home and embrace a pro-American message (Chavez 2006; Navarrette 2006; Pineda and Sowards 2007, "The Power of Symbols" 2006). By April 1, Latino elites clearly articulated a new theme: "We Are America." Throughout the month, this message was disseminated nationally, with leaders distributing US flags to participants at large-scale events (Epstein and Steingold 2006) and Spanish-language radio personalities reiterating that Latinos represent part of what it means to be American (Ramírez 2013).

Because I am interested in understanding the effects of the protests with the "We Are America" frame, and this message came to prominence only after the first wave of March protests, I use April 1, 2006, as a cutoff date to divide the LNS into "control" (pre-protest) and "treatment" (post-protest) groups.[6] Accordingly, the pre-protest group consists of 3,646 interviews (42.2 percent), whereas the post-protest group includes 4,988 respondents (57.8 percent). Given that the protests started prior to April 1, that US flags began to increase in prominence at some isolated events in late March, and that the patriotic frame took time to resonate across the Latino community, this date choice is likely to underestimate the treatment effect. As a result, if anything, my results are biased toward presenting a more conservative estimate about the effects of these events on the Latino population.

States experienced differing levels of political activity during the 2006 events, and surveying occurred at different rates across the states; although respondents in the majority of states are split somewhat evenly between the treatment and control groups, in several states, considerable variation exists in the proportion of respondents who were "treated" (see Appendix B, Table B.4). More generally, unobserved characteristics such as political, legal, and historical context all vary across states.[7] In multivariate models testing the natural experiment, state-level fixed effects are used to control for these differences.

Although the data collection for the LNS occurred before, during, and after the 2006 protests, this coincidence was unexpected. As a result, no questions were included about whether individuals themselves actually participated in the protests, nor were respondents asked about exposure to press coverage of these events. Thus, as with all observational research, I am limited in my ability to establish a clear causal link between the observed shifts in attitudes and participation in these events. For example, while I provide strong theoretical expectations for how framing shapes immigrants' identities, and I present clear evidence in support of my hypotheses, this research design does not allow me to identify the exact causal mechanism that engendered a sense of inclusion and belonging among Latinos after the 2006 protests.

Although a controlled experiment would be necessary to establish the precise mechanism underlying the observed shifts, the results obtained from this quasi-experimental approach offer external (or real-world) validity and demonstrate that changes will also occur beyond a laboratory setting. Moreover, my findings are consistent with experimental research demonstrating the importance of the frame of the 2006 protests for the *majority* population; using a survey experiment, Wright and Citrin (2010) demonstrate that among whites, visual and verbal associations of Latino protesters with US flags were less likely to evoke hostility than comparable representations featuring Mexican flags. Finally, because no information is available about protest attendance, I cannot ascertain if actual participation in the protests was necessary to bring about a shift in attitudes or if exposure to press coverage, for example, was sufficient to change individual attitudes.

Given the limitations of the quasi-experimental design, I hope that future research will expand upon these findings to investigate whether the relationships identified here are causal or if they are mediated by other intervening factors. For instance, future research could use laboratory or survey experiments to examine whether frames—such as the "We Are America" frame used in the 2006 protest—cause shifts in attitudes or self-identification among Latinos similar to those in Wright and Citrin's findings about white Americans. A research design of this nature could compare pre- and post- attitudes of a treatment group of Latinos exposed to this specific message and a control group exposed to protests with no mention of identity claims or with a pan-ethnic frame.

Toward an Understanding of the Relationship between Politics and Identity Choices

Scholarship in US politics frequently assumes that the relationship between identity and politics moves in one direction, asking how identity relates to certain political outcomes. As Lee (2008, 458) explains, this literature primarily assumes an "identity-to-politics" link, implying that "individuals who share a label—e.g., African American, Latino, Asian American, Arab American—will also share common political goals and interests and act in concert to pursue them." Here, I develop a theory of identity acquisition that posits a politics-to-identity link whereby a particular political debate can influence one's social identity in unexpected ways.

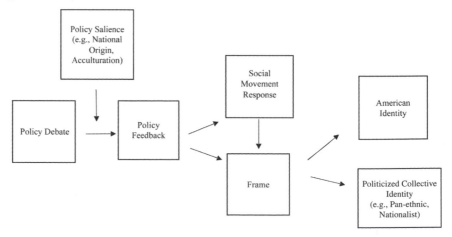

Figure 2.1 The Politics-to-Identity Link

Much research assumes that perceived discrimination will lead minority groups to unite around a counteridentity fueled by feelings of marginalization. For instance, traditional models of Latino politics suggest that immigration-related protests and experiences with discrimination will result in the rejection of an American identity and a heightened sense of pan-ethnicity. My theory presents a more nuanced view. As Figure 2.1 demonstrates, a different frame, such as the "We Are America" theme that emerged in 2006, can instead promote political incorporation through the emergence of an American identity. In other words, contentious political debates can spark a process of policy feedback leading to social movements, protests, and new identity frames that result in *varied* outcomes in terms of self-identification and political incorporation.

My theory emphasizes the importance of a collective response in the form of social movements or protests, with the effects of these movements contingent upon several factors. First, *framing* can influence whether the policy feedback process leads to a greater sense of political incorporation or heightened feelings of alienation. Additionally, this larger process is conditional upon the *salience* of the policy being debated. Generally speaking, within the Latino population, the immigration debate is more salient for some subgroups (for instance, less acculturated individuals as well as those of Mexican, Dominican, or Salvadoran origin/ancestry) and less salient for others (for example, more acculturated individuals as well as those of Puerto Rican or Cuban origin/ancestry). Moreover, in the modern media age, both *direct participation* and *observing mass participation* can spark this larger process. Indeed, given that the patriotic theme of the 2006 protests was widely repeated by the Spanish-language media, movement participants and observers alike stood to be influenced by this distinctive identity frame.

Chapter 3 turns to the question of policy salience, a key intervening variable in my model. To better understand later arguments about the conditional effects of the immigration policy debate within the Latino community, I present brief histories of the five largest national origin groups in the United States, followed by a discussion of the varied ways in which Latino social movements have politicized identity over time. Later chapters further develop these ideas by examining the ways in which the spring 2006 immigration protests affected Latino policy attitudes and self-identification both across and within the Latino population.

3 | From Assimilation to Nationalism to "We Are America"

Immigration Law, Social Movements, and Identity Frames, 1900s–2006

> *We have a choice, all of us, now: we can be part of thirty different minority groups, or we can be the largest minority group in the United States in the twenty-first century. What do you want? What do you want? Show our power. Let them hear our voice.*
> —Talk show host and Latino activist Geraldo Rivera, October 1996

Alternating between Spanish and English, Geraldo Rivera spoke these words to tens of thousands of participants rallied at the first major Latino protest in the nation's capital in the fall of 1996 (CSPAN 1996; translation by the author). As in 2006, this monumental gathering took place to object to immigration-related legislation then advancing in the US Congress. As the above quote reflects, Rivera and other speakers at the event emphasized the need for pan-ethnic unity within the Latino population.

The 1996 quest to bring this diverse population together in response to an immigration policy proposal represented a shift in both the politics and the politicization of identities by Latino organizations. In the face of significant discrimination, the first Latino organizations formed in the early 1900s. These groups frequently distanced themselves from new immigrants, focusing instead on the rights of established US citizens. Indeed, only in the past forty years have these organizations fully embraced what is now assumed to be a "pro-Latino" stance on immigration issues.

Throughout this book, I argue that the 2006 immigration protests, and their distinct frame that Latinos represent America, influenced the identity of group members in counterintuitive ways, fostering a sense of inclusion in the United States rather than one of difference. Chapter 2 outlines the core theoretical foundations of this argument, including the importance of policy feedback, social movements, and frames, which help individuals interpret the world and shape individual attitudes and opinions (Chong and Druckman 2007; Klar, Robison, and Druckman 2013). I also underscore the varied salience of the immigration policy debate to the Latino population based on factors such as national origin and level of acculturation.

Below, I provide important background for these arguments by placing the 2006 immigration debate and ensuing protests in historical and political context in order to establish the distinct substantive focus of these events as well as their unique framing. This chapter is divided into three parts. I begin by highlighting major milestones in contemporary immigration law through the 2006 debate. Next, to better understand the varied role that national origin plays in this process, I present a brief synopsis of the historical experiences of the five major Latino subgroups in the United States—Cubans, Dominicans, Mexicans, Puerto Ricans, and Salvadorans. An individual's national or ancestral origin (McClain, Carew, Walton et al. 2009; Portes and Zhou 1993) and premigration experiences (Waldinger, Soehl, and Lim 2012; Wals 2011) influences their political attitudes in the United States. These descriptions provide important background for later arguments about the varied salience of the immigration policy debate by national origin subgroup.

The final section of this chapter describes the ways in which Latino organizations have politicized identity over time. In the early twentieth century, these groups represented largely middle class US citizens, mobilizing around an assimilation frame. In the 1960s, framing shifted toward cultural difference; by the end of the twentieth century, the emphasis switched to pan-ethnic unity, as exemplified by the opening quote of this chapter. In 2006, the predominant frame echoed the patriotic themes of a century prior. This time, however, Latino organizations represented a much broader range of community members, fighting for the rights of noncitizens and the inclusion of even undocumented immigrants as American.

Contemporary Developments in US Immigration Policy

On some level, US history has been characterized by a continual cycle in which outsiders struggle for inclusion. In fact, the federal government has sought to delineate lines of inclusion and exclusion virtually since its inception. In 1790, the fledgling US government enacted the Naturalization Act, which provided citizenship to any "free white person" of good character residing in the United States for at least two years (First Congress 1790). Over the next century, immigration policy became increasingly federalized, eventually leading to a series of quotas, or caps, on the number of newcomers who could enter the United States based on national origin.

National origins quotas first emerged in the 1880s, and formed the foundation of US immigration policy until 1965 (see Appendix C, Table C.1, for details as well as a chronology of major immigration laws through 2006; for a full discussion of national origin quotas, see Tichenor 2002; Ngai 2004). Notably, individuals from the Western Hemisphere were omitted from these formal restrictions, largely in response to concerns of the business community. Yet, in regard to Mexico, the US State Department worked to limit Mexican immigration through other means. As Ngai (2004, 55) explains, "Consular officials used the ban on contract labor, the literacy test, and the provision excluding persons 'likely to become a public charge' to refuse visas."[1] During this period, the difference between legal and illegal migration to the United States increasingly solidified.

Between the 1940s and 1960s, hundreds of thousands of Mexicans also came to the United States under the *bracero* program, through which Mexican workers were employed in the agriculture and railroad sectors (Calavita 1992; Massey, Durand, and Malone 2002). The program was consistently plagued by concerns over exploitation of workers, low pay, and illegal employment practices (Hardy-Fanta 1993). Following the program's 1964 termination and subsequent immigration reforms, Mexicans were subject to formal visa caps for the first time and were forced to compete with nationals from other Latin American and Caribbean countries for entry into the United States. The *bracero* program established a culture of seasonal employment migration within a portion of the Mexican population that persisted even after the formal program ended. In the aftermath of the *bracero* program, undocumented immigration grew substantially (Massey, Durand, and Malone 2002).

The 1965 Reforms

Contemporary immigration policy is grounded in the 1965 Immigration and Nationality Act (P.L. 89-236), which repealed the national origin quotas that had guided US immigration policy for decades. This legislation, also known as the Hart-Celler Act, introduced a new approach to immigration, prioritizing the principles of family reunification and the employment needs of US companies rather than emphasizing national origin.[2]

At the time of its passage, lawmakers thought that the 1965 immigration reforms would have little impact on immigrant demographics. In contrast to these expectations, these new principles had dramatic consequences on the composition of immigrants in the United States.[3] In 1960, 74 percent of foreign-born residents in the United States originated in Europe. By 2010, that figure had shifted considerably, with 81 percent of the foreign-born population from Latin America and Asia (Wasem 2013b). As these numbers suggest, the 1965 reforms significantly changed the face of newcomers to the United States (for a full discussion of the 1965 reforms and their consequences, see Chin and Villazor 2015).

The 1986 Reforms

In the wake of the 1965 Immigration and Nationality Act, both legal and unauthorized immigration in the United States increased significantly (Smith 2011). According to the Department of Homeland Security, unauthorized immigrants include "all foreign-born non-citizens who are not legal residents" (Hoefer, Rytina, and Baker 2010, 1). The majority of these individuals either arrived with a temporary authorization for admission and overstayed this period or came to the United States outside of proper legal channels. By the early 1980s, an estimated 5 million people were living in the United States without legal status (Plumer 2013).

As in the more recent battle over comprehensive immigration reform, the federal government sought a legislative solution for undocumented immigrants that would balance stricter enforcement measures, which sought to prevent any further growth of this population, with a path to legalization for those living here without authorization. In 1986, after five years of trying, Congress finally passed a comprehensive immigration policy, the Immigration Reform and Control Act (IRCA, P.L. 99-603), which was signed into law by Republican president Ronald Reagan. A bipartisan compromise, the legislation was also known as the Simpson-Mazzoli Act, after Senator Alan Simpson (R-WY) and Representative Romani Mazzoli (D-KY), who chaired the immigration subcommittees in the Senate and the House, respectively. The law developed procedures through which undocumented residents living continuously in the United States since 1982 could eventually apply to receive US citizenship ("amnesty") and created a new visa category (H-2A) for temporary agricultural workers.[4] To balance these new programs, IRCA increased staffing and surveillance along the US-Mexico border and initiated a sanctions program under which employers who hired undocumented workers could be fined anywhere from $250 to $10,000. Additionally, the legislation provided four years of funding assistance to states to alleviate any new social services costs incurred from a growing number of residents. As a result of the 1986 reforms, an estimated 2.7 million people, mostly Mexicans, attained legal status (McCabe and Meissner 2010).

Congressional support for the proposal was divided and did not fall along traditional ideological or party lines.[5] Then-Representative Charles Schumer (D-NY), who described the final legislation as "a left-center bill," was widely credited with saving the legislation by negotiating a compromise regarding agricultural workers that would meet the needs of Western industry while also protecting workers' rights (Pear 1986c). In both the House and the Senate, opponents included liberals who feared that the employer sanctions of the bill would lead to increased discrimination against all Latinos as well as conservatives who opposed the "amnesty" and guest-worker provisions (Zolberg 2006). By and large, Latinos were divided in response to the 1986 IRCA. Although many supported the law because of its path to citizenship, others shared the concern that the employer sanctions would result in increased discrimination (Pear 1986c).[6] The Congressional Hispanic Caucus, founded in 1976 as a forum for Latino members of Congress to advance initiatives important to their community, had firmly opposed previous iterations of the bill. On the final vote for the 1986 legislation, caucus members were divided, with five of eleven supporting the legislation (Chavez 1986).

The 1986 IRCA, and congressional modifications in 1990, increased the number of legal immigrants arriving in the United States from less-represented countries. The provisions embodied in IRCA, including an unprecedented path to citizenship for unauthorized immigrants balanced by employer sanctions and new border security initiatives, provided a potential road map for policy changes in later debates over comprehensive immigration reform. Most subsequent bipartisan proposals have sought to balance some element of "amnesty" along with increased security and enforcement. Yet, the law failed to reduce the number of undocumented immigrants, mostly Mexicans, coming to the United States. In fact, in subsequent years, the unauthorized population grew rapidly, from an estimated 3.5 million in 1990 to an estimated 12.2 million in 2007, before leveling off during the 2007–2009 recession (Passel and Cohn 2015).

By the 1990s, some residents of receiving states became increasingly frustrated with the growing immigrant population. Although the Supreme Court has long held that immigration policy is the domain of the federal government, some states also began to consider their own legislation related to immigrants.

The 1990s and the Social Services Debate

In 1975, the state of Texas passed a law that would have prevented state education funds from being used on undocumented immigrant children. The Supreme Court overturned this law in *Plyer vs. Doe* (1982), which reaffirmed the right of all children to attend public schools through twelfth grade regardless of legal status. Despite the Court's earlier ruling, nearly twenty years after Texas' original efforts, California's Proposition 187 sought to ban undocumented immigrants from accessing a much wider range of social services, including public education and healthcare.[7] Approved by the state's voters on November 8, 1994, the proposal also called for service providers to verify the legal status of applicants for benefits and to report suspected undocumented immigrants to the California attorney general's office and the Immigration and Naturalization Service (INS).

Up until this point, the national debate over immigration had been largely bipartisan, characterized by atypical political alliances such as those formed to pass the 1986 IRCA. In California, most Democrats opposed Proposition 187. Although Republicans were somewhat split in their support for the proposal, then-governor Pete Wilson, a Republican, was a vocal proponent of Proposition 187. His strong support for the proposition marked a significant shift in the partisan nature of the immigration debate.[8]

By 1996, the heightened polarization around immigration politics in California began to appear at the national level. Politicians increasingly debated what it means to be American and who deserves citizenship rights in the United States. For instance, the Republican-led Congress introduced English-only legislation, and the party's platform that year included language seeking to strip the citizenship rights of children born to parents living illegally in the United States, which are currently guaranteed under the fourteenth amendment of the US Constitution. (Pear 1996). Moreover, a Republican provision in that year's welfare reform bill (the Personal Responsibility and Work Opportunity Reconciliation Act, PL 104-193) drew on themes from California's Proposition 187 by imposing restrictions on benefits for undocumented immigrants as well as non-naturalized legal immigrants.

After months of heated congressional debate, in September of that year, Democratic president Bill Clinton signed the Illegal Immigration Reform and Immigrant Responsibility Act (IIRIRA, PL 104-208) into law. This bill contained some of the toughest measures against illegal immigration in history, including further restrictions on immigrant admissibility and asylum law, creating new categories of aliens subject to removal (deportation) from the United States,[9] doubling the size of the border patrol over five years, tightening penalties on smugglers, and calling for the construction of a fence in the most heavily trafficked border areas. Importantly, the new law meant that legal permanent residents could now be deported for smaller legal violations, and these violations were retroactive, allowing for deportation for a crime even after individuals had completed a prison sentence (Hagan, Castro, and Rodriguez 2009). Although deportations were not entirely new in the United States, prior to the 1996 law, most immigration efforts focused on the border. The 1996 changes expanded immigration enforcement to include "interior removals," with IIRIRA and subsequent legal changes resulting in an increase in deportations of more than 600 percent by 2008 (De Genova 2002; Hagan, Castro, and Rodriguez 2009).

The final version of IIRIRA did not include earlier, more controversial provisions, including efforts to deny access to public education to the children of undocumented immigrants or to deport legal immigrants who used public assistance for more than twelve months over a seven-year period. Nevertheless, Republican advocacy of such provisions further sparked the ire of the Latino community.

2000–2007: Failed Attempts at National Reform and the Path to "We Are America"

By 2000, some Republicans had begun to moderate their positions on immigration. That year, Democratic president Bill Clinton signed the bipartisan Legal Immigration Family Equity (LIFE) Act, which included provisions to extend the 1986 amnesty to certain immigrants. By 2001, however, estimates of the undocumented population had risen to 8 million (Jachimowicz 2004). When Republican president George W. Bush took office that year, he emphasized the need to improve the US relationship with Mexico and the importance of comprehensive immigration reform. However, the terrorist attacks of September 11, 2001, stymied the issue (McCabe and Meissner 2010). In response to those attacks, the bureaucratic apparatus responsible for immigration issues was transformed. The INS, which had overseen immigration law and enforcement under the auspices of the Department of Justice since 1941, was dissolved, with authority for immigration issues transferred to the new Department of Homeland Security (DHS).[10]

After several years of silence, President Bush raised the issue of comprehensive immigration reform again in January 2004. Seeking to fix gaps from the 1986 reforms, Bush asked Congress to create a temporary program for foreign guest workers and undocumented immigrants. Two congressional proposals for comprehensive immigration reform emerged in response, both of which were referred to committees but never considered by the full House or Senate.[11]

THE SENSENBRENNER BILL AND THE 2005–2006 DEBATE

In May 2005, the late senator Edward M. Kennedy (D-MA) and Senator John McCain (R-AZ) introduced the Secure America and Orderly Immigration Act (S. 1033). Among other provisions, their proposal for comprehensive reform would have allowed for temporary visas for unskilled workers and a new path to legalization through which undocumented workers could ultimately apply for legal status after paying a substantial fine (Patterson 2005). Although this bill failed to advance out of committee, a revised and expanded version of this legislation was introduced the following year with additional cosponsors (S. 2611). The Comprehensive Immigration Reform Act of 2006 (CIRA) passed the Senate with a bipartisan vote of 62–36 on May 25, 2006.

In the interim, however, the House of Representatives undertook a far more partisan approach. On December 6, 2005, Representative James F. Sensenbrenner, Jr. (R-WI), then chair of the House Judiciary Committee, introduced the Border Protection, Anti-Terrorism, and Illegal Immigration Control Act (H.R. 4437). Sensenbrenner's proposal had a number of key provisions, including increased penalties for illegal immigration, expanded construction of a nearly 700-mile fence along the US-Mexico border, increased cooperation between the Homeland Security Department and local law enforcement officials, and classification of unauthorized immigrants and anyone helping them enter or stay in the United States as felons. This final provision was particularly far reaching, threatening anyone who aided undocumented immigrants in any way with criminal penalties and up to five years in prison.[12] In contrast to the Senate's bipartisan proposal, nearly all cosponsors of the House bill were Republicans. The broad scope of the legislation, and the wide range of people who would have been subject to punishment under its provisions, incited deep opposition across the Latino community.

In the House of Representatives, members of the Congressional Hispanic Caucus, the Congressional Black Caucus, and the Congressional Asian Pacific American Caucus united to oppose the bill. During the floor debate over H.R. 4437, several members of the Hispanic Caucus, which represents Latino Democrats, invoked ideas about American values as they expressed opposition to the bill's extensive measures.[13] For instance, Congresswoman Lucille Roybal-Allard (D-CA) argued, "Our great nation serves as a model for democracy, fairness, and the rule of law. Unfortunately, this bill takes us away from these ideals upon which our nation was founded" (Roybal-Allard 2005). No Members of the Hispanic Conference, which represents Latino Republicans, spoke about the bill during the floor debate.

The Sensenbrenner bill passed on December 16, 2005, just ten days after it was introduced, by a vote of 239–182. Of those who voted on the bill, 92 percent of Republican representatives supported the legislation, while 82 percent of Democrats opposed it (2005). All voting members of the Hispanic Caucus opposed the bill, whereas the Hispanic Conference was more divided.[14]

National Origin Groups

The discussion above focuses on major immigration policies at the national level. Importantly, however, there are also policies specific to certain Latino national origin subgroups. To better understand the varied salience of immigration policy for Latinos as well as the diversity of experiences encompassed within this broad pan-ethnic group, the following section presents a brief history of the five largest national origin groups presently in the United States: Cubans, Dominicans, Mexicans, Puerto Ricans, and Salvadorans. Individuals from these groups currently constitute over 80 percent of the Latino population (Ennis, Rios-Vargas, and Albert 2011). Although the accounts below are limited, they provide a preliminary basis for understanding one of the cleavages underlying Latino attitudes toward immigration policy (for a more comprehensive historical analysis of the different Latino national origin groups, see García Bedolla 2014).

Puerto Ricans: Conquest, Citizenship, and Territorial Status

Puerto Ricans became Americans "by conquest" in 1898, when the island was awarded to the United States under the Treaty of Paris in the aftermath of the Spanish-American War. In the early twentieth century, Puerto Rico officially became a US territory. All Puerto Ricans were granted US citizenship by statute under the 1917 Jones Act.

Although Puerto Ricans from the island arrived in New York in the early twentieth century, migration to the mainland began in force in the 1940s and 1950s as employers in the Northeast began to actively recruit workers from the island. Most subsequent migration to the US mainland has been the result of labor flows. As Portes and Grosfoguel (1994) observe, Puerto Rican migrants to the mainland were typically from the lower economic strata, whereas historically, middle- and upper-class Puerto Ricans remained on the island.[15] Consequently, Puerto Ricans on the mainland have consistently demonstrated higher levels of poverty in comparison with other Latino groups (de la Cruz and Ramirez 2003). Because Puerto Ricans are automatically granted US citizenship and can move freely between the island and the mainland, immigration politics are generally less salient for this community than for other national origin groups. Instead, Puerto Rican politics on and off the island is frequently dominated by debates over Puerto Rico's commonwealth status and whether this unique status should be maintained.

Cuban Exiles in the United States

Cubans in the United States historically have seen themselves as an exile community rather than as long-term settlers (de los Angeles Torres 1999; Rieff 1995). The first big wave of Cubans arrived in the United

States starting in January 1959, when communist leader Fidel Castro rose to power on the island, and lasted through the 1960s. Within the broader international context of the cold war, the US government collaborated extensively with Cuban exiles during this period. President John F. Kennedy's Cuban Refugee Program, one of the most generous assistance packages ever awarded by the United States, also provided direct financial and relocation assistance to an estimated 250,000 Cubans (Portes and Grosfoguel 1994; Wilson and Portes 1980).

A second wave of arrivals began in the spring of 1980, after Castro declared that anyone wishing to leave for the United States could do so. The 1980 exodus soon became known as the Mariel Boatlift, after Mariel Harbor, from which the boats departed. In the months that followed, an estimated 125,000 Cubans arrived in Florida, including many from Cuban jails and mental health facilities (Glass 2009).[16]

Regardless of cohort, Cuban exiles have maintained a distinct advantage with respect to US immigration policy. Under an amended version of the 1966 Cuban Adjustment Act (CAA), most Cubans who arrive in the United States become eligible for legal resident status after 366 days regardless of whether they enter through proper legal channels.[17] In the 1990s, President Clinton enacted several changes in Cuban immigration policy, including implementation of what is now known as the "Wet Foot/Dry Foot" policy in 1995. Under this policy, Cubans who are found at sea are returned to Cuba unless they have sufficient evidence for an asylum claim. However, most Cubans who reach US soil are allowed to stay (for details about this and other policy changes enacted during this time, see Wasem 2009). In practice, these policies have allowed nearly all Cubans who come to the United States to eventually achieve legal permanent resident status, a special benefit applying to no other country or national origin group (Wasem 2009). Consequently, although Cubans do not have the citizenship rights of Puerto Ricans, they do receive preferential legal treatment in comparison with other national origin groups.

In addition to these provisions, early collaboration and resettlement assistance, especially for the first wave of arrivals, led Cubans to have a uniquely positive relationship with the US government. The distinct treatment of Cuban Americans, the impossibility of returning to Cuba for most group members, and the specific political concerns of this exile community have historically distinguished this group's political attitudes and interests from the broader Latino population, with Cubans supporting Republicans more than members of other Latino national origin groups.[18]

Mexican Americans: Conquest, "Amnesty," and Enduring Migration

The migration of Mexicans to the United States is notable both for its extended history as well as for the large number and duration of arrivals. Under the 1848 Treaty of Guadalupe Hidalgo, Mexico ceded to the United States the territory that now constitutes California, Nevada, and Utah as well as parts of Arizona, New Mexico, and Wyoming. Existing residents of those states were given the choice of staying in the United States or returning to Mexico. This territorial acquisition changed the demographics of an expanding nation; nearly 75,000 of the Mexicans who remained on this land pursued US citizenship as a result of this conquest (Smith 2011).

Mexican migration to the United States ebbed and flowed through out the twentieth century, with the first major wave arriving in the 1910s–1920s (García Bedolla 2014). Although Mexicans were not included in the congressionally established quotas that governed federal immigration policy during that time, the US Consul in Mexico began to limit the number of Mexican nationals receiving visas through administrative means. Additionally, with Mexican migrants in mind, in 1929 Congress approved legislation deeming illegal entry into the United States a felony offense; the enduring association between illegal immigration and Mexicans first emerged at this time (Ngai 2004).

Prior to the civil rights movement, many Mexicans living in the United States experienced significant discrimination and violence. Under the Mexican "repatriation" program of the 1930s, as many as 1 million people, both US citizens and noncitizens, were forcibly removed from the United States (Balderrama and Rodriguez 2006; García Bedolla 2014; but see U.S. Citizenship and Immigration Services 2014). Thousands more were victims of lynching in the southwestern United States (Carrigan and Webb 2013).

As described above, one of the main reforms of the 1965 Immigration and Nationality Act included the provision of a large number of visas based on family preference, allowing family members living in the United States to sponsor relatives living abroad. The 1986 IRCA also provided a path to citizenship for nearly 3 million people, mostly Mexican (Zolberg 2006). As a result of these developments, coupled with the large number of Mexicans living in the United States with family abroad, in recent years Mexicans have constituted the largest group of legal immigrants to the United States. In 2008, for instance, nearly 94 percent of Mexican immigrants who received lawful permanent residence status did so under the family-based immigrant provision, including 111,703 immediate relatives of US citizens and 66,693 who received family sponsorship (Terrazas 2010a). However, this process is plagued by significant backlogs. For instance, the US State Department's August 2014 Visa Bulletin indicated that for Mexicans, for most categories of family members, applications were then being processed from 1993 or 1994 (U.S. Department of State Bureau of Consular Affairs 2014).

Beyond these legal pathways, significant numbers of Mexicans arrive or remain in the United States without legal status. As of 2011, an estimated 6,800,000 unauthorized Mexicans lived in the United States, constituting approximately 59 percent of the overall undocumented population (Hoefer, Rytina, and Baker 2012). These figures suggest that the issue of immigration reform will be especially salient for many in the Mexican population.

The uniquely long history of Mexican Americans in the United States also underscores another key area of division with respect to the salience of immigration issues: established versus new arrivals. Indeed, more incorporated immigrants often distance themselves from newcomers, supporting more restrictive immigration policies (Branton 2007; de la Garza, DeSipio, Garcia et al. 1992; García Bedolla 2005; Hood, Morris, and Shirkey 1997; Rouse, Wilkinson, and Garand 2010; Sanchez 2006a). Given the extensive history of Mexicans in the United States, generational differences are particularly important within this subgroup. Although I focus extensively on the role of national origin throughout this book, I also underscore the importance of other markers of acculturation, including language preference and immigrant generation, as additional factors driving variation within the Latino population. The long and complicated history of Mexican Americans in the United States highlights the importance of examining a range of cleavages in order to better understand the heterogeneous Latino population.

Dominican Republic

Dominican migration to the United States began in earnest in the late 1960s, following President Joaquin Balaguer's 1966 ascent to power in that nation. The first decade of Balaguer's rule was characterized by significant repression, and Dominicans coming to the United States in this period were primarily political exiles. These newcomers received assistance from the US government and settled primarily in the New York area (Itzigsohn 2009). These early political migrants and their descendants, however, represent only a fraction of Dominicans currently living in the United States.

The worsening economy in the Dominican Republic resulted in large-scale migration to the United States in the 1970s and 1980s. In contrast to earlier arrivals, only a small number of these immigrants were political asylees (Grieco 2004; Portes and Grosfoguel 1994). The pace of economic migration to the United States continued to increase in subsequent decades, with new arrivals driving much of the population growth within the Dominican community. Between 1990 and 2000 alone, more than 300,000 Dominicans migrated to the United States (Grieco 2004); this figure represented more than one-third of the total Dominican population living in the United States in 2000 (Ennis, Rios Vargas, and Albert 2011). An estimated 83 percent of Dominicans in the United States reside in the Northeast, with nearly half of this community concentrated in the New York City metropolitan area (Grieco 2004).

In recent decades, Dominican migrants have received neither special preference nor targeted restrictions under immigration law, with nationals who entered legally doing so primarily through the work certification process or family sponsorship. Between 2000 and 2010, the Dominican population in the United States nearly doubled, growing from 765,945 to 1,414,703 (Ennis, Rios-Vargas, and Albert 2011). As of 2004, an estimated 109,000, or 13–15 percent of the Dominicans living in the United States, were unauthorized (Grieco 2004). Dominicans have also been disproportionately impacted by the 1996 legislative changes in IIRIRA making it easier to deport legal permanent residents who had committed minor crimes. According to 2009 estimates, between 36,000 and 50,000 Dominicans had been deported since the law's enactment (Northern Manhattan Coalition for Immigrant Rights 2009). Consequently, much Dominican mobilization around immigration reform has focused on the possibility of changing the laws surrounding deportations (Zepeda-Millán 2014).

El Salvador

Immigrants from El Salvador have a more complicated history. In the 1980s, the nation experienced a bloody civil war, fueled by the era's cold war adversaries. During the war, which spanned from 1980 until 1992, the United States contributed more than $6 billion in military and economic aid to the Salvadoran government. In turn, the opposition, an alliance of left-wing insurgents, received substantial assistance from the countries of the cold war's Communist bloc (Buergenthal 1994). Estimates indicate that more than 75,000 Salvadorans were killed during the war, with the US-backed Salvadoran government responsible for the majority of fatalities (Benjamin-Alvarado, DeSipio, and Montoya 2009). The conflict also created an estimated 500,000 internally displaced people as well as more than 1 million emigrants, primarily to Mexico and the United States (Wood 2008; Zolberg 2006).[19]

By 1987, roughly 10 percent of El Salvador's population had fled to the United States, with the largest concentration in Los Angeles; between 1980 and 1990 alone, the number of immigrants from El Salvador surged from an estimated 94,000 to 465,000 (Terrazas 2010b). Migrants to the United States came for both political and financial reasons, as the extreme violence in their country precluded economic opportunities.

In the peak years of the Salvadoran civil war, President Reagan tried to downplay the violence occurring in the region (García Bedolla 2014). Because the United States provided support to these governments overseas, the Reagan administration denied asylum claims from refugees of El Salvador and other Central American nations, classifying them instead as economic migrants who were subject to deportation. Ultimately, because of pressure from activists, religious leaders, and journalists, the US government changed course and provided asylum or relief to hundreds of thousands of Salvadorans (for details, see Coutin 2000).[20]

Legislatively, the first steps toward resolving Salvadoran asylum claims were included in the 1990 Immigration Act (P.L. 101-649). This law established Temporary Protected Status (TPS), providing a renewable safe haven for individuals unable to return home because of extraordinary circumstances such as natural disaster or civil war.[21] Technically, TPS is short term, requiring federal renewal every six to eighteen months, and the status applies only to those who have lived in the United States continually since each country's original designation. Since 2001, the US government repeatedly renewed TPS status for individuals from El Salvador, with an estimated 217,000 Salvadorans in the United States under this policy as of 2011 (Wasem and Ester 2011). Hundreds of thousands of nationals from El Salvador have also gained lawful status through the Nicaraguan Adjustment and Central American Relief Act (NACARA), a 1997 law providing immigration benefits and relief from deportation to certain individuals from Central America and the former Soviet Union as well as through political asylum proceedings and suspension of deportation (Gammage 2007; Wasem and Ester 2011). Yet, despite these provisions, legal status remains a consistent concern within this popluation. The 1986 IRCA legislation covered only undocumented immigrants arriving in the United States prior to January 1, 1982. Because many Salvadorans arrived after this date, they were excluded under this earlier policy solution (Menjívar 2000).

Salvadorans represent one of the fastest-growing Latino communities in the United States. The 2010 US Census counted 1,648,968 Salvadorans, representing an increase of more than 150 percent since 2000 (Ennis, Rios-Vargas, and Albert 2011). Some estimates suggest that Salvadorans may have already surpassed Cubans as the third-largest national origin group in the United States (Lopez and Gonzalez-Barrera 2013). Yet, despite this rapidly growing presence, research on the Salvadoran American community remains limited (Menjívar 2000).

After Mexicans, Salvadorans constitute the second-largest undocumented population in the United States, totaling approximately 660,000 (Hoefer, Rytina, and Baker 2012). Although this number is significantly smaller than the estimated 6.8 million undocumented immigrants in the United States from Mexico, this figure represents a larger *proportion* of Salvadorans in the United States without legal status; based on the 2010 census figures above, an estimated 40 percent of the Salvadoran community might be in the United States without legal status. Indeed, in an analysis of interviews and surveys focusing on the Los Angeles Salvadoran community, Menjívar asserts, "Legality is crucial for Salvadorans—no other issue among the people with whom I spoke was more important than having proper documentation" (2000, 84). Between 2000 and 2008, the number of unauthorized immigrants from El Salvador grew by an estimated 35 percent (Terrazas 2010b).[22]

As the above account suggests, Salvadorans have had a more tumultuous relationship with the US government than most other Latino groups, and Salvadoran immigrants are more likely to have experienced extreme levels of violence prior to their arrival. The complicated history of Salvadorans in the United States and the large percentage of this community that does not have legal status contrasts starkly with the experiences of other subgroup members. In sum, the distinct histories of these five national origin groups, as well as the different relationship each group has had with the US government and their varied treatment under US immigration law, suggest that the immigration debate will resonate with individuals from different national origin groups in distinct ways.

Latino Social Movements and Identity Frames

My politics-to-identity theory emphasizes the importance of both issue salience and framing to understand the varied ways in which policy debate can influence social identities. In the previous section, I situate the 2006 immigration debate within the historical context of US immigration policy and describe the treatment of the five largest Latino national origin groups under US citizenship and immigration law. This discussion presents the foundation for subsequent arguments that the 2006 protests had varied salience for members of different subgroups. Below, I present historical background to support the final part of my theoretical argument: that the 2006 protests and their unique, patriotic frame influenced Latinos' sense of belonging in the United States. To do so, I trace the evolution of Latino social movements (see Table 3.1) and their distinct identity frames over time and then describe the emergence of the "We Are America" frame in 2006.

Mexican American Organizing in the Early Twentieth Century

The first Mexican American organizations emerged in response to the extreme violence and discrimination experienced by this population at the start of the twentieth century. By the 1930s, nearly 1.5 million Mexicans lived in the United States (Balderrama and Rodriguez 2006). On paper, these new citizens were given rights to land and political representation through treaties, yet many of these rights were subsequently violated in practice (DeSipio 2006; García Bedolla 2014). As described above, countless Mexicans were also victims of lynching and forced deportations during this time. Within this political context, Latino organizing took root.

The first Mexican American activist organizations sought to defend the civil rights of this community. Most of these organizations limited their membership to native or naturalized US citizens fighting for inclusion (San Miguel 1983). They typically represented the middle class,

Table 3.1   Latino Social Movements over Time

Period	Organization(s)	Message and Defining Characteristics
1910s–1950s	Order of Sons of America	Assimilation, patriotism, English only
	League of United Latin	Civil rights for Mexican Americans
	American Citizens (LULAC)	Membership limited to US citizens
	American GI Forum	
1960s–1970s	*Chicano* Movement	Cultural difference
	Puerto Rican Nationalists/	Nationalism
	Young Lords Party	Spanish language and heritage
	United Farm Workers	Workers' rights (initially on behalf of
	Organizing Committee	immigrants with legal status only)
	Chicana Feminist Movement	Gender Inequality
1980s	Sanctuary Movement	Advocacy for Central American refugees
		Alliances with churches
1994	California Protests against	Student-led protests against ballot
	Proposition 187	proposition to restrict immigrant access to social services
		Prominent Mexican flags
		Voter backlash against "foreign" symbols
1990s	National Council of La Raza	First Latino protests in Washington, DC
	National Coordinating	Emphasis on Latino unity/
	Committee for Citizenship	"One Latino family"
	and Participation	Minimum wage, affirmative action,
	(*Coordinadora 96*)	amnesty for immigrants
2006 and Beyond	Protests against H.R. 4437, *"Ya es Hora"* (The Time Is Now) and others	We Are America, Today We March, Tomorrow We Vote
		American flags and other patriotic symbols
		Immigration reform, including rights of the undocumented

promoting increased civic participation within this group. These early organizations fought for the rights of US citizens, and generally did little to advocate for the less-established immigrant population.

The Order of Sons of America (OSA), established in 1921, was one such organization. The group sought "to realize the greatest enjoyment possible of all the rights and privileges and prerogatives extended by the American Constitution"; for instance, the organization fought against discrimination by business owners and landlords and worked for the inclusion of Mexican Americans on Texas juries (Orozco 2010). As with other groups of the era, OSA emphasized patriotic messages, adopting

"America" as their song and "For Our Country" as their motto. These themes and slogans were designed to promote the inclusion of Mexican Americans within the greater polity.

In 1929, OSA and two related organizations merged to form the League of United Latin American Citizens (LULAC), which remains the oldest and largest Mexican American civil rights organization (Marquez 1993). As with its predecessors, LULAC's initial membership was restricted exclusively to US citizens (San Miguel 1983). The organization sought reform within the existing social, political, and legal order, arguing that social change should occur at the individual level rather than the group level.

As described above, in the 1940s, the United States initiated the Mexican *bracero* program in an attempt to respond to labor shortages in the agricultural and construction industries. During this period, Republican President Dwight Eisenhower also established a border control program, Operation Wetback.[23] These early efforts at securing the border were associated with both a decline in undocumented immigration and an increase in anti-Latino discrimination.

LULAC fought to end racism and discrimination against *braceros* and other migrant workers. Yet, the organization opposed illegal immigration, which it saw as "an obstacle to Mexican American integration" (Tichenor 2002, 230). Instead, the organization emphasized Americanism and assimilation as a means of upward mobility (Beltrán 2010). Highlighting a tension between different immigrant generations that persists to this day, many established Mexican Americans in this period distanced themselves from newer arrivals, with some arguing explicitly for limits to further immigration in an attempt to counter any stigma against their community (Smith 2011).

Consistent with other early Mexican American organizations, LULAC took great pains to emphasize its commitment to US culture. For instance, it made English the group's official language and continued with the tradition of OSA by adopting "America" as its song. Indeed, as Marquez (1989, 369) describes, "LULAC's call for loyalty to the United States Government, '100% Americanism,' and the adoption of the English language were attempts to placate a hostile Anglo American majority and demonstrate that the Mexican American people could become loyal and productive citizens of the United States."

Early Latino activism was also closely linked to the labor movement, particularly in the southwestern United States. For instance, in California in 1938, Luisa Morena, a labor leader active in the United Cannery, Agricultural, Packing, and Allied Workers of America (UCAPAWA-CIO), spearheaded the formation of *El Congreso del Pueblos de Habla Española* (the Congress of Spanish-Speaking Peoples). Unlike other groups of this period, *El Congreso* sought to promote Latino unity across different national origin groups regardless of legal status, fighting for the rights of documented and undocumented workers alike (Rosales 2006). In contrast to LULAC's embrace of American values, *El Congreso* worked to preserve Latino culture (Rosales 2006). These views were seen as radical during an era emphasizing the Communist threat, and *El Congreso* faced numerous challenges, including FBI surveillace. Despite goals for national expansion, the organization was unable to grow beyond local chapters, and a major meeting planned for 1939 ultimately did not take place, signaling the group's subsequent decline (Rosales 2006, García Bedolla 2014).

Another major organization to emerge during this time period was the American GI Forum (AGIF), established after World War II to fight for the rights of returning Latino veterans. Similar to LULAC, the group strategically emphasized Americanism, opting to exclude any reference to Mexico in their name and using the American flag in their logo (Ramos 2014). Because the group was comprised of soldiers who had fought on behalf of the U.S., their patriotism could not be questioned; while their early activism focused specifically on veterans' rights, the organization soon expanded their work into areas including educational access and civil rights.[24]

The emphasis that LULAC, AGIF, and other early organizations placed on being American foreshadowed the message of the 2006 protests, when organizers once again mobilized around the theme that Latinos are American. A century later, this revived message of inclusion was extended to a much broader population: citizens, noncitizens, and even the undocumented. First, however, Latino activism would travel down a far different path, emphasizing cultural nationalism and ethnic differences with the Anglo majority.

1960s–1970s: The Rise of Cultural Nationalism

Latino mobilizing in the 1960s was influenced by the 1965 Immigration Act as well as other major national political events. Within the context of the civil rights movement, important legal milestones included the

1964 Civil Rights Act, which prohibited discrimination on the basis of race, color, or national origin, and the 1965 Voting Rights Act, which was designed to protect the rights of minority voters. These legal victories coincided with the emergence of identity-based social movements within a number of minority communities.

By the 1960s, LULAC had achieved a number of significant legal accomplishments.[25] However, still facing discrimination despite these advances, many Latinos grew increasingly frustrated with the organization's emphasis on Americanism and assimilation. Turning to the civil rights movement for new inspiration, the rhetoric of Latino organizations also began to shift. In particular, the black nationalist movement, with its emphasis on separatism, racial pride, and national identity, helped to guide a new generation of activists. The Chicano and Puerto Rican nationalist movements that emerged during this period stood as a counterpoint to earlier Latino organizations. In contrast to their predecessors, these organizations emphasized difference rather than similarity with the dominant US culture.

CHICANISMO AND THE UNITED FARM WORKERS

In the 1960s and 1970s, the Chicano movement developed around the ideology of cultural nationalism, or *Chicanismo*, which emphasized that Mexicans are united by a shared historical struggle and indigenous past. Drawing on the literary, visual, and performing arts, *Chicanismo* helped unite different segments of the Mexican American community, including activists, cultural figures, and intellectuals (García 1997). Diverse in membership and scope, a number of organizations emerged across the southwestern United States under the umbrella of *Chicanismo*, focusing on a range of issues related to the community's fight for social justice.

As Barreto, Manzano, Ramirez et al. (2009, 747) explain, in contrast to more recent Latino advocacy, the Chicano movement focused "not on Latinos as an immigrant group but rather as an ethnic minority suffering from institutional neglect and systematic exploitation."[26] Some organizations within the Chicano movement even went as far as advocating for the physical separation of races, arguing that Mexican Americans had distinct needs and interests (Marquez 2001).

Yet, even as members of the Chicano movement sought to unite the Mexican American community and strongly emphasized preservation of Mexican culture, members of the movement did not embrace the fight for undocumented immigrants for many years. This division within the Latino community represents an example of "secondary marginalization," in which elites of a marginalized group prioritize the interests of dominant group members and neglect or "make invisible" issues that affect the most vulnerable group members (Cohen 1999, 27).

The work of another prominent group during this time further illustrates this trend. Union organizers César Chávez and Dolores Huerta collaborated in the early 1960s to form the United Farm Workers Organizing Committee (UFWOC), which led widely publicized strikes to improve conditions for migrant workers in California. Chávez and Huerta participated in the 1965 Delano grape strike, helping to unite Filipino and Mexican farmworkers. In 1966, the UFWOC initiated the *perigrinacion*, or pilgrimage, a 300-mile march across California to bring attention to the low wages paid by grape growers. These efforts extended into a nationwide boycott of table grapes spanning four years, ultimately resulting in significant concessions by grape growers that improved both the salary and the working conditions of farmworkers (for more on these events, see Shaw 2008 and Ganz 2009). Yet, even as the UFWOC fought for farmworkers, its early advocacy efforts were largely on behalf of legal immigrants. Indeed, for much of his advocacy career, Chávez, a third-generation immigrant, strongly criticized undocumented immigration, which he saw as a threat to the efforts of US workers seeking better pay and working conditions (Ferriss and Sandoval 1998; Gutiérrez 1995).

In addition to immigration, another line of division developed around gender. In the early 1970s, a Chicana feminist movement emerged, emphasizing themes of nationalism as well as gender inequality (Garcia 1989). Although significant diversity existed within this movement, in general, Chicana feminists fought against what they perceived to be oppression and exploitation within the Chicano movement and mobilized around issues including women's employment, income, and childcare (Garcia 1997; NietoGomez [1976] 1997). Further highlighting intragroup divisions, conflict arose between Chicana feminists and women who were "loyalists" to the Chicano movement (for details, see Beltrán 2010). The rise of the Chicana feminist movement underscores gender as another important cleavage within the Latino population.

By the beginning of the 1970s, younger members of the Chicano movement began to push more senior leaders to support immigrant rights. Chicano organizations began openly advocating for undocumented immigrants for the first time in the mid-1970s (Gutiérrez 1995; Tichenor 2002). After decades of activism by Mexican American organizations, this new position represented a decisive move away from the more exclusive organizing of years past.

PUERTO RICAN NATIONALISM

The 1960s also marked *el Nuevo Despertar*, or the "New Awakening," of Puerto Rican nationalism. Given the island's unique status as a US commonwealth, the theme of Puerto Rican independence featured prominently in Puerto Rican social movements of this period, with activists seeking self-determination and liberation of Puerto Ricans both on the mainland and on the island.

As with the Chicano movement, the Puerto Rican nationalist movement emphasized ethnic pride and identity, highlighting various aspects of cultural heritage. The movement also had a distinct socialist message, protesting the exploitation of their people and culture by US "colonizers." Although the broader Puerto Rican nationalist movement included a number of groups, by far the most widely known and active of these organizations was the Young Lords Party, which modeled itself on the Black Power movement (Beltrán 2010). Founded in Chicago, the organization had active groups in New York, New Jersey, Pennsylvania, Connecticut, and the island of Puerto Rico as well as ties to Massachusetts, Ohio, and Michigan. Nationally, the Young Lords Party provided a range of social services for the Puerto Rican community. In contrast to the efforts of LULAC and earlier movements to "Americanize" Latinos, the Young Lords also taught Spanish and Puerto Rican culture classes, designed to help participants embrace their distinct Puerto Rican identity (Melendez 2003).

Similar to that of the Chicano movement, throughout the 1960s and 1970s, the message of Puerto Rican national pride was emphasized in a variety of formats. Although the Chicano and Puerto Rican nationalist movements did not encompass all of the views within these communities, the emphasis they placed on Mexican and Puerto Rican culture as well as the Spanish language marked a significant departure from the assimilation frame that dominated Latino organizing in the first half of the twentieth century.[27] Instead, these organizations shifted their strategy to one of "playing the ethnic card," in which participants embraced differences rather than seeking to blend into the dominant culture.

1980s: Playing the Pan-Ethnic Card and Seeking Sanctuary

Although civic organizations in the 1960s and 1970s mobilized by "playing the ethnic card," a confluence of forces began to refocus this narrative toward the "pan-ethnic card." By the late 1970s, the Southwest

Council of La Raza, a Chicano group established a decade prior, broadened its focus, eventually transforming into the National Council of La Raza (NCLR). The NCLR became the first national Latino organization to represent Puerto Ricans, Mexican Americans, and Cuban Americans, advancing pan-ethnic interests at the federal level (Mora 2014).[28] During this period, the federal government and the private sector also worked to promote a pan-ethnic category (Mora 2014; Rodriguez 1999).

By this time, Latino organizations had largely embraced the cause of unauthorized immigrants. However, the issue did not inspire the same type of mobilization that it has in contemporary politics. Although the 1986 IRCA contained major changes to US immigration policy, nationally, there was little public mobilization of Latinos surrounding this policy debate. The lack of a Latino response to this legislation contrasts starkly with the unprecedented protests of 2006. NCLR's response to the 1986 bill exemplified the ambivalence that many Latinos felt about the proposal. Although the group declined to support the proposal, a spokesman acknowledged it was "probably the best immigration legislation possible under current political conditions" (Pear 1986c).

During this time, organizing around Latino issues also acquired a new focus. As described above, at the same time that immigration reform was debated nationally, a separate battle was being waged over the fate of hundreds of thousands of Central American refugees fleeing violent wars in their home countries. In response, Latino organizations developed on another front, with the emergence of the sanctuary movement. This movement was led by religious organizations and social activists united to provide safe communities for Central American asylum seekers (Coutin 2000). This specific focus distinguished these groups from other Latino civic organizations. Activists of this era engaged in civil disobedience against President Reagan's policies in the region (Bloemraad, Voss, and Lee 2011), with protesters building transnational ties and collaborating closely with the religious community.

The Proposition 187 Debate: Mexican Flags and the Nativist Backlash

The next big push in Latino organizing occurred in response to the 1994 debate over Proposition 187 in California. This proposal was a popular referendum, meaning that California voters cast ballots to decide whether to enact it. In the final months before the vote, Latino students spearheaded much of the activity against Proposition 187, organizing petition drives, operating phone banks, and leading highly visible protests. By some accounts, in Los Angeles alone, an estimated seventy thousand people marched in the streets against the proposal (Gutiérrez 1999). During the California protests, many advocates returned to nationalistic messages. Participants carried signs in Spanish and widely displayed flags of Mexico as well as other Latin American nations. Some of these events also demonstrated a fusion of cultures; for instance, at one protest in Los Angeles, participants sang a mariachi-style rendition of "The Star-Spangled Banner" (McDonnell and Lopez 1994).

After the events, many newspapers published letters to the editor that criticized the predominance of Spanish words and foreign symbols at these events and particularly the prominence of the Mexican flag (Gorman 2006; Gutiérrez 1999; Miller 1998). Even many opponents of Proposition 187 later conceded that the protests were counterproductive, arguing that the pervasiveness of the Mexican flag "scared" undecided citizens into supporting the proposition at the voting booth, the result of a backlash against these foreign symbols (Martin 1995).

This critique would resurface following some of the early protests in 2006 in which Mexican flags were prominent. The 1994 backlash in California presented a clear warning for subsequent Latino leaders; invoking the electoral victory of Proposition 187, protest organizers in 2006 sought to refocus around a pro-American message.

The 1994 events also reinforced other divisions within the Latino community. Echoing the position of Mexican American activists from nearly a century before, in a political context in which immigrants were stigmatized, many established, US-born Latinos sought to distance themselves from newer arrivals (García Bedolla 2005). This "selective dissociation" underscores that when immigration issues emerge at the forefront of political debate, areas of fissure appear in Latino opinion upon several grounds (García Bedolla 2003).

1996 Reforms and Latino Unity

As the opening quote to this chapter describes, in response to Republican proposals and rhetoric about immigrants in 1996, in October of that year, thousands joined in the Latino and immigrants' rights march on Washington, DC. This event, the first major Latino protest in the nation's capital, was organized by the National Coordinating Committee for Citizenship and Participation, also known as *Coordinadora '96*. This network of organizations first developed to fight Proposition 187, but later spanned across the United States.

The 1996 protest emerged in response to the increasingly polarized congressional debate over IIRIRA, with participants calling for an end to discrimination against Latinos. In line with the broader goals of *Coordinadora '96*, protesters also advocated for a wider range of reforms, including increased legal protections for agricultural and domestic workers, a higher minimum wage, maintenance of affirmative action programs, and an amnesty program for undocumented immigrants arriving in the United States prior to 1992 (Milloy 1996).

The event began with a protest march from Malcolm X Park down to the Ellipse, with participants chanting in Spanish, "We are here; we're not going away" (Constable 1996) and "United, we will never be defeated" (Eisenstadt 1996). Protesters arrived from around the country, with crowd estimates ranging from 25,000 to 100,000 (Gonzalez 1996). Once again, the event featured an adaptation of patriotic symbols, as the rally began with a choir singing "The Star-Spangled Banner" in Spanish. Attendees ranged from longtime legal residents carrying US flags to more radical students carrying Mexican flags and even banners of the Mexican Zapatista rebel army (Constable 1996).

Many participants spoke of their opposition to Governor Wilson and House Speaker Newt Gingrich (R-GA) for their attacks on immigrant rights. Overall, however, protesters and speakers emphasized that Latinos must end intraethnic division and promote pan-ethnic unity (Holmes 1996). In addition to Geraldo Rivera, Congresswoman Nydia Velázquez (D-NY), who was born in Puerto Rico, and Congressman Ed Pastor (D-AZ), president of the Congressional Hispanic Caucus, asserted that Republican rhetoric had united Latinos, with Pastor emphasizing that Latinos are one family regardless of national origin (CSPAN 1996). These events are consistent with scholarly arguments about the emergence of a pan-ethnic identity in the face of political adversity and discrimination (Padilla 1985). The protests were framed around Latinos' minority status, and the importance of pan-ethnic unity and strength.

In contrast to these events, more recent Latino activism has largely been characterized by a shift away from the messages of difference that have dominated social movements for the past half century. Instead, similar to the pro-American messages advanced by LULAC and other early Mexican American organizations, in the spring of 2006, Latino leaders and Spanish-language news personalities consciously returned to a frame emphasizing inclusion and patriotism. Yet, whereas membership of earlier groups was limited to US citizens, more recent activists asserted that Latinos—native born, immigrant, and even undocumented—all had a stake in this identity claim. The remainder of this book explores this claim and its varied consequences.

Opposition to H.R. 4437: The Spring 2006 Protests

The Sensenbrenner Bill (H.R. 4437) passed the House of Representatives in December 2005. In February 2006, hundreds of Latino leaders and activists first convened in Riverside, California, to coordinate action against the proposal (Bloemraad, Voss, and Lee 2011). By the time the Senate moved to consider its version of an immigration bill that spring, a prolonged series of protests was already underway. The protests quickly catapulted across the United States.[29] In all, somewhere between 3.5 and 5.1 million people, mainly of Latino descent, took to the streets to protest the provisions of H.R. 4437 (Barreto, Manzano, Ramirez et al. 2009; Bloemraad and Trost 2008).

Although Latinos are certainly not the only group affected by the immigration debate, the 2006 protests were largely a Latino affair. Asian Americans represent the second-largest immigrant group in the United States, and H.R. 4437 also would have affected millions of individuals from that community. Yet, although some Asian Americans mobilized around H.R. 4437, overall, their participation in the 2006 protests was far lower than that of Latinos, largely because of the Latino-specific framing of these events (Rim 2009; Zepeda-Millán 2014).

The protest movement began on the East Coast, with three early demonstrations in February of 2006 (for a chronology of the protests, including location, date, and crowd estimates, see Appendix C, Table C.2). By March, the movement began to grow in earnest; according to a database of protests compiled from newspaper accounts by Bada, Fox, Zazueta et al. (2006), nearly seventy protests occurred that month alone. One early, well-attended gathering in Chicago had an estimated 100,000–300,000 participants, whereas attendance estimates at a Los Angeles protest on March 25 ranged from 200,000 to 1 million (Félix, González, and Ramirez 2008).

Across the United States, the National Day of Action for Immigrant Justice, or *La Marcha*, was planned for Monday, April 10. Beginning on

Sunday, April 9, and continuing through the next day, rallies occurred in an estimated 120–140 cities (Pineda and Sowards 2007). These events marked an unprecedented mobilization of immigrants, primarily Latino, across the nation, demonstrating an unexpectedly high level of organization within this community (Cordero-Guzman, Martin, Quiroz-Becerra et al. 2008; Martinez 2011; Pantoja, Menjívar, and Magaña 2008). The final large day of coordinated action occurred on May 1, when an estimated seventy protests took place across the United States, from Anchorage, Alaska, to Boston, Massachusetts. As part of the "Day without Immigrants" demonstrations, participants skipped work and school and vowed not to make any purchases for twenty-four hours. The selection of May Day, or International Workers' Day, was designed to draw attention to both immigrants' rights and workers' rights issues (Heiskanen 2009).

In March, the early demonstrations were generally concentrated in areas with high Latino populations. By April, the protests spread across the United States, even expanding to areas where the proportion of Latinos was quite low. Indeed, the extensive reach of the demonstrations illustrates the growing geographical diversity of Latino immigrants. The protests quickly spread far beyond traditional immigration centers to new host communities across the United States (Bloemraad, Voss, and Lee 2011; Massey 2008), with Latinos in new immigrant destinations equally as likely to participate as those in more established communities (Benjamin-Alvarado, DeSipio, and Montoya 2009). By May, the protests began to taper off, with the number of events resembling those of March more than April.

As the protests evolved, so did their message. Many March protests featured Mexican flags or a combination of Mexican and US flags. By April, these images had been supplanted. Instead, organizers reframed these events, emphasizing that Latinos are American and urging participants to demonstrate their patriotism.

From Mexican Flags to American Flags: Framing, the Press, and the 2006 Protests

A key part of my theoretical argument is that the patriotic framing of the 2006 events led Latinos to *feel* more patriotic. How did the frame of these protests evolve to emphasize that Latinos are American? Research on framing emphasizes that frames emerge out of an iterative process, underscoring the interplay between social movements, political elites, and the media. In this case, both English- and Spanish-language media played a significant role in this shift.

Many early protests featured a preponderance of Mexican flags and images. These events were widely criticized in the English-language press (see, e.g., Epstein and Sterngold 2006; Hendricks and Garofoli 2006). For example, following the March 25 protest in Los Angeles, an op-ed in the *San Francisco Chronicle* called on demonstrators to "Forget the Mexican Flags" (Navarrette 2006); a similar message was echoed in the editorial pages of the *New York Times,* the *Omaha World-Herald,* and beyond (Chavez 2006; Pineda and Sowards 2007, "The Power of Symbols" 2006). At a March 25 demonstration in Denver, Colorado, protesters also brought both Mexican and US flags, carrying signs in Spanish and English. Following that protest, opponents portrayed marchers as "anti-American." After these early events, both locally and nationally, organizers realized that they needed to retool their message (Martinez 2011).

In April, by the time the wave of mass protests began in earnest, organizers had refined their framing, coalescing around a patriotic narrative. At events across the United States, marchers were specifically instructed to emphasize being American, underscoring their loyalty to the United States. Two mantras highlighted this new theme: "We Are America" and "Today We March, Tomorrow We Vote." As hundreds of thousands of protesters assembled throughout the country, organizers distributed US flags to participants, explicitly asking them to leave their Mexican flags at home. In Washington, DC, for instance, during a rally that lasted more than three hours, protesters were guided in the pronunciation of the "Pledge of Allegiance" and repeatedly chanted, "USA, USA" (Epstein and Sterngold 2006). More than a dozen Latino organizations also united under the banner of the We Are America Coalition.

Spanish radio personalities are widely credited with building popular support for the protests. In general, Latinos listen to radio more than any other news source, and Spanish radio stations have become increasingly pervasive in recent years (Ramírez 2013).[30] In Chicago, deejay Rafael Pulido (*el Pistolero,* or the Gunman), actively promoted the March 10 protest. Likewise, weeks before the Los Angeles protests, popular radio hosts such as Renán Almendárez Coello (*el Cucuy,* a mythical character roughly translated as "the Boogeyman")[31] and Eduardo Sotelo (*el Piolín,* or Tweety Bird) enthusiastically promoted the events on air.

In Los Angeles, Sotelo also spearheaded the formation of the March 25 Coalition, an organization of more than a dozen rival deejays collaborating to mobilize Latinos for the March 25 protest in Los Angeles. The coalition was credited with driving the unexpectedly large crowds at this event (Watanabe and Becerra 2006) as well as subsequent protests across the country (Starr 2006).[32]

The Spanish-language media also promoted and reiterated this patriotic frame. They encouraged protesters to be peaceful, clean up after themselves, and bring US flags to events (Navarro 2006). In an interview with the *Los Angeles Times* at the end of March, Sotelo explained, "We wanted them to show that we love this country. Bringing the U.S. flag, that was important. There are so many people who say, 'I'm glad my parents came here and sacrificed like they did for us'" (Watanabe and Becerra 2006). Sotelo's comments suggest that this framing was both strategic and heartfelt. *La Opinion*, a Spanish-language newspaper based in Los Angeles, ran an editorial in support of the protests In urging its readers to participate, the paper noted, "We cannot forget the counterproductive effects that national flags had in the historical march against Proposition 187. This was skillfully used by critics to delegitimize that protest" (2006, quoted in Baker-Cristales 2009). Event organizers and Spanish-language media personalities both emphasized that Latinos were not a Mexican or Hispanic "other," as movements of previous decades had suggested. Rather, Latinos represented another face of "America." These efforts continued through the May 1 "Day without Immigrants" events, referred to by many deejays as the "Great American Boycott" (Félix, González, and Ramirez 2008).

Religious organizations were also active in building support for the protests, and likewise, for their emphasis on the "We Are America" frame. At one rally in Los Angeles, for instance, Cardinal Roger Mahony asked those carrying flags from other countries to roll them up so that only US flags were visible (Chander 2007). As these efforts reflect, the message of the protests followed in the path of Mexican American social movements from a century before, highlighting US symbols to demonstrate solidarity with the majority. However, this time organizers sought to appeal to a much wider constituency, including citizens, noncitizens, and even those without legal status. This approach was highly effective in building non-Latino support for the protests; existing research finds that the most successful frames of the marches emphasized core American values, family, and work, whereas appeals emphasizing pride in one's country of origin or even human rights issues were widely perceived to be too "foreign" (Bloemraad, Voss, and Lee 2011, 31; see also Wright and Citrin 2010). The remainder of this book explores the effects of these protests on the Latino population.

Conclusion

By examining key developments in contemporary immigration policy, this chapter presents important background about the history and politics that led to the 2006 debate over immigration reform. I also explore the distinct experiences of the five major Latino national origin subgroups, highlighting differences in the ways that members of these subgroups are affected by the immigration policy debate.

The final part of the chapter examines the changing identity frames advanced by Latino social movements over time. In the early twentieth century, activists fought discrimination by framing their movement in a way that emphasized similarity with other Americans. This movement, however, was limited in both scope and constituency, representing primarily middle-class Mexican American citizens. Over time, and in response to the politics of the day, the message of Latino groups shifted. In the 1960s, spearheaded by the Chicano and Puerto Rican nationalist movements, these organizations emphasized national difference. By the 1990s, in response to a contentious immigration debate, movement organizers shifted their frame once again, highlighting Latino unity.

The spring 2006 events represent a marked shift away from these frames of difference. Indeed, when millions of people took to the streets to protest immigration reform, the frame shifted back to similarity. Latino activists and Spanish-language radio personalities emphasized that Latinos are among the many faces of America, highlighting core American values and symbols. Yet, in contrast to the exclusive organizations of the early twentieth century, this time, activists fought for the rights of undocumented immigrants rather than established citizens. The identity claim of Latinos being American extended even to this highly marginalized population.

My politics-to-identity theory asserts that the 2006 protests, and their patriotic frame, were well positioned to shape broader ideas and attitudes within the Latino population. Yet, this chapter also outlines political cleavages within this heterogeneous population based on national origin, level of acculturation, and to a lesser extent, gender. I suggest that the immigration policy debate is likely to have varied salience based on these categories. Chapter 4 examines this claim by testing whether these cleavages materialize in individual attitudes toward immigration policy and whether intragroup differences persist after the 2006 events.

4 | The Immigration Paradox

Latino Policy Priorities and the Limits of Pan-Ethnic Unity

> *Immigration is not the only issue on which Hispanics or Asians vote.*
> *But it is a gateway issue. Republicans have much in common with*
> *immigrants—beliefs in hard work, enterprise, family, education,*
> *patriotism, and faith. But for their voice to penetrate the gateway,*
> *Republicans need to cease being the obstacle to immigration reform and*
> *instead point the way toward the solution.*
> —Former governor Jeb Bush (R-FL) and Clint Bolick, vice
> president for litigation at the Goldwater Institute, June 2013

In the summer of 2013, in an effort to persuade their Republican colleagues to act on comprehensive immigration reform, former governor Jeb Bush and Clint Bolick penned an op-ed in the *Wall Street Journal* in which the above quote appeared (Bush and Bolick 2013). Describing immigration as a "gateway issue," Bush and Bolick contend that in order to connect with Latino and Asian American voters on any other issue, immigration reform must first be addressed.

Since the early 2000s, the immigration policy debate has become increasingly divisive, as has the use of anti-Latino rhetoric (Chavez 2008; Gimpel and Edwards 1999; Wong 2006). In response, some scholars and pundits have argued that this shift in tone would unite all Latinos. This claim was particularly common following the 2006 immigration protests, in which millions of Latinos across the United States took to the streets to demonstrate their opposition to H.R. 4437.

Yet, the perceived primacy of the immigration issue appears at odds with the background presented in Chapter 3. Indeed, only since the 1970s have Latino organizations mobilized around questions related to immigration reform, and significant variation exists in the extent to which Latinos are affected by this political debate. For instance, later-generation Latinos, including individuals with parents, grandparents, or other ancestors born in the United States, are much less likely to be personally affected by any policy changes. As Chapter 3 describes, although some national origin groups have large undocumented populations, for other groups (for instance, Puerto Ricans and Cubans), legal status is virtually a nonissue. Moreover, over the past few decades, Latinos have consistently emphasized that education, the economy, and health care—not immigration reform—are their primary policy concerns (Rouse 2013). Yet, as Bush and Bolick suggest, the ongoing debate over immigration policy is uniquely poised to shape the political attitudes and opinions of some community members. This chapter examines this "immigration paradox," with a particular focus on the variation that underlies it. Specifically, I examine differences in Latino attitudes toward immigration policy, establishing the varied salience of this issue.

Consistent with the differences outlined above, existing scholarship finds variation in Latino attitudes toward immigration reform based on country of origin as well as level of acculturation (Branton 2007; de la Garza, DeSipio, Garcia et al. 1992; García Bedolla 2005; Hood, Morris, and Shirkey 1997; Rouse, Wilkinson, and Garand 2010; Sanchez 2006b). However, most existing research predates the 2006 protests, which marked a significant polarization of the immigration debate. In this chapter, I update our understanding of the variation in Latino attitudes toward immigration policy using two national surveys conducted after these events.

Central to the debate over immigration reform is the question of what to do with the estimated 11 million undocumented immigrants currently living in the United States. Drawing on existing literature, and consistent with the varied histories outlined in Chapter 3, I hypothesize that Mexicans, Dominicans, and Salvadorans will have more liberal attitudes toward immigration reform, whereas Puerto Ricans and Cubans will hold more conservative views. More liberal policy options include an eventual path to citizenship for these individuals, typically following a waiting period, financial penalty, and other requirements. More conservative approaches have traditionally included a guest-worker program for undocumented immigrants instead of a path to citizenship, as well as a range of policies designed to enforce existing immigration law or make the lives of undocumented immigrants so difficult that they decide to leave the United States on their own ("self-deportation"). In the 2016 election, Republican presidential candidate Donald Trump espoused even more extreme policy options, including the mass deportation of all undocumented immigrants living in the United States and the construction of a wall across the entirety of the US-Mexico border. To date, no major national survey of Latinos includes these policy options, so the analysis below focuses only on traditional policy choices. Chapter 8 uses limited data from smaller, more recent surveys about Trump's candidacy to extend some of the arguments outlined below.

Additionally, I evaluate the claim that the 2006 immigration debate and ensuing protests would unite the Latino population. Existing research finds that after the protests, Latinos were more likely to rank immigration as a top policy priority (Carey, Branton, and Martinez-Ebers 2014) and express more support for immigrant-friendly policies, particularly in areas where large numbers of protests occurred (Branton, Carey, Martinez-Eberset al. 2015). Recall, however, that my theory contends that the 2006 policy debate and protests were likely to influence the attitudes and self-identification of certain Latino subgroups more than others. In the second half of this chapter, I evaluate the varied salience of the immigration protests in two ways. First, I discuss data about participant demographics in the 2006 protests to establish distinct levels of participation within the Latino population. Then, taking advantage of the natural experiment that occurred during data collection for the Latino National Survey (LNS), I test whether intragroup differences in attitudes persist even in the wake of these events.

The Immigration Paradox

Despite the frequent assumptions of political pundits, immigration is not Latinos' stated policy priority. In fact, in response to national surveys administered over the past few decades, Latinos have consistently prioritized other issue areas over immigration reform. For instance, in the Pew Hispanic Center's 2014 preelection poll of Latinos, respondents were asked the perceived importance of a range of issues. Education was ranked either extremely important or very important by 92 percent of those surveyed, followed by jobs and the economy (91 percent) and health care (86 percent). By contrast, only 73 percent of Latinos placed immigration reform into one of these two categories (Lopez, Gonzalez-Barrera, and Krogstad 2014). Notably, immigration policy consistently placed fourth, behind these social policy issues, over many years of polling (Pew Hispanic Center 2012).

Yet, as the unprecedented mobilizations of 2006 reflect, immigration holds a singular position in contemporary Latino politics: although not always a stated priority issue, the debate over immigration reform has the unparalleled power to mobilize large facets of the Latino population. By comparison, no similar mobilizations have occurred in response to proposals for universal health care, job creation, or education reform. As Chapter 3 notes, it is only in recent decades that Latino civic organizations have come to widely embrace the issue of immigration reform, making this paradox all the more striking.

What accounts for the unmatched influence of the immigration debate? Many Latinos feel a strong emotional connection to this issue (Rouse 2013), and the polarizing rhetoric over the past two decades has exacerbated such feelings. For many Latinos, politicians' use of language such as "illegals" or "anchor babies" or references to Mexicans as criminals, rapists, and drug dealers (Lapidos 2013; "Full Text" 2015) signifies a lack of respect and cultural understanding toward their community regardless of one's own legal status or ancestral origin. Since 2005, immigration initiatives have also become increasingly expansive, extending far beyond the undocumented population. For instance, H.R. 4437, which inspired the 2006 protests, contained language that would have classified unauthorized immigrants and anyone helping them enter or stay in the United States as felons. The provisions of this legislation would also have subjected any individuals aiding undocumented immigrants to criminal penalties and up to five years in prison. A 2011 survey conducted by Latino Decisions found that an estimated 53 percent of Latinos knew someone who was an undocumented immigrant. These figures suggest that the ramifications of H.R. 4437 would have been far-reaching across this community (Sanchez 2011), broadening the base of opposition to this proposal far beyond the undocumented population.

In large part because of the expanded scope of the immigration debate, many journalistic and scholarly accounts assumed that the 2006 protests would unite all Latinos. Yet, as history suggests, not all Latinos respond to the immigration debate in the same way. Indeed, at both the mass and the elite levels, questions of immigration reform have often highlighted divisions among Latinos. Below, I seek to understand the variation that underlies this paradox.

Variation in Latino Attitudes toward Immigration Policy

In recent years, a growing number of states have considered policies thought to be anti-immigrant. The Latino community's mixed support for these bills demonstrates the extent of intragroup variation in attitudes. For instance, when California voters cast ballots in 1994 on Proposition 187, an initiative that would have prohibited the provision of certain public services to undocumented immigrants, nearly one-quarter of the state's Latino population reportedly voted for the proposal, and a far higher number initially expressed support for the referendum (García 2003). In 2004, Arizona voters considered Proposition 200, which required proof of citizenship for voter registration, photo identification for voting, and verification of immigrant status to receive certain public benefits. About half of that state's Latino voters reportedly supported the initiative as well as several subsequent, related proposals (Leal, Nuno, Lee et al. 2008). Moreover, when Arizona passed S.B. 1070, an expansive law including provisions that would punish individuals who aided undocumented immigrants, polls found that nearly 24 percent of Latinos supported the legislation (Cable News Network 2010).

What accounts for this variation in Latino views on immigration policy? Below, I focus primarily on the idea of an individual's personal distance from the immigration process, which is thought to correlate with more conservative attitudes on immigration policy. Specifically, I operationalize this concept by focusing on national origin as well as level of acculturation. Drawing on intersectionality literature, I also anticipate that Latinas will hold more liberal views on immigration policy than Latino men.

With respect to national origin, as the previous chapter recounts, members of different national origin groups have had widely varied experiences both before and after arrival in the United States. This diversity of experience is likely to influence individuals' understanding of US politics (Wals 2011). Moreover, as a result of a patchwork quilt of immigration, citizenship, and asylum provisions, some national origin groups have fared far differently than others with respect to immigration and citizenship status, leading to significant variation in the percentage of undocumented immigrants by national origin group. For instance, as of 2011, approximately 6,800,000 Mexicans and an estimated 660,000 individuals from El Salvador were living in the United States without legal status (Hoefer, Rytina, and Baker 2012). Based on 2010 US Census estimates, these figures represent approximately 33 percent and 40 percent, respectively, of Mexicans and Salvadorans residing in the United States. Although the percentage of undocumented Dominicans is significantly lower, as noted in Chapter 3, Dominicans have been disproportionately affected by 1996 legal changes that led to significant increases in deportations from the United States. Consequently, Dominican responses to the immigration debate have also been motivated by the desire to enact legal changes about deportation policy (Northern Manhattan Coalition for Immigrant Rights 2009; Zepeda-Millán 2014).

In contrast to these experiences, all Puerto Ricans are born US citizens. Cubans who arrive in the United States have received preferential treatment under US immigration law for decades, such that few Cubans reside in the United States without proper legal status. As a result, I anticipate that the immigration policy debate will have varying importance to members of different Latino subgroups.

Existing research about the relationship between national origin and policy attitudes focuses primarily on Mexican Americans, Puerto Ricans, and Cubans, finding that Mexican Americans have the most liberal policy preferences, whereas Puerto Ricans hold the most conservative views (Branton 2007; Rouse, Wilkinson, and Garand 2010). However, research on the attitudes of members of other ancestral subgroups varies. For instance, some scholars find that Central Americans espouse more liberal policy positions (Branton 2007), yet others reach a different conclusion (Knoll 2012; Rouse, Wilkinson, and Garand 2010).

Based on the different histories outlined in Chapter 3, *I hypothesize that Puerto Ricans and Cubans will hold more conservative views on immigration policy than will respondents of Mexican, Dominican, or Salvadoran ancestry.* In particular, given the unique history of Salvadoran immigrants described in Chapter 3, the relatively recent arrival of many Salvadorans to the United States, and the high percentage of undocumented immigrants within this community, *I expect that Salvadorans will hold the most immigrant-friendly views.*

In addition to national origin, level of acculturation—measured by indicators including immigrant generation and language preference—also significantly influences immigration policy preferences, with more acculturated individuals and later-generation immigrants holding more conservative policy views (Branton 2007; de la Garza, DeSipio, Garcia et al. 1992; García Bedolla 2005; Hood, Morris, and Shirkey 1997; Jiménez 2009; Rouse, Wilkinson, and Garand 2010; Sanchez 2006b). Consistent with this research, *I hypothesize that more acculturated respondents will be less likely to support liberal policy options;* following existing literature, language preference is used as an indicator of acculturation in the United States (Abrajano 2010; Bloemraad 2006; Leal 2007; Portes and Rumbaut 2006). Immigrant generation is also included in multivariate analyses below.

With respect to gender, in the general population, women are more likely to take liberal positions on social issues than are men (Andersen 1997; Shapiro and Mahajan 1986; Swers 2002). Yet, a growing body of research questions whether this gap also persists within minority populations. Some scholars find that Latinas are more liberal than Latino men (Cain and Kiewiet 1985; Welch and Sigelman 1992), but other research suggests that these differences are conditional upon country of origin (García Bedolla, Lavariega Monforti, and Pantoja 2007; Montoya, Hardy-Fanta, and Garcia 2000). Focusing specifically on immigration issues, some scholars finds that Latino men and women hold similar views toward immigrants and immigration policy (Binder, Polinard, and Wrinkle 1997; Hood, Morris, and Shirkey 1997; Knoll 2012; Wrinkle 1991), whereas others conclude that Latinas have either more restrictive (Rouse, Wilkinson, and Garand 2010) or more liberal (Farris 2013) policy attitudes compared with Latino men.[1] *Consistent with research on women and politics in the general population, I hypothesize that Latinas will be more likely to support immigrant-friendly policies than Latino men.*

To test the hypotheses outlined above, I analyze two major national surveys of the Latino population. First, I use data from Phase 1 of the LNS (2006), conducted at a time when the immigration debate was highly politicized. Because the survey contains more than 400 respondents from each of the five largest Latino subgroups (Mexicans, Puerto Ricans, Cubans, Dominicans, and Salvadorans), the data provide an opportunity to compare opinions across nationalities in a way not possible in previous research. Additionally, data collection for the LNS occurred before, during, and after the spring 2006 immigration protests, facilitating the natural experiment used at the end of this chapter. Using this research design, I test whether immigration policy preferences change both within and across groups after the protests (see Chapter 2 for a full description of the research design).

I am also interested in understanding whether Latino attitudes toward immigration policy vary at a time when immigration issues are less politicized. To do so, I examine data from Pew's 2008 National Survey of Latinos (NSL), administered when the immigration debate was no longer at the forefront of the policy agenda. The NSL was conducted by International Communications Research (ICR) between June 9 and July 13, 2008, and includes 2,015 Latino respondents aged eighteen and older. Although this survey also includes respondents from the five largest immigrant groups, sample sizes range from 51 Dominicans to 1,220

Mexicans, limiting the extent to which inferences can be drawn about these groups. Taken together, however, data from the LNS and the NSL demonstrate that in both politicized and nonpoliticized contexts, variation in immigration attitudes persist across Latino subgroups consistent with the hypotheses outlined above.

National Origin, Acculturation, Gender, and Immigration Policy Attitudes

I begin to test these hypotheses by using bivariate analysis to explore variation in Latino attitudes toward immigration policy. The LNS gauges opinions on immigration reform by asking respondents about approaches for addressing the legal status of undocumented immigrants, the most contentious aspect of the immigration reform debate. Specifically, individuals were asked, What is your *preferred* policy on undocumented or illegal immigration? Should there be immediate legalization of current undocumented immigrants, a guest-worker program leading to legalization eventually, a guest-worker program that permits immigrants to be in the country but only temporarily, an effort to seal or close off the border to stop illegal immigration, or none of these? These responses range from liberal to conservative policy preferences.

Figure 4.1 reflects preliminary support for the national origin hypotheses outlined above. In response to this question, Salvadorans demonstrate the most liberal attitudes toward immigration reform, with 62.2 percent supporting immediate legalization for the undocumented population. A majority of Dominicans (51.2 percent) and a plurality of Mexicans (49.2 percent) and Cubans (39.1 percent) also prefer this policy choice. In contrast, just 24.8 percent of Puerto Ricans express support for this solution. A plurality of Puerto Ricans (47.1 percent) advocate a guest-worker program leading to eventual legalization, whereas 15.8 percent support a guest-worker program without a path to citizenship. On the more restrictive end, only a small minority of respondents support the most conservative policy option of closing the border. Notably, however, more Puerto Ricans (12.3 percent) and Cubans (10.3 percent) prefer this option than members of other subgroups.

The Pew Hispanic Center's NSL (2008) asks respondents their opinions on several specific programs intended to enforce current immigration law. These provisions include workplace raids to discourage employers from hiring undocumented immigrants, a requirement that

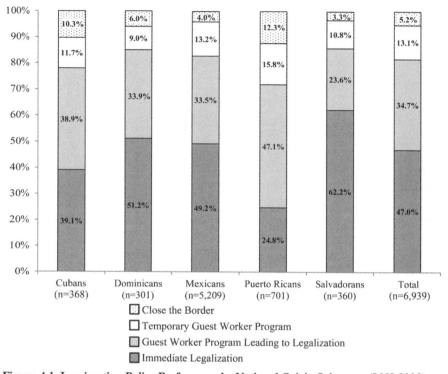

Figure 4.1 Immigration Policy Preferences by National Origin Subgroup (LNS 2006)

The relationship between national origin and immigration policy attitudes is statistically significant, $\chi 2$ (12, N = 6,939) 262.44, p <0.00.

employers check with a federal government database to verify the legal immigration status of any potential employee (e-verify), criminal prosecution of employers who hire undocumented immigrants, and criminal prosecution of undocumented immigrants working without authorization. Table 4.1 presents responses to this series of questions. As these data reflect, across all issues, Puerto Ricans were most supportive of the enforcement measures and were followed by Cubans in three out of four categories. Although the order varies, in general, Mexicans, Salvadorans, and Dominicans demonstrate the least support for restrictive immigration enforcement measures. These data present preliminary support for the national origin hypotheses outlined at the start of this chapter. Across the Latino community, a majority of respondents support liberal immigration policy options. However, compared with

Table 4.1   Percentage of Respondents Approving of Immigration Enforcement
Provisions by National Origin Subgroup (Pew NSL 2008)

Policy	Cubans (n=86)	Dominicans (n=46)	Mexicans (n=1166)	Puerto Ricans (n=145)	Salvadorans (n=60)	Total (n=1,912)
Workplace Enforcement	17.44%	19.57%	16.12%	29.17%	15.00%	18.57%
E-Verify	60.50%	47.73%	37.48%	64.03%	41.38%	43.69%
Employer Prosecution	25.61%	15.22%	21.35%	39.13%	18.97%	24.37%
Prosecution of Undocumented Workers	23.81%	15.22%	19.78%	27.59%	20.34%	21.40%

Note: The n in each column refers to the total number of individuals indicating either approval or disapproval for the relevant provision. The percentage included in the table reflects the portion of respondents expressing support for these provisions, with all other respondents indicating disapproval. For each policy, a small number of respondents in each group did not express an opinion and were omitted from the data presented above. The n included at the top of the table represents the highest n for each national origin group, with slight fluctuation depending on the specific policy. Boldface labels signify that in that row, the relationship between national origin and attitudes toward those enforcement provisions are statistically significant, $\chi^2 < 0.01$.

Salvadorans, Mexicans, and Dominicans, Cubans and Puerto Ricans are less likely to support these policies, suggesting that immigration reform is less salient to these subgroup members.

Latino attitudes toward immigration, and immigrants more generally, also vary based on an individual's level of acculturation or assimilation (Branton 2007; García Bedolla 2005; Knoll 2012; Rouse, Wilkinson, and Garand 2010; Sanchez 2006a). To some extent, this variation might be a result of personal distance from the immigration process. Indeed, as immigration issues become more politicized, some more established immigrants selectively dissociate themselves from the negative stereotypes surrounding newer arrivals (García Bedolla 2003). Existing research employs a range of measures for acculturation, including immigrant generation, self-identification, and language preference. The importance of immigrant generation has been studied at length elsewhere (Branton, Carey, Martinez-Ebers et al. 2015; García Bedolla 2003, 2005; Hood, Morris, and Shirkey 1997), and variables for immigrant generation are included in multivariate models below.[2] Consistent with this book's broader focus on the process of incorporation, however, in the descriptive data that follow, I focus instead on language preference as a measure of acculturation. Traditionally, English speakers have held restrictive views on immigration policy (Binder, Polinard, and Wrinkle 1997; Branton 2007; Hood, Morris, and Shirkey 1997; Leal 2007), with the immigration debate of greater importance to Spanish speakers.

Using the language in which an individual completed the survey as a proxy for language preference, I analyze more recent data to examine differences in opinion among English and Spanish speakers toward a range of immigration-related policies. Both the LNS and the NSL confirm the relationship between this marker of acculturation and Latino attitudes toward immigration policy. Indeed, Figure 4.2 demonstrates substantial variation toward policy options based on language preference, with an estimated 62.2 percent of Spanish speakers preferring immediate legalization for undocumented immigrants, compared with just 21.7 percent of English speakers. Likewise, drawing on data from the

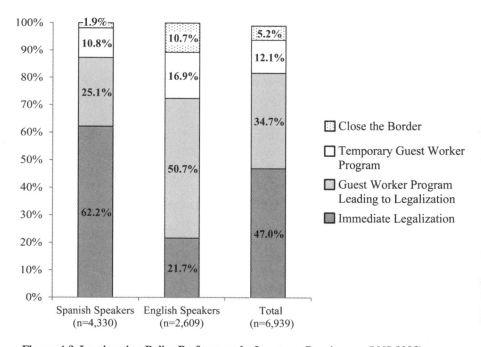

Figure 4.2 Immigration Policy Preferences by Language Dominance (LNS 2006)

The relationship between language preference and immigration attitudes is statistically significant, $\chi2$ (3, N = 6,939) 1.2e+03, p <0.00.

Table 4.2 Percentage of Respondents Approving of Immigration Enforcement Provisions by Language Dominance (Pew NSL 2008)

Policy	Spanish Speakers (n=1,095)	English Speakers (n=829)	Total (n=1,912)
Workplace Enforcement	9.68%	30.48%	18.57%
E-Verify	34.64%	55.07%	43.69%
Employer Prosecution	14.43%	37.15%	24.37%
Prosecution of Undocumented Workers	16.65%	27.54%	21.40%

Note: The n in each column refers to the total number of individuals indicating either approval or disapproval for the relevant provision. The percentage included in the table reflects the portion of respondents expressing support for these provisions, with all other respondents indicating disapproval. For each policy, a small number of respondents did not express an opinion and were omitted from the data presented above. The n included at the top of the table represents the highest n for each category, with slight fluctuation depending on the specific policy in question. Boldface labels signify that in that row the relationship between language preference and attitudes toward those enforcement provisions are statistically significant, $\chi 2$ <0.00.

NSL, Table 4.2 shows that English speakers are considerably more likely to support a range of enforcement policies than their Spanish-speaking counterparts.

With respect to gender, I hypothesize that Latinas will hold more liberal policy attitudes than Latino men. This expectation is consistent with research on gender and policy attitudes in the general population, although this relationship is far less conclusive within the Latino population (Binder, Polinard, and Wrinkle 1997; Farris 2013; Hood, Morris, and Shirkey 1997; Knoll 2012; Rouse, Wilkinson, and Garand 2010; Wrinkle 1991). Consistent with my hypothesis, data from both the LNS and the NSL suggest that Latinas have slightly more liberal attitudes about immigration policy than their male counterparts. For instance, as Figure 4.3 reflects, Latinas are more likely to support immediate legalization for the undocumented population (49.5 percent) than are Latino men (43.9 percent), whereas men are more likely to support conservative policy options. Less variation is evident in the NSL questions about immigration enforcement, shown in Table 4.3. To the extent that distinctions do exist, however, once again Latino men are generally more likely to support the enforcement provisions, consistent with the gender hypothesis.

Collectively, the results presented above indicate that although

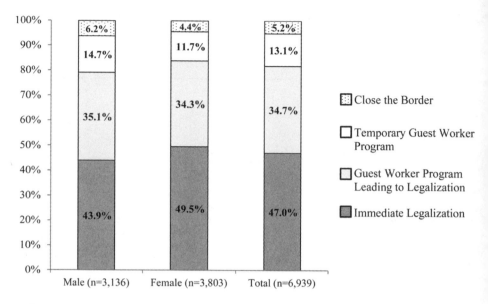

Figure 4.3 Immigration Policy Preferences by Gender (LNS 2006)

The relationship between gender and immigration attitudes is statistically significant, $\chi 2$ (3, N = 6,939) 33.52, p <0.00.

Table 4.3 Percentage of Respondents Approving of Immigration Enforcement Provisions by Gender (Pew NSL 2008)

Policy	Male (n=922)	Female (n=990)	Total (n=1,912)
Workplace Enforcement	21.04%	16.26%	18.57%
E-Verify	43.82%	43.57%	43.69%
Employer Prosecution	26.23%	22.63%	24.37%
Prosecution of Undocumented Workers	22.07%	20.78%	21.40%

Note: The n in each column refers to the total number of individuals indicating either approval or disapproval for the relevant provision. The percentage included in the table reflects the portion of respondents expressing support for these provisions, with all other respondents indicating disapproval. For each policy, a small number of respondents in each group did not express an opinion and were omitted from the data presented above. The n included at the top of the table represents the highest n for each group, with slight fluctuation depending on the specific policy. Boldface labels signify that in that row the relationship between gender and attitudes toward those enforcement provisions are statistically significant, $\chi 2$ <0.05.

immigration is an important issue for a majority of Latinos, it is clearly more salient for some segments of this population than for others. The largest differences appear when examining divisions by level of acculturation, with support for liberal policy options much higher among Spanish speakers than English speakers. Generally speaking, among the national origin groups, Salvadorans are most likely to favor liberal policy solutions, followed by Mexicans and Dominicans. Compared to these subgroups, Cubans and Puerto Ricans have more conservative policy views. Although male and female attitudes are similar overall, slightly higher numbers of Latinas support more liberal policy options. Below, I place these findings within the context of the 2006 immigration debate and test these hypotheses in multivariate analysis.

Immigration Attitudes and the 2006 Protests

At the start of this chapter, I point to an "immigration paradox": even though Latinos rarely cite immigration reform as a priority issue, this policy debate is uniquely positioned to mobilize group members. Throughout this book, I further develop these ideas by arguing that the immigration policy debate and unprecedented protests of 2006 also influenced the attitudes and self-identification of Latinos through the process of policy feedback.

Yet, an important part of my theory emphasizes that these effects are contingent upon the extent to which the immigration policy debate is salient for different segments of the Latino population. Above, I establish intragroup variation in attitudes about immigration policy during two periods: one in which the immigration debate is highly polarized and one in which the issue has left the political spotlight. These findings suggest that the immigration debate is likely to have varied salience for group members, particularly across national origin group and level of acculturation.

Following the 2006 protests, many suggested that these events would unify the Latino community. Below, I extend the previous analysis by testing whether Latino attitudes toward immigration policy converged, or if intragroup variation persisted even after the 2006 protests. I approach this question in two ways. First, I examine who in the Latino community was most likely to participate in these events. Next, using the research design outlined in Chapter 2, I treat the coincidence of the 2006 protests and the data collection for the Latino National Survey as a natural experiment in order to evaluate the effects of these events on Latino attitudes toward immigration policy. I hypothesize that overall, Latinos will hold more liberal policy attitudes following the 2006 protests. Yet, in contrast to expectations that these events will unify the Latino community, I anticipate that intragroup divisions will persist, consistent with the cleavages outlined above.

Who Participated in the 2006 Protests?

Because the coincidence between the LNS and the 2006 protests was unplanned, that survey did not include any questions about whether respondents attended these events. Limited data does exist from other sources, however, regarding the demographics of protest participants. Consistent with the bivariate findings presented above, this evidence indicates that Spanish speakers and Mexicans were most likely to participate in the 2006 events, confirming the varied salience of the immigration reform debate to the broader Latino population.

One set of data comes from a unique survey conducted by the University of Illinois at Chicago's Immigrant Mobilization Project during Chicago's March 1, 2006, protest. At this event, which included an estimated 400,000 to 700,000 protesters, a team of professors, graduate students, and undergraduates interviewed 410 people in an attempt to capture participant demographics (Flores-González, Pallares, Herring et al. 2006). When asked to self-identify, 52 percent of respondents indicated they were Mexican, whereas another 24 percent used a Latino pan-ethnic identifier. Among foreign-born respondents, 81 percent reported being of Mexican origin, with just 10 percent from other Latin American countries (Flores-González, Pallares, Herring et al. 2006).[3]

Although this data might reflect, in part, the large percentage of Mexican Americans that constitute Chicago's Latino community, the predominance of Mexicans in the 2006 protests is widely supported by other research. For instance, Barreto, Manzano, Ramirez et al. (2009) analyze data from a Latino Policy Coalition survey conducted in late April 2006. They find that individuals of Mexican origin, those who speak Spanish at home, and younger respondents are more likely to report having participated in these events than other Latino respondents. Likewise, Abrajano and Alvarez (2010) cite data from a Democracy Corps survey of 984 likely Latino voters conducted between May

18 and June 4, 2006, in which respondents were asked whether they or someone they know participated in the protests. A majority of Mexicans answered yes, followed by Central and South Americans. Puerto Ricans and Cubans were least likely to report participation, with fewer than 20 percent of Cubans indicating that they or someone they knew attended a protest. Spanish speakers and women were also more likely to have participated or known a participant in these events. Focusing specifically on protests in New York City, Zepeda-Millán (2014) finds that the protests were largely a Mexican and Dominican affair, with members of these groups participating at much higher rates than other immigrant groups in the city. Collectively, this information about the demographics of protest participants reiterates support for my hypotheses about the varied salience of immigration issues within the Latino community based on national origin, level of acculturation, and gender.

Did the Protests Change Latino Attitudes about Immigration Policy?

I now turn to the question of whether Latino attitudes toward immigration policy converged after the protests, or whether the differences outlined above persisted even after these events. Although many suggested that the 2006 protests would lead to pan-ethnic unity, the public opinion data presented above as well as the limited data about who mobilized in response to this debate suggest a different story. To test whether Latino attitudes about immigration policy changed—and became more unified—following the 2006 protests, I treat the LNS as a natural experiment, comparing the opinions of respondents interviewed before and after April 1, 2006, on immigration policy options. This approach provides the opportunity to examine Latino attitudes about immigration reform before and after the protests to see whether comparable respondents held similar views, or if Latino attitudes shifted following the 2006 protests.

Consistent with research that suggests Latinos were more likely to express support for liberal policy options after the protests (Branton, Carey, Martinez-Ebers et al. 2015), across the survey, the number of respondents who preferred immediate legalization for unauthorized immigrants increased slightly (from 46.1 percent to 47.6 percent). However, this aggregate figure masks much larger increases in support for legalization *within* different Latino subgroups. For instance, as Figure 4.4

reflects, with the exception of Mexican Americans, support for the most liberal policy option increased by an estimated 10 percentage points or more across all subgroups, including Puerto Ricans.

Yet, despite these increases, significant intragroup variation persists when comparing across the national origin groups. For example, even as support for immediate legalization grew among Puerto Ricans, less than one-third of this subgroup supported this policy option after the protests, compared with more than two-thirds of Salvadoran Americans. Substantial differences also occur when looking at the data by language preference. Among Spanish speakers, support for legalization increased from 57.6 percent before the April protests to 65.8 percent after these events. In contrast, among English speakers, the increase is from 13.6 percent to just 24.8 percent. Again, both groups are more likely to prefer liberal policy preferences after the protests, but large differences remain between these populations, with the percentage of Spanish speakers who support immediate legalization more than double the percentage of English speakers preferring this option.

To test these results more closely, and to examine whether the differences outlined at the start of this chapter persist when control variables

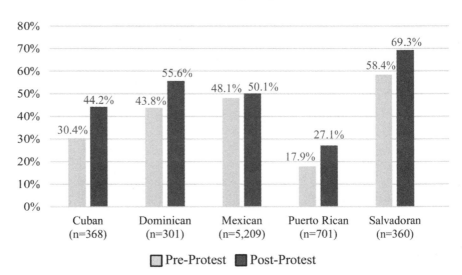

Figure 4.4 Percentage of Respondents Supporting Immediate Legalization of Undocumented Immigrants before and after 2006 Protests, by National Origin (LNS 2006)

The relationship between national origin and immigration policy attitudes is statistically significant both before and after the 2006 protests, $\chi2 < 0.00$.

are introduced, I conducted multivariate analysis on the LNS data. Model 1 in Table 4.4 presents these results for the full sample.

Again, the dependent variable reflects the respondent's preferred immigration policy option, ranging from liberal (immediate legalization of undocumented immigrants = 1) to conservative (secure the border = 4).

Table 4.4 Latino Opinions on Immigration Reform Policy before and after April 2006 Protests (LNS 2006)

	Full Sample (1)	Cubans (2)	Dominicans (3)	Mexicans (4)	Puerto Ricans (5)	Salvadorans (6)
Post-Protests	−0.51***	−0.35**	−0.64**	−0.51***	−0.25	−0.95*
	(0.07)	(0.13)	(0.21)	(0.07)	(0.20)	(0.42)
Female	−0.25***	−0.47*	−0.29	−0.29**	−0.10	0.02
	(0.07)	(0.24)	(0.16)	(0.09)	(0.18)	(0.18)
Spanish Speaker	−1.10***	−0.86**	−0.80**	−1.01***	−1.11***	−1.72***
	(0.09)	(0.26)	(0.24)	(0.08)	(0.18)	(0.32)
Skin Color	0.46**	0.63*	0.25	0.42**	0.72	0.18
	(0.13)	(0.27)	(1.24)	(0.13)	(0.49)	(0.86)
Age	0.84***	1.02***	−2.79*	0.63**	0.80	1.01
	(0.18)	(0.21)	(1.42)	(0.19)	(0.60)	(0.95
Years of Education	0.43	1.49***	−0.34	0.26	0.79	−0.76
	(0.24)	(0.42)	(0.67)	(0.29)	(0.52)	0.52
Household Income	0.34**	0.41	1.26***	0.34*	0.13	0.08
	(0.12)	(0.22)	(0.27)	(0.13)	(0.25)	(0.62)
Immigrant Generation						
Newcomer	0.26	−1.74**	−0.69	0.43**	−0.39	0.35
(in US < 5 years)	0.13	(0.64)	(0.41)	(0.16)	(0.71)	(0.62)
Second Generation	0.51***	−0.32	−0.49	0.67***	−0.11	1.06
	(0.11)	(0.33)	(0.43)	(0.13)	(0.32)	(0.56)
Third Generation	0.74***	−0.03	−1.32	0.98***	−0.01	2.11**
and Above	(0.11)	(0.54)	(0.76)	(0.15)	(0.32)	(0.61)
Pseudo R-Squared	0.08	0.08	0.08	0.09	0.04	0.12
N	5,127	277	220	3,837	544	249

Note: Ordered logistic regression with robust standard errors. The dependent variable is a respondent's preferred immigration policy option, ranging from the most liberal to the most restrictive as follows: 1 = Immediate legalization of current undocumented immigrants; 2 = a guest worker program leading to legalization eventually; 3 = a guest worker program that permits immigrants to be in the country, but only temporarily; 4 = an effort to seal or close off the border to stop illegal immigration. All continuous variables are rescaled from 0 to 1. For the first model, state-level fixed effects are used, with respondents from DC, Maryland, and Virginia combined as one category representing the DC metropolitan area. In subsequent models, the standard error is clustered by state.

*p < 0.05, **p < 0.01, ***p < 0.001.

Because the variable is ordinal, meaning that the distance between the categories is impossible to define, I use ordinal logistic regression. A positive coefficient indicates a more restrictive policy preference.[4]

In addition to the core variables of interest, existing research establishes that other individual-level characteristics are also associated with Latino policy preferences on immigration (Branton and Dunaway 2008; Ellison, Echevarría, and Smith 2005). Drawing on this literature, the models include a number of demographic control variables, including skin color, years of education, income, and age, to test whether the hypotheses outlined above persist even when other factors are taken into account. All of the control variables are coded continuously as described in Appendix A.

Above, I present preliminary support for the hypothesis that the immigration policy debate has varied salience for different Latino subgroups. A growing body of research on intersectionality emphasizes the importance of understanding differences *within* broadly defined groups such as Latino/Hispanic (Beltrán 2010; García Bedolla, Lavariega Monforti, and Pantoja 2007). Consistent with this emphasis, I anticipate that these variables are likely to operate differently across the national origin groups; in other words, I expect that the factors that shape Puerto Rican attitudes on immigration policy, for instance, are likely to be distinct from those that influence Mexican or Salvadoran opinions on this topic. To capture this variation, models 2 through 6 replicate the multivariate model presented in the first column for each of the five largest national origin groups. This approach of limiting the sample to different subgroups of a larger population follows literature on gender in politics, which commonly uses split samples in order to better understand the ways in which differences between subgroups are constructed (Burns, Schlozman, and Verba 2001; Masuoka and Junn 2013; Welch 1977).

The results in Table 4.4 confirm that respondents interviewed after the protests are more likely to support liberal immigration policies than those interviewed before. This result obtains across the full sample and in the split samples for each national origin group. Yet, although the number of Puerto Ricans supporting immediate legalization increases by 10 percentage points after the protests, this difference is not statistically significant in the multivariate analysis.

With respect to gender, the analysis confirms that women are more likely to prefer liberal policy options to a high degree of statistical significance across the survey. Within the different national origin groups, however, gender retains statistical significance among only Cubans and Mexicans. This finding points to the importance of better understanding the interaction between gender and national origin in shaping Latino policy attitudes (García Bedolla, Lavariega Monforti, and Pantoja 2007).

Speaking Spanish is the only variable to reach statistical significance in the full model and across all of the national origin groups. In all cases, Spanish-dominant respondents are more likely to support liberal immigration policy choices. This finding suggests that as respondents acculturate in the United States and gain more distance from the immigrant experience, their attitudes toward immigration policy are likely to shift. In fact, for Salvadorans, who express the strongest support for immediate legalization of undocumented immigrants, being interviewed after the protests and language preference are two of the *only* variables associated with immigration policy attitudes to any degree of statistical significance.

As for skin color, in the survey, respondents were asked to report their own skin color on a scale from 1 (very dark) to 5 (very light).[5] Individuals who indicated having lighter skin were more likely to prefer restrictive policy options. As with the acculturation variables, this finding suggests that the ability to blend in with the dominant culture in the United States—real or perceived—is associated with more conservative attitudes toward newer arrivals. Within the national origin groups, these results hold only for Cubans, who are more likely than other respondents to report having lighter skin, and Mexicans.

The age variable is highly statistically significant, with older Latino respondents less likely to support citizenship for undocumented immigrants. This finding is consistent with existing research that finds older Latinos are more likely to express anti-immigrant attitudes (Knoll 2012). Interestingly, however, although the age variable is significant across all national origin groups, among Dominicans, the relationship moves in the opposite direction, with older respondents supporting less restrictive policies. This anomaly reiterates the varied experiences of the national origin groups as well as the need to better understand the differences within these populations.

Among the general US population, existing scholarship debates whether economic threat or culture and ethnocentrism are more likely to shape attitudes toward immigration policy (Brader, Valentino, and Suhay, 2008; Citrin, Green, Muste et al. 1997; Hainmueller and Hiscox

2010; Hainmueller and Hopkins 2014; Kinder and Kam 2012; Scheve and Slaughter 2001). Focusing specifically on Latinos, Rouse, Wilkinson, and Garand (2010) find no correlation between socioeconomic status and immigration attitudes, whereas Knoll (2012) concludes that native-born Latinos with lower incomes are slightly more likely to hold anti-immigrant attitudes.[6] The findings in Table 4.4 suggest that as socioeconomic status increases, Latinos are likely to adopt more restrictive immigration policy attitudes. When looking at the full sample, individuals with a lower income are more likely to support immediate legalization to a high degree of statistical significance. Among the different national origin groups, however, income retains significance for Dominicans and Mexicans only. Although education does not reach statistical significance in the full sample, when income is omitted from the model, education becomes highly statistically significant. The education variable is also significant among Cubans, with more educated respondents supporting more restrictive policies. Collectively, these results suggest that less-educated, lower-income individuals are more likely to feel kinship with undocumented workers than competition.

As for length of time in the United States, in addition to immigrant generation, I also explore whether recent arrivals hold different policy attitudes, looking separately at respondents who have been in the United States for less than five years. Interestingly, this variable operates differently across the national origin groups. Although the newcomer variable does not reach statistical significance in the full sample, it is associated with more restrictive policy attitudes among Mexicans and more liberal policy attitudes among Cubans, who face less adversity in attaining legal status. This variation reiterates the importance of understanding the relationship between an individual's premigration experiences in shaping postmigration policy attitudes (Portes and Rumbaut 2006; Wals 2011).

Looking more broadly at immigrant generation, compared with non-natives (first generation immigrants), individuals with at least one parent or grandparent born in the United States (second generation or third generation immigrants, respectively) prefer more restrictive policies. However, these generational differences are concentrated primarily among Mexican Americans, reflecting the uniquely long history of this population in the United States as well as the very large sample of this subgroup.

Conclusion

In repeated polls over many years, Latinos have indicated that social policy issues such as jobs, education, and health care are of greater importance to their community than immigration reform. Yet, a paradox exists: even as Latinos say they prioritize other issues, the unprecedented protests of 2006 suggest that the contemporary immigration debate is uniquely situated to mobilize the Latino population. The effects of this debate on Latino mobilization are all the more striking given that only in recent decades have Latino organizations embraced the cause of immigration reform.

As I argue throughout this book, the 2006 policy debate and ensuing protests were also poised to influence Latino attitudes and self-identification, particularly given their patriotic frame emphasizing Latino belonging in the United States. Importantly, however, my theory about the effects of the 2006 protests emphasizes that the process of policy feedback is contingent upon the salience of the immigration policy debate. This chapter establishes the foundation for these arguments by updating our understanding of variation in Latino attitudes toward immigration policy. Using data from the LNS as well as Pew's National Survey of Latinos (2008), I test three hypotheses about immigration policy attitudes. Specifically, I anticipate that Dominicans, Mexicans, and Salvadorans will support more liberal approaches to immigration reform than Cubans and Puerto Ricans. I also hypothesize that less-acculturated respondents and women will be more likely to support these policy choices. My findings illustrate support for these hypotheses in both politicized and nonpoliticized contexts.

Importantly, although this chapter underscores divisions within the Latino community, the survey data presented above indicate that a large majority of group members support policies leading toward the legalization of undocumented immigrants. Likewise, Latino activists of all backgrounds have advocated for policy change.[7] Comparing attitudes across national origin groups, however, the immigration debate is clearly more salient for some groups than for others.

Focusing specifically on the 2006 protests, I also outline variation in Latino responses to the immigration policy debate by looking at data about who participated in these events. Finally, treating the LNS as a natural experiment, I demonstrate that although respondents in general were more likely to support liberal immigration policy options following the 2006 protests, significant intragroup variation in attitudes persisted even after these events. These findings suggest that the 2006 protests, with their unique framing and message of "We Are America," were positioned to influence certain subsets of the Latino community more than others. Chapter 5 extends this analysis by exploring variation in the ways in which Latinos perceive what it means to be American, including whether understandings of this identity category changed after the 2006 protests, while Chapter 8 explores Latino attitudes in the wake of the increasingly hostile rhetoric toward immigrants espoused by Republican presidential candidate Donald Trump.

5 | Defining American

Identification, Political Socialization, and Protest Politics

WE ARE AMERICANS.*
**Just Not Legally.*
—*Time* magazine cover story by Jose Antonio Vargas,
June 25, 2012

On June 22, 2011, Pulitzer Prize–winning journalist Jose Antonio Vargas revealed in a *New York Times* article that for nearly two decades, he had been living as an undocumented immigrant in the United States. In the article, Vargas described his years working for high-profile news organizations including the *Washington Post* and the *Huffington Post* without having legal authorization to reside in the United States. A year later, Vargas appeared on the cover of *Time* magazine along with dozens of other undocumented immigrants, under the above headline. In the image and related article, Vargas sought to assert his "American-ness" despite his lack of legal status. In an effort to "elevate" the debate over immigration policy, Vargas also began an advocacy organization, Define American, to collect stories and testimonials about what it means to be American (Vargas 2011).

As Vargas suggests, different definitions of what it means to be American influence the legal debate over immigration policy by establishing parameters for inclusion or exclusion in the United States. Indeed, throughout history, debates over immigration policy have been defined by differing interpretations of national identity and what it means to be American. Such debates typically focus on ascriptive categories such as race/ethnicity or birthplace (Tichenor 2002). Vargas's story and his organization emphasize that identifying as American has both legal and cultural components. As his example reflects, in the context of the ongoing immigration debate, individuals without formal legal status have repeatedly sought to define themselves as American. Indeed, in the 2006 protests, even undocumented Latinos asserted claims of belonging in the United States.

This chapter explores individuals' understandings of these subjective identity claims. My politics-to-identity theory emphasizes that through the process of policy feedback, protests and their frame can shape the extent to which Latinos in the United States adopt an American identity. Yet, whether an individual sees oneself as American depends in part on the prior question raised by Vargas and his organization: What does it mean to be American in the first place? Here, I examine *intergroup* variation in perceptions of what it means to be American by testing whether Latino views differ from those of African Americans and whites. Drawing on intersectionality theory, I also examine *intragroup* variation by evaluating whether differences exist within the Latino population. In the process, I build on research emphasizing varying perceptions between core (center) and peripheral (marginalized) group members as well as individuals in the near- and far-periphery (Masuoka and Junn 2013; Pickett and Brewer 2005). The final part of the chapter returns to the politics-to-identity theory advanced throughout this book by examining whether the 2006 protests, and their unique frame, influenced Latinos' understanding of this identity category.

The Meaning of "American"

For centuries, scholarship and public discourse have emphasized two primary, competing myths about what it means to be American, one emphasizing ideology and the other focusing on ascriptive features. These two approaches represent rival understandings over the "content," or meaning, of a collective identity (Abdelal, Herrera, Johnston et al. 2006, 2009; Brubaker 1999; Citrin and Sears 2014).

The ideological approach to American identity relies heavily on ideals. From the founding fathers to the present day, being American has consistently been equated with equality of opportunities, freedom, and the pursuit of success. In his early observations of life in the United States, for instance, Alexis de Tocqueville famously observed, "Americans were born equal without having to become so" ([1848] 1969). Discussions of liberalism (Hartz 1950), the American dream (Hochschild 1995), individualism (Morone 1990), and the American creed (Huntington 1981) all emphasize the centrality of ideological pursuits to the character of America. By their very nature, these ideological terms suggest that "American" is an open category to which all individuals may aspire.

Over time, however, American has also been defined by ascriptive features such as skin color, birthplace, language, and religion (Citrin and Sears 2014; Davos and Banaji 2005; Schildkraut 2011; Silber Mohamed 2014; Theiss-Morse 2009). From John Jay to Joseph McCarthy to John McCain, political leaders throughout US history have repeated assertions that the United States is a Christian nation (Theiss-Morse 2009). Debates over whether the United States should accommodate languages other than English in places ranging from classrooms to the ballot box have arisen at the local, state, and national levels (Schildkraut 2005a; Schmidt 2000; Tatalovich 1995). With respect to race and ethnicity, being white remains central to individual ideas about what it means to be American across racial and ethnic groups (Davos and Banaji 2005).

Throughout history, these ethnocultural definitions decisively shaped US approaches toward immigration policy (Smith and Edmonston 1998; Tichenor 2002), with nativists advancing a conceptualization of American based on religious, racial, and other restrictive grounds (Citrin, Reingold, and Green 1990; Higham 1955). The national origin quotas that guided US immigration policy in the early twentieth century specifically privileged white, Anglo-Saxon immigrants over other groups, with the laws of this time emphasizing the centrality of certain ascriptive features (King 2001; Ngai 2004).[1]

Although such considerations no longer guide federal law, ethnocultural definitions of American continue to shape arguments against immigration reform. For instance, in a provocative series of writings, Samuel Huntington (2004a, 2004b) asserts that early settlers in the United States initially defined America with their own ascriptive characteristics: white, English-speaking, and Christian. He argues that the modern-day influx of Latino immigrants threatens these key aspects of US culture; in describing the "Hispanic Challenge," he expresses particular concerns over the persistence of Spanish rather than English, the potential departure from an "Anglo" society, and the "Hispanicization" of the southwestern United States. Ethnocultural arguments about what it means to be American likewise resurfaced repeatedly in the 2016 presidential campaign of Republican nominee Donald J. Trump (Porter 2016; Tesler 2016a; 2016b).

In contrast to ideological definitions of American, which describe an open, accessible category to which anyone might aspire, a focus on ascriptive characteristics suggests that full membership to the group is inaccessible to most minorities and immigrants. In other words, greater emphasis on ascriptive characteristics suggests a restrictive or impermeable definition of American. In contrast, definitions of American that do not emphasize ascriptive traits can be viewed as open, porous, or more accessible to outsiders (Masuoka and Junn 2013; Silber Mohamed 2014).

The extent to which an individual defines American as an open or closed group is closely connected to positions on public policy (Citrin, Green, Muste et al. 1997; Citrin, Wong, and Duff 2001; Schildkraut 2005a) as well as political knowledge and participation (Huddy and Khatib 2007). Indeed, the way an individual defines American can shape policy attitudes and opinions as much as partisanship and ideology (Schildkraut 2011), with perceptions of group boundaries correlating closely to attitudes on immigration policy across racial and ethnic groups (Masuoka and Junn 2013). Below, I explore whether an individual's race/ethnicity correlates with his or her varied perceptions of the boundaries of American.

Intergroup and Intragroup Variation: The Core and the Periphery

Much of our understanding about the ways in which individuals define the boundaries of identity categories is grounded in social identity theory, which emphasizes the importance of differentiation between one's own in-group and a contrasting out-group (Tajfel 1982). As part of this process, individuals perceive similarity with other members of their in-group and seek to distinguish themselves from members of the out-group. Relatedly, self-categorization theory underscores the importance of a "prototype" group member, real or imagined, who exhibits a range of attributes or characteristics common to the group. Perceived proximity to this prototypical person influences whether an individual self-categorizes as a member of that group (Lakoff 1987; Turner, Hogg, Oakes et al. 1987). This research suggests that a strong relationship exists between self-identification and perceived boundaries of an identity category.

Consistent with these theories, focusing on the Anglo population, Theiss-Morse (2009) finds that the more strongly an individual identifies with the national group, the more likely he or she is to establish clear boundaries for membership in that group. In other words, individuals who express high levels of patriotism have more restrictive views about what being American means and are more likely to understand

"American" as an exclusive category associated with ascriptive features. By emphasizing characteristics that outsiders are unlikely to possess, this process enables strong identifiers to more easily distinguish themselves from non–group members. Similarly, Davos and Banaji (2005) find that among white Americans, a positive correlation exists between strongly identifying as American and defining this identity category in terms of being white.

A growing body of research has also begun to examine minority views on what it means to be American. Until recently, such assessments were not possible because of limited data; the General Social Survey, for instance, did not begin to target large numbers of Spanish speakers until 2006. With respect to *ideological* definitions of American, minority groups hold similar views to white Americans (Citrin and Sears 2014; Schildkraut 2011). Yet, the research on minority attitudes about *ascriptive* definitions of American is less conclusive, particularly with respect to the Latino population. Given this gap in the literature, *I advance our understanding of both intergroup and intragroup attitudes about the boundaries of being American and test whether political events influence these definitions.*

Focusing on a range of different potential group memberships, Pickett and Brewer (2005) distinguish between members of a group's "core," or center, and members of the "periphery," or marginalized group members. Because the standing of peripheral members is more tenuous vis-à-vis the in-group, these group members are more likely to emphasize differences between the in-group and the out-group. As a result, marginal group members' "perception of the in-group may differ dramatically from those who are core members. Put differently, the view from the edge of a group may be quite different than the view from the center" (Pickett and Brewer 2005, 103). In order to protect their in-group status, peripheral group members establish stricter boundaries for group membership than core group members do and are more likely to define a group in terms of stereotypical qualities.

Masuoka and Junn (2013) extend these ideas in their analysis of the ways in which members of different minority groups perceive national belonging in the United States. Their account emphasizes the importance of the racial hierarchy, which places whites at the top (core) and other racial/ethnic groups in the periphery to varying degrees, with Asian Americans and Latinos in the middle and African Americans at the bottom, furthest from the core. They test whether a group's standing in the racial hierarchy is consistent with Pickett and Brewer's work, which suggests that marginalized group members will see the boundaries of group membership as less permeable than do those in the core.[2] Consistent with this theory, African Americans, whose status is most marginalized, define American with more rigid ascriptive boundaries than members of other racial and ethnic groups (Citrin and Sears 2014; Masuoka and Junn 2013; Silber Mohamed 2014; Theiss-Morse 2009). As Masuoka and Junn (2013, 98) describe, "Because national identity is a social-group identity, members will associate their own personal characteristics as valuable to being American." In particular, compared with white respondents, African Americans are more likely to emphasize the importance of ascriptive characteristics that group members possess themselves, including being a Christian and being born in the United States.

The analysis below begins by revisiting the comparison between intergroup perceptions of what it means to be American, focusing on whites, African Americans, and Latinos. Specifically, my *intergroup hypothesis* anticipates that, consistent with the racial hierarchy theory advanced by Masuoka and Junn, Latino perceptions of what it means to be American will fall in between those of whites (most porous, meaning respondents are less likely to define American in ascriptive terms) and African Americans (most restrictive, with respondents placing greater emphasis on ascriptive traits).

In addition to distinguishing between the core and the periphery, Pickett and Brewer also differentiate between individuals who reside in the near-periphery, or those in the periphery who are closest to the core, and the far-periphery, or those in the periphery who are most different from core group members. Within the Latino population, our understanding of the differences between the near- and far-periphery has been hindered by limited data. Both Masuoka and Junn (2013) and Schildkraut (2011) use data from the Twenty-First Century American Survey (2004) to examine intragroup attitudes about what it means to be American. Yet, this survey has a limited Latino sample (n = 441), all of whom are US citizens. Moreover, only a small number of respondents completed the survey in Spanish, and these responses are not analyzed separately. As a result, the sample is biased toward Latinos who are most similar to the white population—in other words, closer to the core. Even within this sample, Schildkraut (2011) finds significant variation, with Mexican Americans and foreign-born respondents more likely to emphasize ethnocultural characteristics in their definition of American.

These intragroup differences underscore the need for further study with a larger Latino sample to better understand these distinctions.

My *intragroup hypothesis* further develops this line of research. Although there are many ways that far- and near-periphery could be operationalized within the Latino community, I focus in particular on level of incorporation, using language dominance as a proxy for this concept. I anticipate that *within* the Latino population, less-incorporated group members (i.e., Spanish-dominant respondents, who occupy the far-periphery) will place *more overall importance* on ascriptive categories than more-incorporated individuals (i.e., English-dominant individuals, who occupy the near-periphery). This hypothesis is driven by expectations that, for individuals in the far-periphery, rigid ascriptive categories will evoke feelings of exclusion or separation from the majority group, with American perceived as an inaccessible category. Compared with these group members, among individuals in the near-periphery, I anticipate *more open attitudes* about what defines American, meaning these individuals will be less likely to define American in ascriptive terms.

Mapping national origin onto the concepts of near- and far-periphery is more challenging. Depending on one's national or ancestral origin, a given Latino immigrant will have had vastly different historical experiences prior to arrival in the United States. As previous chapters describe, different subgroups have additionally developed distinct legal and political relationships with the US government, guided largely by federal immigration policy. These experiences also correlate with varied attitudes toward immigration policy, with Puerto Ricans and Cubans holding the most conservative attitudes and Salvadorans expressing the most liberal views (see Chapter 4).

As a preliminary step toward connecting national origin with the concepts of near- and far-periphery, I use these distinct attitudes and experiences as a proxy. Accordingly, I place Cubans, who have received preferential treatment by the US government, and Puerto Ricans, who are born US citizens, in the near-periphery. I anticipate that Mexicans and Dominicans would fall in the center of the periphery, with Salvadorans in the far-periphery. As the third chapter describes, during the 1980s, the US government was involved in El Salvador's bloody civil war, with the conflict resulting in a shift in political identities that persists over time and space (Wood 2003). Refugees who fled to the United States to escape this conflict also faced significant challenges upon arrival. These challenges, combined with the high proportion of undocumented Salvadorans currently living in the United States, contribute to this group's placement in the far-periphery.

I also draw on intersectionality theory as an additional lens for understanding intragroup differences in Latino perceptions of what it means to be American. Intersectionality theory highlights the compounding effects of multiple disadvantages such as race/ethnicity, national origin, class, and gender (Crenshaw 1989; García Bedolla 2007; Hancock 2007a). Because these disadvantages shape and reinforce each other, people who are marginalized in multiple ways have distinct life experiences (Carter, Sellers, and Squires 2002). Consistent with this approach, across national origin groups, I anticipate that characteristics such as immigrant generation, skin color, and socioeconomic status will serve as mediating factors, pushing individuals closer to or further from the core.

Intersectionality theory also suggests that Latinas and Latino men will have distinct understandings of what it means to be American. Similarly, existing research on immigrant incorporation emphasizes the different experiences of Latino men and women (Hardy-Fanta 1993; Jaramillo 2010; Jones-Correa 1998b; Menjívar 2000), indicating that Latinas are less likely than Latinos to self-identify as American (Golash-Boza 2006, Silber Mohamed 2015). These factors suggest that compared with Latino men, Latinas are located in the far-periphery. I test whether these varied experiences translate into more restrictive definitions of what it means to be American among Latinas in comparison to their male counterparts.

As in other chapters, I begin by presenting a bivariate analysis to identify general trends across subgroups. Importantly, however, further variation is likely to exist within subgroups. Accordingly, in multivariate analysis, I include other indicators of incorporation associated with one's placement in the periphery.

At the end of this chapter, I return to the natural experiment begun in Chapter 4 to test the *political events hypothesis*. Recall that my politics-to-identity theory anticipates that the 2006 protests, and their frame of Latino belonging, led to greater feelings of inclusion and political incorporation among Latinos in the United States. Here, I explore whether these events influenced the extent to which Latinos *define* American in ascriptive terms. Consistent with my broader theory, I hypothesize that the protests, and their unique patriotic frame, resulted in more open attitudes about what it means to be American, with respondents interviewed after these events placing less emphasis on ascriptive categories than comparable respondents interviewed before.

General Perspectives on Defining "American": GSS Baseline

As a first step toward understanding Latino perceptions of what it means to be American, I study whether Latinos define this category in the same way as whites and African Americans. To answer this question, I use a combination of data from the General Social Survey (GSS 2004; Davis and Smith 2004) and the Latino National Survey (LNS; Fraga, Garcia, Hero et al. 2006). The GSS is a long-standing national survey that interviews two samples of an estimated 1,500 people on a biannual basis. Ideally, I would have used GSS data collected in the same year as the LNS for the best possible comparison. Unfortunately, however, the 2006 version of this survey did not include relevant questions regarding ascriptive definitions of American. Instead, I use data from the 2004 GSS, which included questions about the importance of birthplace, religion, and language to being American. Specifically, respondents were asked, "Some people say the following things are important for being truly American. Others say they are not important. How important do you think each of the following is?" Respondents were then given a number of characteristics to evaluate, including: to be a Christian; to have been born in America; and to be able to speak English. Race was not included among the list of ascriptive characteristics.[3]

The GSS data allow for comparison between a large population of Anglos (n = 971) and a smaller sample of African Americans (n = 164) and English-speaking Latinos (n = 112).[4] Given the limited Latino sample in the GSS, I supplement this data with responses from the LNS (2006).[5] The large sample size of this survey and the diversity of respondents facilitate a broader examination of what it means to be American for different subsets of the Latino population, providing the opportunity to test hypotheses about the attitudes of far- and near-periphery group members.

Specifically, I focus on four ascriptive features commonly associated with being American: race, religion, language, and birthplace. When respondents place greater emphasis on these characteristics in their definition of American, this suggests a restrictive category more likely to be closed to outsiders. In contrast, respondents who place less emphasis on these characteristics hold a more porous view of what it means to be American, suggesting a category that is open or permeable to outsiders (Masuoka and Junn 2013; Silber Mohamed 2014). Notably, of these four ascriptive categories, race and birthplace are fixed, or impossible for individuals to change, whereas language proficiency and religion are relatively more mutable.

Although an analysis using both ascriptive and ideological definitions of American would have been ideal, unfortunately, questions in the LNS do not lend themselves to the study of American as an ideological category. Moreover, in comparison to ideological definitions of American, beliefs surrounding ascriptive categories are especially consequential for the political and social incorporation of immigrants and their descendants; whether American is described in ascriptive terms is likely to influence the extent to which newcomers feel able to integrate into US society.

To gauge Latino definitions of identity, LNS respondents were asked, "When you think of what it means to be fully American in the eyes of most Americans, do you think it is very important, somewhat important, or not important to: have been born in the United States? speak English well? be white? be Christian?" Responses included not important (1), somewhat important (2), and very important (3). The phrasing of the LNS question is less straightforward than the GSS, encompassing both individual opinions and perceptions of others. Unfortunately, given this wording, it is impossible to know whether respondents are referring to their own description of what it means to be American or a more prescriptive opinion about what being American *should* mean in the eyes of others. Yet, claims of group membership depend upon both an individual's self-perception as well as one's perceptions of the ways in which ascriptive characteristics influence *other people's* categorizations of that group (McClain, Carew, Walton et al. 2009). In other words, a combination of these factors shapes perceptions of identity boundaries, and the phrasing of the LNS question captures both of these aspects. Given the unmatched sample of the LNS, this question represents the best opportunity to study intragroup variation within the Latino population. The similar responses between Latinos in the GSS and the LNS across two out of three ascriptive categories (see Table 5.1) likewise confirm the validity of this measure, despite the ambiguous question phrasing.

Table 5.1 presents a comparison of responses from the GSS and the LNS. As the table illustrates, using raw data from both surveys, Latino

Table 5.1 Percentage of Respondents Emphasizing the Importance of Ascriptive Characteristics for Being American (GSS 2004 and LNS 2006)

Ascriptive Characteristic	GSS, Whites	GSS, Blacks	GSS, Latinos	LNS
Speak English	N=971	N=164	N=112	N=9,834
Very Important	82.2%	90.2%	90.2%	85.0%
Somewhat/Fairly Important	14.5%	7.9%	8.0%	11.0%
Not Important	3.3%	1.8%	1.8%	4.0%
Christian	N=948	N=159	N=104	N=9,834
Very Important	47.3%	75.5%	35.6%	42.2%
Somewhat/Fairly Important	17.2%	6.9%	26.0%	21.9%
Not Important	35.6%	17.6%	38.5%	35.9%
Born in United States	N=961	N=157	N=107	N=9,834
Very Important	55.9%	70.1%	60.8%	44.84%
Somewhat/Fairly Important	22.0%	12.7%	24.3%	25.16%
Not Important	22.1%	17.2%	14.9%	30.00%
White				N=9,834
Very Important				19.1%
Somewhat/Fairly Important				18.9%
Not Important				62.0%

Note: In the GSS, respondents were given four options (very important, fairly important, not very important, not important at all), whereas in the LNS, respondents were given three choices (very important, somewhat important, and not very important). In the table above, the GSS categories "not very important" and "not important at all" have been combined to facilitate comparability between the datasets.

respondents consistently place even more importance on speaking English than do whites. These numbers defy the fears of Samuel Huntington (2004a, 2004b) and other nativists who argue that Latinos in the United States do not wish to learn English.

With respect to being a Christian, Latinos are less likely to think this attribute is "very important" than other groups. Across both surveys, a similar minority of white and Latino respondents think Christianity is *not* important for being defined as American. Comparatively, the very high percentage of African Americans emphasizing the importance of Christianity is consistent with existing research on this topic (Citrin and Sears 2014; Masuoka and Junn 2013; Silber Mohamed 2014; Theiss-Morse 2009).

Turning to birthplace, looking only at the GSS data, African Americans are most likely to emphasize the importance of being born in the

United States, followed by Latinos and then whites. Comparing Latino respondents across the surveys, significant differences are evident, with 60.8 percent of Latinos interviewed in the GSS placing high importance on birthplace compared with 44.8 percent doing so in the LNS. The varied samples in these surveys likely account for much of this discrepancy; whereas a majority of LNS respondents was born outside the United States (64.6 percent), only a minority of GSS respondents was born abroad (30.5 percent). In actuality, the Latino population falls between these numbers, with an estimated 53 percent of adults born outside the United States (Lopez and Taylor 2010).[6] The greater emphasis placed on birthplace by GSS respondents suggests that more incorporated group members (i.e., those in the near-periphery) are more likely to emphasize characteristics that they themselves possess.[7] Although the data from the LNS broaden our understanding of Latino attitudes, the differences between the LNS and the GSS samples highlight the limitations of comparing across different surveys to fully understand intergroup variation.

With the exception of the birthplace question in the LNS, Latino and white respondents demonstrated similar perspectives on what it means to be American, even across surveys. When variation did exist, Latino and white perceptions of American were generally closer to each other than to the views of African Americans. Overall, these findings are consistent with Masuoka and Junn's (2013) theory of a racial hierarchy, reiterating support for the idea that African Americans have a more restrictive understanding of what it means to be American than does the Anglo majority, with Latino views being more ambiguous (see also Citrin and Sears 2014; Theiss-Morse 2009). The similarities between white and Latino attitudes suggest that theories focusing only on the core and the periphery must be more nuanced to accommodate Latino views. The analysis below advances our understanding of these differences by looking at varying attitudes *within* the Latino population.

Divergent Pasts, Convergent Present?

As Chapter 4 demonstrates, more-established Latinos have significantly different attitudes about immigration policy and who should be included in the United States when compared to those less incorporated. Below, I explore whether this variation translates into different understandings of what it means to be American.

The *intragroup hypothesis* emphasizes the importance of placement within the periphery for understanding variation in Latino attitudes about what it means to be American. I anticipate that those in the far-periphery (operationalized as Spanish speakers, respondents from El Salvador, and Latinas) will place greater emphasis on ascriptive categories than group members who are more incorporated into US life. Likewise, I anticipate that members of the near-periphery (in particular, English speakers, Latino men, and individuals from Puerto Rico and Cuba) will generally hold more open attitudes about what it means to be American, with ascriptive features having less significance for this group.

I begin by subdividing the LNS sample to compare attitudes by level of incorporation, national origin, and gender. Using data from both phases of the LNS, Figures 5.1 through 5.3 explore whether variation exists in the extent to which individuals define American in ascriptive terms. The data suggest much similarity among Latinos. However, consistent with the intragroup hypothesis outlined above, a few cleavages do appear. The foremost of these differences is with respect to language preference: across all categories, Spanish speakers were more likely to emphasize ascriptive characteristics than their English-speaking counterparts were. This finding suggests that Spanish speakers are more likely to perceive American as a category impermeable to admission.

With respect to national origin, Salvadoran attitudes about the importance of ascriptive characteristics also demonstrated support for the intragroup hypothesis. Compared with other national origin groups, members of this far-periphery group were much more likely to emphasize birthplace, religion, and language skills in their understanding of what it means to be American and were second-most likely to emphasize skin color.

Given the privileged legal status of Cubans and Puerto Ricans, and the distinctive attitudes that members of these national origin groups have about immigration policy (see Chapter 4), I tentatively placed these groups in the near-periphery. Accordingly, I anticipated that group members would have more porous attitudes about what it means to be American, meaning they would be less likely to emphasize ascriptive characteristics. Figure 5.2 demonstrates mixed support for this hypothesis. Interestingly, differences emerge around the most distinctive features of each population, but operate in different directions, with Cubans more likely to emphasize skin color than other national origin groups and Puerto Ricans least likely to emphasize birthplace. Cuban exiles included only a very small number of nonwhite immigrants

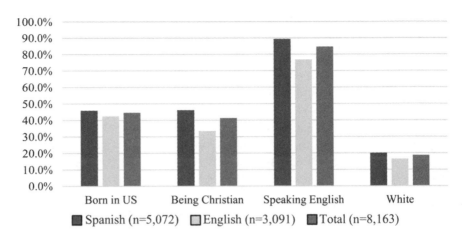

Figure 5.1 Importance of Ascriptive Characteristics for Being American, by Language Preference (LNS 2006)

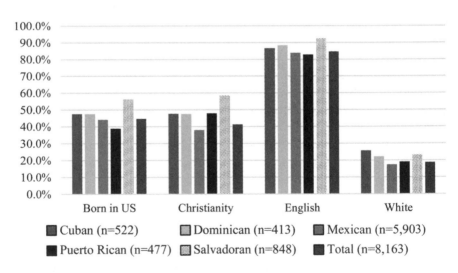

Figure 5.2 Importance of Ascriptive Characteristics for Being American, by National Origin (LNS 2006)

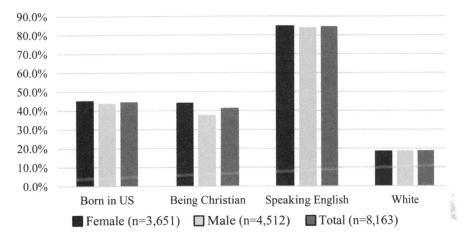

Figure 5.3 Importance of Ascriptive Characteristics for Being American, by Gender (LNS 2006)

prior to 1980, and Cubans in the United States generally have lighter skin than members of other national origin groups (Rieff 1995). Similar to the high emphasis placed by African Americans on Christianity (Masuoka and Junn 2013), group members appeared to place greater emphasis on characteristics they themselves possessed. In contrast, regardless of birthplace, Puerto Ricans are unique in that all group members are granted US citizenship at birth, regardless of birthplace. The relatively low emphasis placed by Puerto Ricans on birthplace suggests that being American means more than a birthright for this population.

Looking at the sample by gender, only minimal differences are evident between Latinas and Latino men across most categories, with women more likely to emphasize being Christian. On one hand, this result is surprising given evidence discussed in Chapter 6 that Latinas are less likely to see themselves as American than Latino men. On the other hand, intersectionality research suggests that gender might be a less strongly held identity, with factors such as language, nativity, and ethnicity likely more important. The multivariate analysis below provides the opportunity to explore these ideas further, testing whether any of the differences described above persist when a range of control variables are introduced. Because the dependent variables are categorical (measured from 1–3, with 3 being most important), ordered logistic regression is employed. To ease in the interpretation of the results, predicted probabilities are included below.[8]

In the models that follow, dummy variables are used for national origin groups. Because Mexicans are by far the largest Latino subgroup in the United States as well as in the LNS, Mexican Americans are used as the reference category. Given the large size and extensive history of the Mexican immigrant population in the United States, research on Latino politics frequently focuses on this subgroup. Using this group as the reference category allows us to test whether the broader Latino population has a comparable perception of what it means to be American. Dummy variables are also included for gender (1 = female, 0 = male) and language preference (1 = Spanish, 0 = English).

In addition to the variables described above, I also test other variables that might be indicators of placement in the near- or far-periphery, including immigrant generation and socioeconomic status. Consistent with the first part of the intragroup hypothesis, I expect that later generation Latinos, in the near-periphery, will be more likely to see American as a permeable category. To measure immigrant generation, respondents are divided into three categories of dummy variables: first generation defined as those born outside of the fifty US states and Puerto Rico, second generation including those born in the United States but with both parents born elsewhere, and third generation and above referring to individuals with at least one parent born in the United States. An additional dummy variable is also included for new arrivals, referring to those who have been in the United States for less than five years. Two measures of socioeconomic status are included: education and income, measured continuously.[9]

I also include control variables in the model related to respondents' personal characteristics. The first of these variables is age. Latinos are the youngest minority population in the United States, with a median age of twenty-seven, compared with forty-one for the white population (Pew Hispanic Center 2009). Within the general population, older Americans define "true American" more narrowly than their younger counterparts, with younger respondents more reluctant to describe American in ascriptive terms (Citrin, Reingold, and Green 1990; Citrin and Sears 2014; Theiss-Morse 2009). Age is measured continuously, with the expectation that among Latinos, younger respondents will also be less likely to define American ascriptively.[10]

Control variables are used for self-reports of skin color (measured 1–5, with 1 being very dark and 5 being very light) and religiosity, measured by attendance at religious services (from 1–5, with 1 being more than once a week and 5 being never). In both cases, I expect that these characteristics are likely to affect responses; consistent with existing findings about African Americans, I anticipate that members of the near-periphery will be more likely to emphasize characteristics they possess that differentiate them from other peripheral group members (Citrin and Sears 2014; Masuoka and Junn 2013). In other words, individuals with light skin will be more likely to emphasize the importance of skin color for being American, and individuals who are more religious will be more likely to emphasize Christianity.

Drawing on literature from African American politics, I employ the concept of linked fate as another measure of being in the far-periphery. Linked fate refers to the perception that one's own life circumstances are connected to that of other group members (Dawson 1994). To measure this concept, respondents were asked how much they believe their fate is linked to other Latinos, with responses ranging from 1 (nothing) to 4 (a lot). Again, consistent with the intragroup hypothesis, I anticipate that respondents who have a high sense of linked fate will have a more restrictive definition of American, placing greater emphasis on ascriptive characteristics.

Table 5.2 presents the results of the multivariate analysis. As expected, compared with English speakers, Spanish-dominant Latinos hold more restrictive views of what it means to be American across three out of four ascriptive categories. These respondents were 23 percentage points more likely to emphasize birthplace, 3 percentage points more likely to emphasize religion, and 9 percentage points more likely to say English skills are very important than were their English-speaking counterparts. These results underscore that those respondents in the far-periphery, who are less integrated into life in the United States, understand American to be a more closed category, placing greater emphasis on ascriptive conditions such as birthplace, religion, and language abilities.

Respondents with higher levels of income and education were generally likely to have less restrictive definitions of what it means to be American. For instance, compared with respondents in the lowest income category, those in the highest category were 8 percentage points less likely to emphasize being born in the United States and 6 percentage points less likely to emphasize Christianity. Similarly, when compared

Table 5.2   Latino Attitudes about the Importance of Ascriptive Characteristics for Being American (LNS 2006)

	Born in the United States	Being Christian	Speaking English	White
Female	0.00	0.04	−0.05	−0.06
	(0.04)	(0.05)	(0.07)	(0.05)
Skin Color	−0.03	−0.02	0.00	−0.02
	(0.02)	(0.02)	(0.03)	(0.02)
Age	**0.07*****	**0.26*****	**0.16*****	**0.06****
	(0.02)	**(0.02)**	**(0.02)**	**(0.02)**
Subnational Groups				
Cuban	0.07	0.19	0.14	**0.48*****
	(0.13)	(0.14)	(0.20)	**(0.14)**
Dominican	0.02	**0.37****	0.35	−0.16
	(0.14)	**(0.14)**	(0.22)	(0.15)
Puerto Rican	**−0.20***	**0.47*****	0.08	**0.25***
	(0.10)	**(0.10)**	(0.14)	**(0.11)**
Salvadoran	**0.35****	**0.56*****	**0.67****	0.11
	(0.11)	**(0.12)**	**(0.20)**	(0.12)
Incorporation				
Income	**−0.18*****	**−0.13*****	−0.06	**−0.08***
	(0.03)	**(0.03)**	(0.05)	**(0.04)**
Years of Education	**−0.03*****	**−0.07*****	−0.01	−0.01
	(0.01)	**(0.01)**	(0.01)	(0.04)
New Arrival	0.04	0.00	**0.32****	−0.14
	(0.07)	(0.07)	**(0.12)**	(0.08)
Second Generation	**0.81*****	0.09	−0.11	−0.07
	(0.08)	(0.08)	(0.10)	(0.08)
Third Generation and Above	**0.72*****	0.13	−0.06	**−0.22****
	(0.08)	(0.08)	(0.10)	**(0.08)**
Prefer Spanish	**0.24*****	**0.19****	**0.71*****	−0.10
	(0.07)	**(0.07)**	**(0.09)**	(0.08)
Linked Fate	**0.11*****	**0.17*****	0.01	**0.10*****
	(0.02)	**(0.02)**	(0.03)	**(0.02)**
Religiosity	−0.02	**−0.32*****	−0.02	−0.02
	(0.02)	**(0.02)**	(0.03)	(0.02)
N	6,401	6,401	6,401	6,401
Pseudo R2	0.02	0.07	0.04	0.01

Note: The unit of observation in an individual respondent. Standard errors in parentheses. Estimation is done using ordered logistic regression, using nationally weighted data from Phase I of the Latino National Survey. Analysis is limited to Cubans, Dominicans, Mexicans, Puerto Ricans, and Salvadorans.

Two-tailed tests, significance levels: *p < 0.05, **p < 0.01, ***p < 0.001.

with the least-educated respondents, those with a graduate or professional degree were 18 percentage points less likely to say birthplace is
very important and 26 percentage points less likely to say Christianity
is very important to being American. Again, individuals closer to the
core were more likely to see American as an open category than one
defined primarily in ascriptive terms. This relationship is consistent with
research on the general population demonstrating that more-educated
adults are more likely to hold multicultural views and less likely to define
American in ethnocultural terms (Citrin and Sears 2014).

With respect to national origin, given the adversity faced by the Salvadoran community in the United States, I placed members of this group
in the far-periphery, with the expectation that they would be more likely
to define American in ascriptive terms. As Table 5.2 reflects, compared
with the reference group (Mexicans), Salvadorans maintained a more
restrictive perspective on what it means to be American in three out of
the four categories. In comparison to the prototypical respondent, Salvadorans were 9 percentage points more likely to think being born in
the United States and speaking English are very important and were 15
percentage points more likely to report that being Christian is very important to being American, with high degrees of statistical significance.[11]
These results support my expectation that members of this far-periphery
group would view the boundaries of American-ness as less permeable.

In the bivariate analysis, I find that Cuban exiles, who historically
have lighter phenotypes than other immigrant groups, also place the
most importance on being white. This result obtains in the multivariate
analysis; compared with Mexicans, Cubans were 6 percentage points
more likely to indicate that skin color is very important to being American. Despite my expectation that members of this near-periphery group
would have more open attitudes, here group members appear more
likely to emphasize characteristics that distinguish them from other peripheral group members.

The results regarding Puerto Ricans demonstrate the importance of
intersectionality in understanding the varied experiences of group members. I hypothesized that Puerto Ricans, in the near-periphery, would be
less likely to emphasize ascriptive characteristics. As noted above, group
members were less likely to emphasize birthplace. Yet, compared with
Mexican Americans, they were more likely to emphasize Christianity
and skin color. Puerto Ricans on the mainland have consistently demonstrated higher levels of poverty in comparison to other Latino groups

(de la Cruz and Ramirez 2003). Although group members meet objective criteria for US citizenship, other factors such as lower socioeconomic status and skin color are also likely to influence the perceptions of group members who might be marginalized in other ways.

Table 5.2 confirms that there are no statistically significant differences in the ways in which Latino men and women define American, at least in ascriptive terms. Yet, as Chapter 6 explores, Latinas were significantly less likely to describe themselves as American than Latino men and were more likely to want to preserve a distinct Latino/Hispanic culture. The findings presented above suggest that these differences in self-perception are not the result of distinct definitions of American, at least in terms of ascriptive categories.

There is a strong correlation between immigrant generation and attitudes about the importance of being born in the United States. Second- and third-generation respondents expressed significantly different opinions from their first-generation counterparts, who were omitted as the reference group. Respondents who are second generation and above were 18 percentage points *more* likely to emphasize birthplace as very important for being American. This finding is consistent with the idea of selective disassociation, in which later-generation immigrants are likely to distance themselves from new arrivals (García Bedolla 2005). It is also consistent with the differences evident between Latino responses to the GSS and the LNS in Table 5.1; respondents to the LNS, which has a much higher percentage of foreign-born respondents, placed far less emphasis on birthplace.

Across the categories, there is no significant relationship between respondents' self-reported skin color and their perceptions of being American. The insignificance of the skin color variable is surprising. However, this result might be attributed, at least in part, to lack of racial diversity reported within the sample. Indeed, just 10 percent of respondents placed themselves in the two darkest categories in response to the self-reported question regarding one's own phenotype. It is unclear, however, whether these results reflect a true lack of diversity among respondents or a larger limitation to using self-reported measures of skin color. Because the LNS was conducted over the phone, the self-reported measure is the only one available for this dataset. However, these results should be interpreted with caution, as Tafoya (2004) demonstrates that self-reports of skin color among Latinos also incorporate socioeconomic status and other measures of belonging.

In addition to skin color, linked fate is commonly used as a measure of racial consciousness (Masuoka and Junn 2013). I placed individuals with a greater sense of linked fate in the far-periphery, with the expectation that they would be more likely to describe American in ascriptive terms, suggesting a less permeable category. Consistent with this expectation, respondents who reported having the highest feelings of linked fate were 9 percentage points more likely to emphasize the importance of birthplace, 11 percentage points more likely to emphasize Christianity, and 4 percentage points more likely to indicate that light skin color is very important to being American when compared to the prototype respondent. The strong significance of the linked fate variable confirms the role of racial hierarchy in shaping individuals' perceptions of what it means to be American.

As expected, the age variable was significant across all four categories, with younger respondents having a far more open interpretation of what it means to be American. As age increased, respondents were more likely to emphasize the importance of each of the ascriptive categories, with the oldest respondents holding the most closed definition of American. Specifically, moving from youngest to oldest, respondents were 10 percentage points more likely to say birthplace and skin color are very important, 16 percentage points more likely to emphasize English skills, and 42 percentage points more likely to emphasize being Christian. It remains less clear, however, whether perceptions of what it means to be American change as respondents age or whether the younger generation of Latinos will maintain a more open view of what it means to be American as they grow older.

Finally, the measure of religiosity is statistically significant in the predictable direction with respect to Christianity: respondents who were more likely to attend religious services were 26 percentage points more likely to see religion as a very important part of being American. As in the African American population, individuals seemed to prioritize attributes that they themselves possess (Masuoka and Junn 2013). Given the important role played by the church in mobilizing and incorporating new immigrants (Wong 2006), the insignificance of the religiosity variable in other categories is unexpected.

In sum, the findings above largely support my intragroup hypothesis that individuals in the near-periphery were least likely to define American in terms of ascriptive categories. These group members, most similar to the core, are also most likely to see American as an open category to which they are eligible for admission. In contrast, for those in the far-periphery, American is more likely to be defined as a closed category with barriers to admission. For instance, Spanish speakers, Salvadorans, and individuals reporting a high degree of linked fate were more likely to place greater emphasis on ascriptive categories when compared with the prototype respondent. Yet, some unexpected findings also appear. For example, Cubans, who are more likely to be white than members of other Latino subgroups, were more likely to emphasize skin color, whereas later-generation immigrants were more likely to emphasize the importance of birthplace than individuals born abroad. These results underscore the concept of selective disassociation as well as the complicated role of race in shaping identity categories. Although a range of research uses large-scale survey data to evaluate the varying ways in which individuals define American, and standardized responses provide the best opportunity to study differences both across and within large populations, inherent limitations also exist in using closed-ended survey questions to define identity categories (Abdelal, Herrera, Johnston et al. 2009). The complexity of these findings suggests the need for future research—and in particular, qualitative research—to better understand the mechanisms behind this intragroup variation.

Defining American and the 2006 Protests

Looking beyond differences between the core and periphery, throughout this book, my politics-to-identity theory focuses on the unprecedented protests that occurred across the United States in the spring of 2006 and their unique "We Are America" frame. In Chapter 4, I find that Latinos interviewed after the 2006 protests were more likely to support liberal policy solutions to the immigration debate. Consistent with the patriotic theme of the protests, I anticipate that as part of the policy feedback process, these events and their message of inclusion will also lead to a shift in Latino understandings of identity categories.

Here, I evaluate whether the protests influenced Latino understandings of what it means to be American. My politics-to-identity theory hypothesizes that the protests and their patriotic frame shaped Latino attitudes about what it means to be American, with individuals interviewed after these events less likely to emphasize ascriptive characteristics and more likely to perceive American as an open, accessible category than those interviewed before. Notably, although language abilities and

Table 5.3 Post-Protest Attitudes about the Importance of Ascriptive Characteristics for Being American (LNS 2006)

	Born in the United States	Being Christian	Speaking English	White
Post-Protests	−0.11*	−0.05	−0.17*	−0.19***
	(0.5)	(0.05)	(0.07)	(0.05)
Female	0.00	0.03	−0.05	−0.05
	(0.05)	(0.05)	(0.07)	(0.05)
Skin Color	−0.03	−0.02	0.00	−0.02
	(0.02)	(0.02)	(0.03)	(0.03)
Age	0.43**	2.21***	1.26***	0.53***
	(0.14)	(0.14)	(0.20)	(0.14)
Subnational Groups				
Cuban	0.13	0.16	0.16	0.42**
	(0.15)	(0.16)	(0.23)	(0.15)
Dominican	0.06	0.47**	0.37	−0.14
	(0.15)	(0.15)	(0.24)	(0.16)
Puerto Rican	−0.16	0.55***	0.08	0.28*
	(0.11)	(0.12)	(0.16)	(0.12)
Salvadoran	0.33**	0.52***	0.56**	0.11
	(0.12)	(0.12)	(0.21)	(0.12)
Incorporation				
Income	−0.18***	−0.13***	−0.06	−0.07*
	(0.03)	(0.03)	(0.05)	(0.04)
Years of Education	−0.68**	−0.07***	−0.01	−0.01
	(0.03)	(0.01)	(0.01)	(0.00)
New Arrival	0.05	0.01	0.34**	−0.15*
(in US < 5 years)	(0.07)	(0.07)	(0.11)	(0.07)
Second Generation	0.78***	0.10	−0.13	−0.06
	(0.08)	(0.08)	(0.10)	(0.08)
Third Generation	0.70***	0.13*	−0.06	−0.20*
and Above	(0.08)	(0.08)	(0.10)	(0.08)
Prefer Spanish	0.22**	0.18**	0.65***	−0.14
	(0.07)	(0.07)	(0.09)	(0.07)
Linked Fate	0.32***	0.51***	0.02	0.32***
	(0.10)	(0.07)	(0.09)	(0.07)
Religiosity	−0.08	−1.30***	−0.06	−0.09
	(0.08)	(0.08)	(0.11)	(0.08)
N	6,401	6,401	6,401	6,401
Pseudo R2	0.02	0.08	0.04	0.01

Note: The unit of observation in an individual respondent. Standard errors in parentheses. Estimation is done using ordered logistic regression, using weighted data from Phase I of the Latino National Survey with state-level fixed effects. Analysis is limited to Cubans, Dominicans, Mexicans, Puerto Ricans and Salvadorans.

Two-tailed tests, significance levels: *p < 0.05, **p < 0.01, ***p < 0.001.

religion may be subject to change, skin color and birthplace are more fixed. Given the protests' emphasis on a multicultural United States and the inclusion of immigrants, I anticipate that in particular, respondents interviewed after these events will be less likely to emphasize these latter categories.

As Table 5.3 demonstrates, comparable respondents interviewed after the protests were less likely to define American in terms of being born in the United States, speaking English, and being white. In other words, after the protests, individuals were more likely to define American in multicultural terms. This broader acceptance of multiculturalism as part of what it means to be American connects to research demonstrating that Latinos interviewed after these events were more likely to "view their 'Americanness' through a racial lens" (Zepeda-Millán and Wallace 2013, 522). Even as Latinos were more likely to see themselves as racialized, they were also more likely to perceive American as a permeable category that allows for such diversity.

Conclusion

Throughout this book, I seek to better understand some of the factors contributing to the acquisition of an American identity by Latinos in the United States. As a first step, this chapter addresses variation in the content, or meaning, of American for this heterogeneous population, comparing perspectives on the boundaries of what it means to be American both across racial and ethnic groups (intergroup) and within the Latino population (intragroup). Specifically, I study the extent to which individuals define an American identity based on the ascriptive characteristics of being white, being Christian, being born in the United States, and speaking English.

Using data from the GSS and the LNS, I find that Latino perceptions of what it means to be American are, overall, similar to those of the white population. However, variation in Latino attitudes about the importance of birthplace across the two surveys, coupled with sampling differences between the GSS and the LNS, highlight the need for new data that allow for further analysis of intergroup variation.

Within the heterogeneous Latino population, I explore different understandings of what it means to be American. Specifically, I focus on the extent to which this category is defined in closed terms, with strong emphasis on ascriptive characteristics, or as open and accessible, placing less importance on ascriptive traits. To understand intergroup and intragroup variation, I build on the idea that group members in the core (center) and the periphery (margins) will develop distinct definitions of the group and that additional differences will arise between individuals in the near- and the far-periphery.

Overall, my results demonstrate support for the idea that individuals in the far-periphery are more likely to perceive American in restrictive terms defined by ascriptive categories. In contrast, those in the near-periphery tend to view American as a more open category. In other words, those furthest from the core are more likely to see American as an inaccessible category. My findings about Spanish speakers, Salvadorans, and individuals with a high sense of linked fate demonstrate support for this hypothesis. My results also underscore the importance of intersectional understandings of the characteristics that influence perceptions of identity as well as the complexities of mapping national origin onto the near- and far-periphery. Indeed, findings with respect to national origin and gender suggest the need for an improved understanding of the ways in which these categories interact with other indicators of incorporation to define the near- and far-periphery.

Finally, I explore the extent to which the contentious political events of 2006 influenced Latino understandings of what it means to be American. Consistent with my politics-to-identity theory, I find that respondents interviewed after the protests were less likely to emphasize the importance of being white, being born in the United States, and speaking English than those interviewed before these events. These results demonstrate that the protests and their identity-based message helped to erase some of the perceived boundaries for inclusion in what it means to be American.

As the quote by Jose Antonio Vargas at the start of this chapter suggests, the ways in which we define American have important consequences for public policy. For marginalized populations, advancing a definition of American that includes one's own characteristics can also influence an individual's broader sense of belonging and citizenship. The findings in this chapter illustrate the need for additional research that allows scholars to better understand the ways in which Latinos define American beyond ascriptive characteristics as well as the perceived permeability of this identity category. In Chapter 6, I further develop some of these connections by focusing on variation in the extent to which Latinos adopt an American self-identification as well as attitudes about changing to blend into the United States.

6 | American Identities

Self-Perception among Latinos in the United States

> *We've begun a debate on the complex and crucial issue of immigration reform. . . . We'll hopefully bring to final passage a comprehensive bill that will strengthen our border security and bring twelve million undocumented Americans out of the shadows and help our economy move strongly.*
> —Senate Majority Leader Harry Reid (D-NV), June 2007

In early June 2007, Senator Harry Reid spoke the above words on the floor of the US Senate, discussing renewed efforts to pass an immigration reform bill. His use of the phrase "undocumented Americans" sparked a firestorm among critics who argued that this term was an oxymoron. As Chapter 5 explores, these comments point to a growing debate about what it means to be American. They also highlight another important question: When do Latinos come to *see* themselves as American?

My politics-to-identity theory advances the claim that policy feedback, social movement mobilization, and framing can shape an individual's attitudes and self-perception. I also underscore the importance of variables such as gender and national origin that help to explain intragroup variation. Before turning specifically to political events, in this chapter, I build on this intersectional framework to study some of the demographic factors that influence the process of acquiring an American identity. Although the majority of Latinos self-identify as American, significant variation persists within this population. Below, I study the ways in which gender, national origin, and language dominance influence the extent to which Latinos adopt an American identifier. In particular, I focus on the relationship between gender and self-identification, as this variable remains understudied in existing research. I also extend the analysis presented in Chapter 5 about what it means to be American by exploring attitudes about changing to blend into the United States and preserving a distinct Latino culture.

Psychologists distinguish between aspects of one's social identity, such as group membership or relationships with others, and personal identity, or private feelings of self and individuality (Cheek and Briggs 1982; Leary, Wheeler, and Jenkins 1986). Consistent with existing research, I treat the acquisition of an American identity as a social identity, representing one facet of a larger process of social and political incorporation into the United States (Schildkraut 2014).

Scholarship on intersectionality emphasizes the interaction between categories such as race/ethnicity, gender, class, and national origin, which leads to multiple marginalizations that uniquely influence an individual's experiences and attitudes (Crenshaw 1989; García Bedolla, Lavariega Monforti, and Pantoja 2007; Hardy-Fanta 2006; hooks 1984; Strolovitch 2007). In this chapter, I am guided in particular by intersectionality theory's emphasis on gender and gendered experiences.

In addition, I build on the distinction described in Chapter 5 between group members in the core, or the center, and those in the periphery, who are marginalized, including racial/ethnic minority groups (Pickett and Brewer 2005; Masuoka and Junn 2013). To understand intragroup differences, I also distinguish between the near-periphery, referring to members of the periphery closest to the core, and the far-periphery, including those furthest from the center (Pickett and Brewer 2005). For instance, although Latinos may generally represent the periphery, within this population, English speakers are closer to the core (near-periphery) than are Spanish speakers (far-periphery). I find that distance from the core, particularly when measured by language dominance, significantly influences Latino understandings of what it means to be American. Here, I extend this research, testing the extent to which these variables correlate with Latino self-identification.

Identities in general, and an American identity in particular, are thought to have important consequences for political attitudes and behavior both in the general population and among Latinos specifically (Citrin, Wong, and Duff 2001; Huddy and Khatib 2007; Lee 2008; Schildkraut 2014, 2005a; Silber Mohamed 2015). Latino National Survey (LNS) data demonstrate a significant relationship between identifying as American and a range of participatory outcomes within the Latino community. For instance, those who very strongly identify as American were far more likely to report having voted in 2004 (73.3 percent) than those who do not at all identify as American (47.9 percent). They were also much more likely to have contacted a public official (43.3 percent compared with 18.9 percent), and more than twice as many respondents who strongly identified as American also identified with a political party (62.1 percent compared with 27.4 percent), suggesting greater engagement with the US political system among this group (Silber Mohamed 2015). This strong relationship between self-identification and political participation demonstrates the importance of better understanding the factors that contribute to the adoption of an American identity.

In addition to studying self-perception, I also examine incorporationist attitudes within the Latino population. Classic assimilation theory envisioned a one-way process in which newcomers gradually lost their own culture and adopted a new "American" one (Alba and Nee 1997, 2003; Glazer and Moynihan 1963; Gordon 1964; Park 1928; Warner and Strole 1945). In contrast, contemporary scholarship increasingly views acculturation as a *two-way process* in which individuals may adapt to a new culture while simultaneously maintaining ties to a previous culture or identity (Fraga, Garcia, Hero et al. 2010; Schildkraut 2011). Evolving out of the identity-based social movements of the 1960s, this incorporationist perspective emphasizes that even as immigrants adapt to American life, they can also maintain their own ethnic or cultural values (Glazer 1997; Hackney 1997; Hollinger 1995; Schildkraut 2007, 2011; Tichenor 2002). Incorporationism suggests that an individual can see oneself as American even while striving to preserve an immigrant legacy.

In surveys of the general population, most Americans agree with the idea that assimilating and maintaining a unique culture are two compatible aspects of being American (Schildkraut 2007, 2011). Similarly, Latino attitudes about blending into the United States and preserving a distinct culture indicate that these ideas are not mutually exclusive (Fraga, Garcia, Hero et al. 2010; Schildkraut 2011). Rather, being American can include a variety of cultural backgrounds and experiences, suggesting a broader interpretation of this category than the ascriptive characteristics discussed in Chapter 5. Here, I examine Latino opinions about incorporationism, including whether Latinos should change to blend into the United States and whether group members should maintain a distinct culture. By exploring Latino perspectives on these questions, my analyses provide important insight into attitudes about the broader process of social and political incorporation into the United States.

Latino Social Identities and Assimilation

Much of our understanding of self-identification derives from social identity theory (SIT), which establishes that group memberships influence how individuals see the world (Brewer 2003; Tajfel 1970; Tajfel and Turner 1986). Yet, this theory contributes far less to our understanding of the adoption of new identities (Huddy 2001).

Historically, Latinos in the United States have self-identified primarily in terms of their national origin, such as Mexican, Puerto Rican, or Cuban (DeSipio 1996b; Fraga, Garcia, Hero et al. 2006b). However, to some extent, Latinos in the United States can also choose among other ethnic "options" (Waters 1990). A pan-ethnic (Latino/Hispanic) identifier represents one such option, with a range of circumstances contributing to the emergence of this identity. For example, pan-ethnic identities develop in situations of exclusion, where unity among different Latino groups would be politically advantageous (Itzigsohn and Dore-Cabral 2000; Padilla 1985).

The adoption of an American identity represents another potential ethnic option. Early literature on immigrants in the United States anticipated that over time, individuals would naturally assimilate, adopting this identity as part of that process (Alba and Nee 1997; Park 1928, 1950; Warner and Strole 1945). Focusing largely on European immigrants arriving in the early twentieth century, this model assumed that the adoption of an American identity would be proportionate to one's time in the United States. Self-identification as American was seen as a hallmark of assimilation (Gordon 1964); as individuals acquired an American identity, they were expected to lose other "ethnic" identities.

The 1965 Immigration Act resulted in an influx of immigrants from Latin America and Asia (see Chapter 3 for details). These new arrivals followed a trajectory distinct from their European predecessors, and scholars began to amend or counter the classic model of assimilation in order to account for these varied outcomes. "New assimilation theory" advocates for the continued relevance of an assimilationist perspective, but emphasizes that both immigrants and the host society continually adapt to each other (Alba and Nee 1997, 2003). One alternative emphasizes a "bumpy" rather than straight line (Gans 1992; Vasquez 2011a, 2011b), and another approach, segmented assimilation theory, highlights the importance of the interaction between individual and contextual variables in the incorporation process. In particular, this theory emphasizes the influence of factors such as human capital, skin color, and language skills in determining the "segment" an immigrant inhabits. This model allows for three possibilities: individuals might assimilate into the US middle class; they might experience downward assimilation into a marginalized underclass; or they might selectively assimilate, achieving economic success while maintaining cultural values (Portes and Rumbaut 2001; Portes and Zhou 1993; Rumbaut and Portes 2001; Zhou 1997). Other research similarly emphasizes the influential role of race/ethnicity and phenotype in the incorporation process (Glazer and Moynihan 1963; Golash-Boza 2006; Lee and Bean 2004; Vasquez 2011a).

Many of the factors that contribute to assimilation or acculturation are also associated with the adoption of an American identity, and the process of integration clearly influences one's self-perception (Kibria 2002). Yet, although related, these variables are also conceptually distinct. Assimilation is frequently measured by indicators such as socioeconomic outcomes, language proficiency, or residential concentration. In contrast, attachment to an American identity represents a psychological connection to the national group.

Variables such as immigrant generation and socioeconomic status influence the adoption of an American identity (Citrin 2007). However, recent literature also emphasizes the need to better understand other factors that contribute to the emergence of this self-perception, particularly among minority groups (Huddy 2016; Schildkraut 2014; Waters and Jiménez 2005). For instance, although scholarship on immigrant incorporation increasingly addresses the importance of gender and national origin, these variables remain understudied in research on the adoption of an American identity (but see Silber Mohamed 2015).

In contrast to the expectations of earlier literature on assimilation, which anticipated that an American identity would replace ethnic identities, most Latinos today are not acquiring this identity at the expense of other identity options. For instance, LNS respondents demonstrated very high levels of support for both national origin and pan-ethnic identities, with 90.3 percent of respondents indicating that they strongly or very strongly identify in pan-ethnic terms, whereas 87.7 percent said the same for national origin identities. By comparison, 67.7 percent reported that they strongly or very strongly identify as American, indicating that this new identity is being adopted *in addition to* other identities, not in place of them. In other words, describing oneself as American does not mean relinquishing a connection to "ethnic" parts of life. Moreover, in contrast to early European immigrants, who incorporated without an ongoing influx of new arrivals from their home countries, contemporary immigrants, and Mexicans in particular, live in a context of immigrant "replenishment" in which coethnics arrive continually.[1]

As a result, today, even later-generation immigrants are perpetually surrounded by ethnic influences, changing the salience of identity choices for this population (Jiménez 2009; Waters and Jiménez 2005). Studying incorporationist attitudes thus enables us to better understand the content, or meaning, of an American identity as well as the ways in which self-identification as American relates to other attitudes about cultural preservation (Abdelal, Herrera, Johnston et al. 2009).

Becoming American: Variation in Identity Acquisition

Below, I outline hypotheses related to the adoption of an American identity among Latinos based on the three cleavages outlined throughout this book. Given that gender is significantly understudied in existing research, I focus in particular on that variable, reordering the hypotheses of previous chapters.

A range of existing literature explores the role played by gender in the broader process of incorporation in the United States (Bejarano 2014; Grasmuck and Pessar 1991; Itzigsohn and Giorguli 2005; Jones-Correa 1998b; Menjívar 2000; Vasquez 2011a, 2011b). This research suggests two possible outcomes for Latina identification. On one hand, Latinas are more likely to participate than Latino men (Bejarano 2014). For example, Latinas are more likely to contribute to their household income in the United States and become involved in their children's school (Grasmuck and Pessar 1991; Hondagneu-Sotelo 1992; Jones-Correa 1998a). In contrast, Latino men are more likely to prefer continuity with their homeland and maintain a "myth of return," holding onto the idea that they will someday live in their home country again (Bejarano 2014; Jones-Correa 1998a). As in the general population, voter turnout is higher for Latinas than Latino men, whereas among immigrants, Latinas are also more likely to naturalize and to pursue US citizenship (Bejarano 2014). This research suggests a greater level of incorporation among Latinas when compared with Latino men.

On the other hand, at the elite level, Latina activists and legislators are more likely to view their roles communally (Bejarano 2013; Fraga, Garcia, Hero et al. 2006b; García, Martinez-Ebers, Coronado et al. 2008; Pardo 1997), emphasizing strong cultural identities and activism on behalf of their ethnic group (García and Márquez 2001; García, Martinez-Ebers, Coronado et al. 2008). Consistent with this group orientation, in Chapter 4, I find that Latinas hold slightly more liberal immigration attitudes than Latino men. Similarly, research from cross-cultural psychology underscores the unique role played by women, who serve as "carriers of the culture," striving to preserve traditional values (Dion and Dion 2001; González, Umaña-Taylor, and Bámaca 2006; Phinney 1990; Phinney, Horenczyk, Liebkind et al. 2001; Warikoo 2006). Focusing specifically on Mexicans, Vasquez (2011a, 2011b) finds that Latinas are more likely to embrace ethnic symbols and traditions, with this connection especially strong among later-generation wives and mothers.

Although existing research establishes that identities are not mutually exclusive, I anticipate that Latinas' strong emphasis on cultural maintenance will be at odds with the emergence of an American identity. Moreover, intersectionality theory emphasizes that minority women are "doubly disadvantaged," which may detract from a broader sense of belonging among Latinas (Orey et al. 2006). Drawing on this literature, I develop the first hypothesis: *Latinas will be less likely to see themselves as American than Latino men and will be more likely to want to maintain a distinct pan-ethnic culture.*

The second hypothesis relates to national origin. A growing body of research suggests that premigration experiences shape Latino attitudes and feelings of belonging in the United States (Rocco 2014; Wals 2011). Similarly, research on segmented assimilation (Portes and Zhou 1993) and intersectionality (García Bedolla, Lavariega Monforti, and Pantoja 2007) emphasizes the important role of national origin in influencing both political attitudes and incorporation into the United States (see also Chapter 4).

Chapter 3 outlines some of the ways in which Latino incorporation experiences vary based on national origin group. For instance, Puerto Ricans are born US citizens, and Cuban exiles have received preferential treatment from the federal government in comparison with other Latino groups. Cubans also tend to have lighter phenotypes, and in general, group members have arrived in the United States with higher levels of human capital. Chapter 5 connects these differing experiences to the concepts of a group's core and periphery. I present a preliminary categorization placing members of these two subgroups—and Cubans in particular—closer to the core (i.e., in the near-periphery). Compared with the other national origin groups studied in this book, Salvadorans have faced significant adversity, including US involvement in their nation's bloody civil war and opposition to asylum claims from Salvadoran nationals in the 1980s. The community also has a large proportion of undocumented immigrants. I placed Salvadorans in the far-periphery (i.e., furthest from the core) and found that members of this subgroup have the most restrictive attitudes about what it means to be American. In line with these differences, I anticipate that *Puerto Ricans and Cuban exiles will be more likely to see themselves as American and that Salvadorans will be least likely to describe themselves as American* when compared with members of other national origin groups.

Language dominance plays an important role in the broader incorporation process, with English speakers having greater access to job opportunities and other avenues of integration in the United States (Portes and Rumbaut 2001; Rumbaut 1994). Likewise, a shared language influences one's identity (DeSipio 1996b; Schmidt 2002); among Latinos, individuals who are Spanish-dominant (far-periphery) are more likely to identify in pan-ethnic terms, whereas those who are English-dominant (near-periphery) are more likely to say that they feel American (Citrin and Sears 2014; Citrin, Wong, and Duff 2001; Golash-Boza 2006). In Chapter 5, I find that Spanish speakers are far more likely to define American in terms of ascriptive categories or characteristics, such as skin color or birthplace. Consistent with existing research, the third hypothesis anticipates that *Spanish-dominant respondents will be less likely to describe themselves as American than their English-dominant counterparts.*

Who Self-Identifies as American?

To better understand *who* self-identifies as American, I return to the LNS. Segmented assimilation theory demonstrates that an American identity and assimilationist attitude are not a given even among later-generation immigrants (Portes and Zhou 1993; Zhou 1997). Accordingly, I include both first-generation and later-generation immigrants in the primary analysis and control for these variables in multivariate models. This approach is consistent with previous research on the emergence of American and pan-ethnic identities (Citrin 2007; Jones-Correa and Leal 1996; Masuoka 2006). Although including the full sample provides the opportunity to understand generational differences in self-perception, I also test the hypotheses outlined above among first-generation immigrants only and note these results separately.

To gauge self-perception among Latinos in the United States, the

LNS includes a series of questions as follows, "In general, how strongly or not do you think of yourself as _____?" The questions were asked in random order, with American, Latino/Hispanic, and a national origin descriptor used separately. Respondents were given four options ranging from not very strongly to very strongly (see Appendix A for a complete list of questions and coding). For this analysis, I focus on the question related to an American identity. I begin by presenting bivariate tests of the hypotheses using this measure as the dependent variable. As in previous chapters, gender is treated as a binary variable (female = 1), language preference refers to the language in which an individual completed the survey (Spanish = 1), and national origin is limited to the five largest Latino national origin groups.

Figures 6.1 through 6.3 present the results of these bivariate analyses, demonstrating preliminary support for the hypotheses outlined above. Consistent with expectations, Figure 6.1 shows that Latinas are less likely to identify as American (38.0 percent) than Latino men (45.5 percent). As for national origin, I hypothesized that Puerto Ricans and Cubans would be most likely to self-identify as American, whereas Salvadorans would be least likely to describe themselves as such. Figure 6.2 indicates that Puerto Ricans (62.4 percent) and Cubans (59.2 percent) are indeed most likely to very strongly self-identify as American, whereas Salvadorans (31.4 percent) are least likely to strongly identify as American. Finally, Figure 6.3 indicates a dramatic difference in self-identification based on language preference, with 67.2 percent of English speakers very strongly identifying as American compared with just 24.9 percent of Spanish speakers. This large gap reflects the strong relationship between language usage and identity. Collectively, these results highlight an important difference in self-identification among individuals in the near- and far-periphery.

Importantly, intersectionality theory also emphasizes variation *within* groups, and the diversity of experiences within heterogeneous populations. Thus, although the bivariate analyses indicate preliminary support for all three hypotheses, multivariate analysis is essential to better capture intragroup variation. Below, I test whether these differences persist when a range of control variables is introduced. For instance, are Puerto Ricans and Cubans really most likely to identify as American? Or, is this apparent difference actually capturing other demographic distinctions between the national origin groups, such as variation in socioeconomic status, citizenship status, or phenotype?

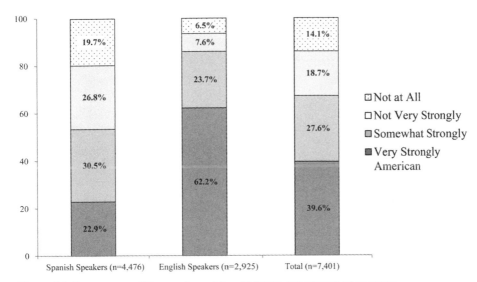

Figure 0.1 Percentage of Respondents Identifying as American by Language Dominance (LNS 2006)

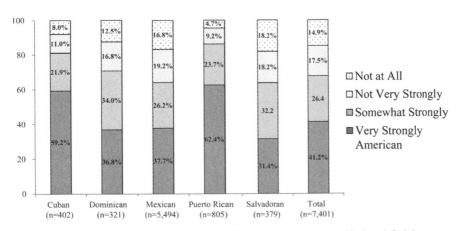

Figure 6.2 Percentage of Respondents Identifying as American by National Origin (LNS 2006)

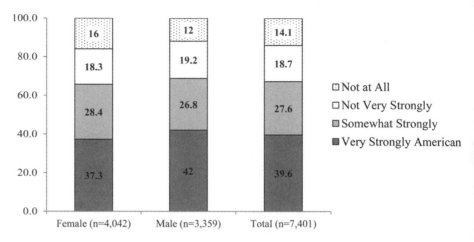

Figure 6.3 Percentage of Respondents Identifying as American by Gender (LNS 2006)

Feeling American and Incorporationist Attitudes: Multivariate Analysis

Below, I use multivariate analysis to test my hypotheses about the relationship between gender, national origin, and level of acculturation with self-identification as American. I also test two additional dependent variables designed to gauge attitudes about social and cultural incorporation, using questions that ask the extent to which an individual thinks it is important for group members to (1) change in order to blend into larger American society, and (2) maintain a distinct Latino/Hispanic culture. These new variables are used, respectively, as potential proxies for feelings of similarity and difference.[2] Notably, these phenomena are not mutually exclusive; rather, in multiple surveys across time, Latinos tend to express support for both measures (Fraga, Garcia, Hero et al. 2006b, 2010). Because all of the dependent variables are categorical, and the responses are ordered from least to most (measured from 1–4 for identifying as American and 1–3 for the incorporationist variables, from not at all important to very important), I use ordered logistic regression.[3]

The models also contain three groups of control variables, for which I outline expectations based on existing literature. Consistent with intersectionality theory, these variables serve to enrich the insights made throughout this chapter, reiterating that significant variation also exists *within* the subgroups described above.

The first series of variables consists of demographic characteristics including skin color (self-reported, 1 [very dark] to 5 [very light]), age, education, and income, all measured continuously. With respect to race, Chapter 5 finds no relationship between skin color and the way that Latinos define American. However, phenotype represents a clear limitation to classic assimilation theory, with skin color significantly altering the opportunities available to immigrants (Glazer 1993; Portes and Zhou 1993; Zhou 1997). Similarly, although Waters's notion of ethnic options emphasizes that later-generation immigrants can choose whether to identify as American or in ethnic terms, she argues that these options are primarily limited to white immigrants of European descent. Other scholars contend that for different immigrant groups, skin color determines how "optional" ethnicity is, particularly among Latinos (Golash-Boza 2006; Lee and Bean 2004; Telles and Ortiz 2008; Vasquez 2011a, 2011b). Based on this research, I anticipate that having lighter skin will be associated with a stronger American identity and greater support for changing to blend into the United States.

As for age, in previous chapters, I demonstrate that older respondents are far more likely to define American in terms of ascriptive characteristics and are less likely to support a path to citizenship for undocumented immigrants. Existing research finds younger Latinos are also more likely to prefer the Hispanic/Latino label (Jones-Correa and Leal 1996; Masuoka 2006), whereas older group members are more likely to identify as American (Schildkraut 2005b; Silber Mohamed 2013; Taylor, Gershon, and Pantoja 2014). Consistent with this research, I expect that older respondents will be more likely to identify as American and more likely to say that Latinos should change to blend into the United States.

Whereas classic models of assimilation frequently equate assimilation with economic success, segmented assimilation theory highlights the centrality of individual characteristics such as human capital for incorporating into the United States (Portes and Rumbaut 2001; Portes and Zhou 1993; Rumbaut and Portes 2001). Similarly, I anticipate that Latinos with a higher socioeconomic status—as measured by education and income—will be more likely to see themselves as American.

The second set of control variables relates to an individual's immigrant status. The analysis includes a series of dummy variables for immigrant generation, with respondents born outside the United States as the excluded category. Dummy variables are included for respondents who are second generation (1 = those born in the United States with parents born elsewhere) and third generation and above (1 = individuals with at least one parent born in the United States).

In earlier chapters, I find that later-generation respondents are more likely to have conservative attitudes toward immigration policy. I also find a weak relationship between immigrant generation and ascriptive definitions of American, with later-generation respondents more likely to emphasize the importance of being born in the United States. Here, I anticipate that later-generation immigrants will be more likely to identify as American. Additionally, a separate dummy variable is included for citizenship status (1 = citizen), with the obvious expectation that citizens will be more likely than noncitizens to see themselves as American. Beyond citizenship, the LNS did not ask respondents about their legal status, meaning that the noncitizen category likely includes a combination of individuals living in the United States legally and undocumented immigrants.

Finally, the third set of control variables incorporates measures of social context. By their very nature, social identities emphasize the way individuals define their identities in relation to others, suggesting a connection between an individual's social relationships and his or her self-identification. Social networks and intergroup contact have long been thought to influence the larger processes of assimilation and acculturation (Gordon 1964; Park 1928; Portes and Rumbaut 2006; Zhou 1997; Zhou and Lee 2007). Similarly, social networks such as friends and family play an important role in shaping attitudes and self-perception (Huckfeldt and Sprague 1987; Portes and Zhou 1993; Zuckerman, Dasović, and Fitzgerald 2007). In a context of ethnic replenishment, when Latinos are consistently surrounded by a new influx of ethnic "raw materials" (Jiménez 2009), I anticipate that intergroup contact will be especially likely to influence the adoption of an American identity.

To better understand the relationship between social networks and self-identification, I include dummy variables indicating whether a respondent's friends are primarily Latino/Hispanic, mixed, or other, with "other" the reference category. I expect that individuals whose friends are predominately Latino/Hispanic will be less likely to identify as American and will place greater emphasis on cultural preservation in comparison to those who have more diverse friendship networks.

In addition to friendship networks, involvement in schools is increasingly thought to be an entry point for Latino civic and political participation in the United States (Holzner 2012; Orr, Wong, Farris et al. 2016). Similarly, working outside the home contributes significantly to the gender gap in the general population as well as among Latinos specifically (Andersen 1975; García Bedolla, Lavariega Monforti, and Pantoja 2007).[4] To capture these aspects of social incorporation, I include dummy variables for whether a respondent has children in school (1 for individuals with children enrolled in elementary, secondary, or high school in the previous year and 0 otherwise) and a job outside of the home (1 if the respondent does not work outside the home and 0 otherwise), with the expectation that both of these variables will be associated with an American identity.

Table 6.1 presents the results of a series of ordered logistic regressions for each of the dependent variables. Because I am most interested in understanding the factors associated with Latinos adopting an American identity, to help interpret these results, Figure 6.4 presents predicted probabilities for this dependent variable. The predicted probabilities are calculated using a prototype respondent with all continuous variables set at their mean and dummy variables set at their modal values, with the exception of gender. In the analyses, independent variables are set to move from their lowest to highest values.[5]

Beginning with gender, controlling for a range of demographic and socioeconomic variables, Latinas were 9 percentage points less likely to very strongly identify as American than Latino men. Moving across the columns, Latinas were also significantly less likely to want to change to blend into the United States and more likely to want to maintain a distinct Latino/Hispanic culture. These results are consistent with research suggesting that females in a range of contexts are more likely to want to retain their culture and traditions (González, Umaña-Taylor, and Bámaca 2006; Phinney 1990; Phinney, Horenczyk, Liebkind et al. 2001; Ullah 1985; Vasquez 2011b; Warikoo 2006). My findings indicate that the gender difference in self-identification is driven, at least in part, by the greater emphasis Latinas place on group orientation and cultural maintenance. As will be discussed below, in many cases, an independent variable associated with a strong American identity is also associated with a *decreased* desire to blend into the United States or an *increased* desire to maintain a distinct culture. The fact that these variables move in the same direction in the case of gender, but in the opposite direction with respect to several other variables, reiterates that among Latinas, identity appears to be more connected to cultural preservation.

With respect to national origin, as expected, Cubans were most likely

Table 6.1 American Self-Identification and Incorporationist Attitudes (LNS 2006)

	American Identity (1)	Blend into the United States (2)	Maintain a Distinct Culture (3)
Female	−0.38***	−0.28***	0.28**
	[−0.52, −0.24]	[−0.43, −0.14]	[0.11, 0.45]
Survey in Spanish	−0.76***	0.75***	0.52***
	[−0.96, −0.57]	[0.56, 0.94]	[0.28, 0.75]
Cuban	0.39*	−0.12	−0.15
	[0.00, 0.79]	[−0.49, 0.26]	[−0.62, 0.33]
Dominican	0.16	−0.15	0.05
	[−0.20, 0.51]	[−0.11, 0.63]	[−0.52, 0.62]
Puerto Rican	0.30	−0.32*	0.30
	−[0.01, 0.61]	[−0.60, −0.04]	[−0.10, 0.70]
Salvadoran	0.08	0.26	0.30
	[−0.24, 0.40]	[−0.11, 0.63]	[−0.19, 0.79]
Skin Color	0.09	0.31*	0.12
	[−0.17, 0.34]	[0.04, 0.60]	[−0.21, 0.45]
Age	1.36***	1.63***	−0.18
	[0.99, 1.73]	[1.25, 2.01]	[−0.64, 0.28]
Years of Education	0.71**	−0.96**	−0.23
	[0.26, 1.16]	[−1.46, −0.46]	[−0.86, 0.39]
Household Income	0.24	−0.02	−0.21
	[−0.02, 0.50]	[−0.27, 0.24]	[−0.51, 0.09]
Second Generation	0.45***	−0.08	0.09
	[0.21, 0.70]	[−0.32, 0.16]	[−0.22, 0.39]
Third Generation and Above	1.37***	−0.41**	−0.13
	[1.10, 1.64]	[−0.64, −0.18]	[−0.41, 0.14]
US Citizen	0.60***	−0.09	0.32*
	[0.42, 0.78]	[−0.30, 0.12]	[0.05, 0.58]
Latino Friends	−0.72***	−0.02	0.79***
	[−1.04, −0.40]	[−0.29, 0.24]	[0.48, 1.10]
Mixed Friends	−0.33***	0.02	0.63***
	[−0.64, −0.03]	[−0.23, 0.26]	[0.35, 0.90]
Kids in School	0.03	0.29***	0.11
	[−0.10, 0.16]	[0.16, 0.43]	[−0.06, 0.27]
No Job Outside Home	−0.24	0.20	0.08
	[−0.51, 0.03]	[−0.09, 0.48]	[−0.29, 0.45]
Pseudo R-Squared	0.14	0.08	0.03
N	5,470	5,403	5,480

Note: Ordered logistic regression with robust standard errors and state-level fixed effects, with California as the excluded state and Mexicans as the excluded national origin group. All continuous variables are rescaled from 0 to 1. Brackets indicate the 95% confidence interval.

***p < 0.00, **p < 0.01, *p < 0.05

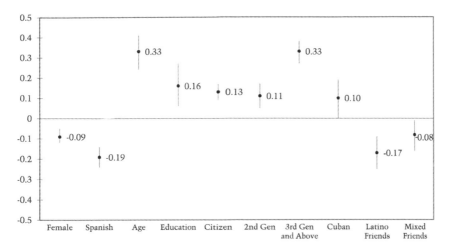

Figure 6.4 Change in Predicted Probabilities, Very Strong American Identity (LNS 2006)

Note: The bullet represents the predicted probability of identifying very strongly as American, with all continuous variables held at their means and dummy variables held at their modal values, except gender. The line on either side of the bullet represents the 95% confidence interval. Prototype respondent is a male, Spanish speaker, first generation US citizen, Mexican from California, with mixed friends, who works outside the home and does not have children in school.

to self-identify as American; compared with Mexican Americans, they were 10 percentage points more likely to describe themselves in these terms. In the full sample, the variable for Puerto Ricans moves in the anticipated direction, but only reaches marginal significance (p < 0.06); when the analysis is limited to first-generation respondents, below, this relationship becomes statistically significant. Compared with the Mexican reference group, however, Puerto Ricans were less likely to indicate that Latinos should change to blend into the United States. In Chapter 5, I find that Puerto Ricans, who receive US citizenship at birth, are least likely to emphasize the importance of birthplace for being American. This apparent contradiction between feeling more American and being less likely to think Latinos should change to blend into the United States reiterates the complex identity calculus for members of this subgroup, and the interplay between subjective identity categories such as citizenship with more objective interpretations of identities.

Although bivariate analysis indicates that Salvadorans were least likely to identify as American, when control variables were added to the model, there was no statistically significant difference between this group and the excluded category. This null finding reiterates that national origin interacts with other variables to influence the incorporation process.

Turning to language preference, the data in Column 1 demonstrates that this variable is statistically significant in the anticipated direction. Indeed, consistent with existing research (García Bedolla 2003; Schmidt 2002), Figure 6.4 indicates that Spanish speakers were 19 percentage points less likely to choose an American identity than their English-speaking counterparts. These results reaffirm the idea that language is a clear measure of one's perceived distance from the core population. Interestingly, looking across the table, respondents who completed the survey in Spanish were more likely to indicate a desire to maintain a distinct Latino culture *and* more likely to express a desire to blend into the United States. These results are consistent with incorporationist ideas emphasizing a *two-way* process in which immigrants and others both adapt, with each group adopting new customs and traditions from the other (Fraga, Garcia, Hero et al. 2010; Hochschild and Mollenkopf 2009).

As for the control variables, as expected, respondents who reported having lighter skin were more likely to indicate a desire to blend into the United States. Surprisingly, however, there was not a statistically significant relationship between skin color and self-identification. This confounding result counters a range of research highlighting the important influence of phenotype on assimilation and self-identification. Yet, much of this existing research relies on the *interviewers'* assessment of an individual's skin color (Golash-Boza 2006; Lee and Bean 2004; Vasquez 2011a, 2011b). In contrast, the LNS uses a self-reported skin color measure. Among Latinos, self-identification as white reflects a combination of perceptions about one's own skin color as well as socioeconomic status and other indicators of belonging (Tafoya 2004). Consequently, this null finding may be more indicative of the limitations of this measure than of the absence of a relationship between these variables.

Consistent with expectations, older respondents were far more likely to strongly identify as American and to express a desire to blend into the United States. With respect to socioeconomic status, although the household income variable did not reach statistical significance in any of the models, more-educated individuals were significantly more likely to identify as American. As expected, second- and third-generation respondents and US citizens were all more likely to identify as American.

In particular, respondents who were third generation and above were 33 percentage points more likely to describe themselves as American compared with the prototypical first-generation respondent.

Turning to the social network variables, the results in Table 6.1 highlight a strong relationship between friendship networks and identification. Individuals whose friendship networks were primarily Latino/ Hispanic, *and* those whose friendships were primarily mixed, were far less likely to indicate that they feel American. Likewise, these individuals—even those with primarily mixed friendships—were more likely to want to maintain a distinct pan-ethnic culture.

In contrast, the other social network variables did not fare as well. Surprisingly, having children in school did not affect identity choice, though these respondents were more likely to express support for changing to blend into the United States. Despite expectations that individuals who do not work outside the home would be less likely to identify as American, there was no statistically significant relationship between these variables; elsewhere, I find that Latinas who do not work outside the home were less likely to self-identify in *pan-ethnic* terms, reiterating that this identity is also acquired while living in the United States (Silber Mohamed 2015).

To further explore the importance of the social network variables, I also ran the identity model using the full sample, but excluding the dummy variable for gender (see Appendix E, Table E.1). With gender absent, the biggest change between the models was the significance of the variable for working outside the home. When gender was excluded, not working outside the home significantly decreased the likelihood of identifying as American. When gender was added back to the model, the work variable lost statistical significance. This distinction suggests that to some extent, the gender variable is capturing the effects of not being exposed to others through work. However, only 15 percent of the female respondents in the LNS did not work outside the home, and gender remains highly significant in separate tests with this group excluded from the sample, demonstrating that employment status is not the only factor driving gendered differences in identification.

To further examine the robustness of these results, I also limited the sample to first-generation immigrants only. As Table 6.2 reflects, the main findings above obtain in this smaller sample. When compared with the Mexican reference group, both Cubans and Puerto Ricans were more likely to self-identify as Americans, with both results highly

Table 6.2 Self-Identification among First Generation Respondents (LNS 2006)

	American Identity (1)	Blend into the United States (2)	Maintain a Distinct Culture (3)
Female	−0.38***	−0.26**	0.10
	[−0.51, −0.24]	[−0.42 −0.10]	[−0.09, 0.30]
Survey in Spanish	−0.60***	0.55***	0.40**
	[−0.79, −0.40]	[0.35, 0.75]	[0.16, 0.64]
Cuban	0.65**	0.13	−0.06
	[0.24, 1.05]	[−0.29, 0.56]	[−0.62, 0.50]
Dominican	0.30	−0.10	0.11
	[−0.03, 0.63]	[−0.53, 0.34]	[−0.49, 0.72]
Puerto Rican	0.49**	−0.41*	0.34
	[0.18, 0.80]	[−0.75, −0.07]	[−0.12, 0.81]
Salvadoran	0.14	0.24	0.33
	[−0.50, 0.18]	[−0.11, 0.59]	[−0.11, 0.77]
Skin Color	0.28*	0.01	0.11
	[0.01, 0.54]	[−0.30, 0.33]	[−0.28, 0.50]
Age	0.81***	1.46***	0.61*
	[0.41, 1.21]	[0.98, 1.93]	[0.02, 1.19]
Years of Education	0.58**	−0.74**	0.12
	[0.16, 1.01]	[−1.25, −0.24]	[−0.50, 0.74]
US Citizen	0.78***	−0.12	0.14
	[0.62, 0.95]	[−0.32, 0.08]	[−0.11, 0.38]
Latino Friends	−0.80***	0.05	0.71***
	[−1.15, −0.45]	[−0.29, 0.40]	[0.33, 1.10]
Mixed Friends	−0.39*	0.01	0.51**
	[−0.73, 0.04]	[−0.32, 0.35]	[0.14, 0.87]
Kids in School	0.01	0.34***	0.08
	[−0.13, 0.15]	[0.19, 0.50]	[−0.11, 0.27]
No Job Outside Home	0.04	0.27	0.19
	[−0.10, 0.17]	[−0.01, 0.55]	[−0.17, 0.56]
Pseudo R-Squared	0.07	0.04	0.02
N	4,591	4,588	4,662

Note: Ordered logistic regression with robust standard errors and state-level fixed effects, with California as the excluded state and Mexicans as the excluded national origin group. All continuous variables are rescaled from 0 to 1. Brackets indicate the 95% Confidence Interval.

***p < 0.00, **p < 0.01, *p <0.05

statistically significant. Again, as expected, Latinas and Spanish speakers were less likely to adopt this identity. In the first-generation model, the skin color variable became statistically significant in the expected direction; respondents with a lighter phenotype were more likely to adopt an American identity. These findings highlight the importance of taking an intersectional approach to understanding identity acquisition in the United States.

Symbolic Ethnicity and Incorporationism

An oft-cited concern of anti-immigrant activists is that Latinos do not want to assimilate in the United States, with immigrants threatening to transform American culture (Chavez 2008; Huntington 2004a, 2004b). In contrast to these claims, I find by a variety of measures that less acculturated Latinos are precisely those who prioritize changing to blend into the United States. For instance, Spanish-dominant respondents were more likely to want to blend. In contrast, in many cases, several of the independent variables that measure acculturation were associated with both a *strong American identity* and a *decreased* desire to blend into the United States or an *increased* desire to maintain a distinct panethnic culture. For example, more-educated respondents and individuals who are second generation and above were less likely to say that Latinos should change to blend into the United States, whereas US citizens were more likely to express support for maintaining a distinct panethnic culture. These findings are consistent with Waters's (1990, 1999) arguments about ethnic options, which emphasize that individuals who blend into the core of society have greater freedom to embrace cultural and ethnic symbols without sacrificing their mainstream identity.

The results described above are also consistent with the idea of "symbolic ethnicity," in which group members who are more incorporated, including later-generation immigrants, and those who are more structurally assimilated seek to preserve their ethnic heritage (Bean, Stevens, and Wierzbicki 2003; Brown and Bean 2006; Gans 1979; Vasquez 2011a, 2011b). Vasquez (2011a, 733) presents one example of this phenomenon in an interview with a third-generation Mexican American who often passes for white and seeks to "return" to his ethnicity. He explains his emphasis on Spanish language and ethnic symbols as follows, "We're all American but it's nice if you can have a little something that kind of separates you out or makes you more insightful." For this respondent, ethnic symbols are seen as an optional add-on to his primary American identity.

My findings also underscore that indicators of structural assimilation, such as socioeconomic status and immigrant generation, are not always associated with attitudes about cultural assimilation (Bean, Stevens, and Wierzbicki 2003; Neckerman, Carter, and Lee 1999; Portes and Zhou 1993). Rather, respondents who were more incorporated by traditional measures were more likely to think that feeling American is possible without sacrificing their *latinidad,* their Latino traditions and culture (Lavariega Monforti 2007). These findings likewise reiterate an incorporationist perspective, which suggests that individuals can adopt an American identity even as they seek to preserve an immigrant legacy. Echoing a finding in Chapter 5, increased time in the United States leads to an understanding of what it means to be American that allows for greater diversity, openness, and cultural difference.

In research on the general population, those who very strongly identified as American were most likely to define American in terms of ascriptive categories; individuals who felt the most American had the most restrictive definition of who qualifies for membership in the national group, thereby limiting access to this category (Theiss-Morse 2009). In contrast, I find that among Latinos, Spanish speakers were significantly more likely to define American in ascriptive terms, but were far less likely to adopt this identity, suggesting an inverse relationship. In other words, individuals in the far-periphery were more likely to perceive American as a closed, inaccessible category, and less likely to describe themselves as such. For both whites and Latinos, ascriptive definitions of American, which emphasize characteristics such as skin color and birthplace, indicate a restrictive understanding of this category. Yet, for the core group members in the Anglo population, this closed definition reaffirms one's sense of belonging. In contrast, for many Latinos in the periphery, the emphasis on ascriptive conditions signifies barriers to entry, indicating that American is an identity or group from which they are excluded.

Conclusion

Throughout this book, I develop the idea of a politics-to-identity link in which political events and framing are poised to influence individual attitudes and self-identification. This chapter addresses a prior question, exploring some of the other factors that contribute to the adoption of an American identity among Latinos. I also explore attitudes about incorporationism, including Latino perspectives about changing to blend into the United States and maintaining a distinct culture. In addition to the concepts of near- and far-periphery developed in Chapter 5, my arguments are also guided by intersectionality theory. In particular, I focus on gender, an understudied variable with respect to the adoption of an American identity. Although many traditional indicators suggest that Latinas are more likely to incorporate in the United States, compared with Latino men, they were less likely to self-identify as American. Consistent with research on cross-cultural psychology that highlights women as the "carriers of culture," I show that women were more likely to want to preserve a distinct Latino/Hispanic culture and less likely to want to change to blend into the United States. For Latinas, incorporation is more likely to occur in a way that emphasizes cultural maintenance. These findings underscore the need for an intersectional understanding of the process of identity acquisition.

Chapter 5 tentatively maps national origin onto the near- and far-periphery, placing Cubans and Puerto Ricans in the near-periphery and Salvadorans in the far-periphery. Among first-generation immigrants, both Cubans and Puerto Ricans were more likely to adopt an American identity than the reference group (Mexicans), indicative of the unique experiences and privileged legal status of these group members. Puerto Ricans were also less likely to think that Latinos should change to blend into the United States. Consistent with existing research, I find that language preference plays a significant role in Latino self-identification, with Spanish speakers less likely to identify as American than their English-speaking counterparts. Notably, however, such categories are multidimensional, and limitations exist in measuring them as binary variables. Although the above analysis demonstrates general trends, the control variables in the model reiterate the importance of exploring the multifaceted nature of these groupings as well as the need for future research that improves our understanding of the ways in which these and other categories interact, resulting in varied experiences for group members.

With respect to incorporationist attitudes, my findings indicate that more-established Latinos feel more comfortable embracing difference. Consistent with arguments about symbolic ethnicity, more-educated Latinos and later-generation immigrants were less likely to think Latinos should change to blend into the United States, whereas US citizens were more likely to think Latinos should maintain a distinct culture. Again, these results build on the findings of Chapter 5, which suggest that individuals in the far-periphery, or those furthest from the core, are more likely to understand what it means to be American in closed, ascriptive terms, whereas those closest to the core perceive American as a more diverse category.

Because identity is, at its core, a relational phenomenon, I also explore the role of social networks in self-identification, finding strong evidence of a relationship between self-identification and the diversity of one's friendship networks. Unfortunately, the questions in the LNS do not allow for further analysis to better understand what underlies this association or the direction of causality. For instance, do networks influence self-perception, or does self-perception guide friendship choices? My results suggest the need for future research to better understand the mechanisms underlying this relationship.

Chapter 7 turns to the relationship between political context and self-identification. Building on the findings presented in this chapter, I return to the natural experiment used throughout this book to evaluate the effects of the 2006 immigration protests on Latino self-identification. By examining the relationships between social movements, framing, and Latino self-identification, I empirically test the politics-to-identity theory advanced throughout this book.

7 | Can Protests Make Latinos "American"?

The 2006 Marches and the Politics-to-Identity Link

> *For all the talk of national security and the economic costs of immigration, the underlying issue driving the current anti-immigrant frenzy is a deep suspicion that this latest group of newcomers won't do what others have before them did [sic]: learn English and embrace American identity. . . . Instead of presenting themselves as an aggrieved, foreign presence, immigration advocates ought to be explaining how similar Latinos are to other Americans in their values, aspirations, and achievements.*
> —Linda Chavez, chair of the Center for Equal Opportunity, March 30, 2006

After the first wave of major immigrants' rights protests occurred in the spring of 2006, Linda Chavez penned an op-ed for the *New York Times,* "American Dreams, Foreign Flags," from which the above quote is drawn (Chavez 2006). In the column, Chavez, who served as Ronald Reagan's director of the US Civil Rights Commission, evoked California's 1994 debate over Proposition 187, which would have prevented undocumented immigrants and their children from accessing a range of social services. Like other Latino advocates, she argued that the sight of tens of thousands of Mexicans in the street, carrying the flag of their home country, had the unintended consequence of *increasing* popular support for that proposition, with the prominence of the Mexican flag scaring Americans into thinking that protesters' allegiances lay with a foreign country.

Much scholarship suggests that ethnic organizing leads to the politicization of collective identities. Similarly, research on social movements emphasizes the ways in which a movement's narrative and framing can alter the identity of participants (Gould 1995; Snow and McAdam 2000; Stryker, Owens, and White 2000). Typically, however, this literature assumes that in times of political turmoil, leaders are likely to "play the ethnic card," attaching increased political salience to racial and ethnic identities (Chandra 2009; Eifert, Miguel, and Posner 2010; Lee 2008). Likewise, new identities that emerge generally emphasize difference with the majority group (Fuchs 1990; Kastoryano 2002; Mora 2014).

Beyond protests, a hostile political context and experiences with discrimination are thought to result in "reactive ethnicity," with individuals more likely to describe themselves in pan-ethnic terms and less likely to identify with the majority group (Aleinikoff and Rumbaut 1998; Bean, Stevens, and Wierzbicki 2003; Massey and Sánchez R. 2010; Neckerman, Carter, and Lee 1999; Rumbaut and Portes 2001; Schildkraut 2005b). Consistent with this research, many scholars assumed that as a result of the contentious debate over immigration reform in 2006, Latinos would *feel* more Latino after the protests (Barreto, Manzano, Ramirez et al. 2009; Benjamin-Alvarado, DeSipio, and Montoya 2009).

Yet, during these events, rather than playing the ethnic card, leaders instead sought to "play the American card," repeatedly and vocally affirming Latinos' claims to being American. Many of the early protests against H.R. 4437 featured a preponderance of foreign flags. As the opening quote of this chapter suggests, this approach quickly led to a backlash. Event organizers and Spanish language radio personalities quickly recast their efforts, shifting to embrace the "We Are America" frame (for details, see Chapter 3).

My politics-to-identity theory argues that reactive ethnicity is not a given during times of contentious political debate. Rather, the policy feedback process can result in varied outcomes depending on the response by social movements and the *framing* of these events. Specifically, given the recasting of the 2006 protests around the "We Are America" frame, I anticipate that Latinos will be more likely to identify as American after these events. This expectation stands in contrast to assumptions that Latinos will be more likely to see themselves in pan-ethnic terms, reactively rejecting an American identity. Additionally, I anticipate that this process of policy feedback will be contingent upon the *salience* of the immigration policy debate, suggesting that the effects of these events will be uneven across the Latino population.

Building on the natural experiment employed in earlier chapters, below, I test my theory by taking advantage of the coincidence between data collection of the Latino National Survey (LNS) and the wave of immigration protests that occurred in the spring of 2006. Specifically, I examine whether respondents interviewed after the protests are more likely to see themselves as American, Latino, or both after these events. To explore the role of issue salience, I also use split samples to separately examine the effects of the immigration policy debate by national origin and language dominance.

Contentious Politics and Latino Self-Identification

Previous chapters demonstrate that compared with respondents interviewed before the 2006 protests, Latinos interviewed after these events are more likely to support liberal immigration policies and less likely to define American in terms of ascriptive characteristics including being white, being born in the United States, and speaking English. This chapter extends these ideas to test whether a politics-to-identity link exists such that, under certain conditions, a major political event framed around a particular identity can shape self-identification in a counterintuitive direction.

Since the mid-1950s, Latino organizations have politicized identities by highlighting cultural differences with the Anglo majority (see Chapter 3 for details). In the 2006 protests against H.R. 4437, however, the narrative returned to one of *inclusion* with the majority. As Latino elites and Spanish-language radio personalities mobilized community members, they encouraged participants to bring American flags to events and emphasized Latino belonging in the United States (Félix, González, and Ramirez 2008; Janiot 2006; Oz 2006). In contrast to the assumption that a reactive ethnicity will automatically emerge in a contentious political context, my politics-to-identity theory emphasizes that the policy feedback process can influence self-identification in *varied* ways. Given the elite emphasis and framing around American symbols, *I hypothesize that respondents interviewed after the spring 2006 events will be more likely to see themselves as American compared with similar respondents interviewed before.*

The racialized tone of the immigration debate in recent years has led scholars to focus renewed attention on the relationship between immigration and ethnicity. As Hero and Preuhs (2007, 499) explain, "Because immigration to the United States over the last generation is so heavily from Latin America, and Mexico in particular, policies regarding 'immigrants' may be viewed effectively as policies regarding 'Latinos'" (see also Hajnal, Gerber, and Louch 2002; Newton 2008). Despite intracommunal divisions regarding immigration policy, scholars and news analysts alike speculated that anti-immigrant sentiment surrounding the 2006 events would likewise unify the Latino community. Anti-Latino rhetoric and "racial profiling" were thought to paradoxically mobilize *all* Latinos, including Puerto Ricans and Cuban Americans as well as those residing in the United States for many generations.

In line with these ideas, surveys conducted after the protests show that Latinos reported increased levels of discrimination after these events. For example, in the Pew Hispanic Center's 2006 National Survey of Latinos (NSL), completed shortly after the protests, a majority of respondents reported an increase in discrimination as a result of the immigration policy debate (Suro and Escobar 2006). Similarly, the LNS contains a series of questions about individual experiences with discrimination by employers, police, landlords, and in a restaurant. Following the protests, reports of discrimination increased across each category; for instance, 15.5 percent of respondents interviewed before the protests reported discrimination while at a restaurant, compared with 20.3 percent of those interviewed after.

Despite elite efforts to frame the 2006 events around the theme of Latinos being American, many political scientists' accounts of the protests assume that feelings of discrimination evoked by these events would lead to an increase in pan-ethnic identification (Barreto, Manzano, Ramirez et al. 2009). For instance, Benjamin-Alvarado, DeSipio, and Montoya (2009, 723) argue, "The rise in national, anti-immigrant, anti-Latino rhetoric and legislative proposals served to reinforce a sense of pan-ethnic identity." These claims are consistent with ideas that discrimination and a contentious political climate lead individuals to reactively adopt an ethnic identity and make them less likely to adopt an American identity (Aleinikoff and Rumbaut 1998; Bean, Stevens, and Wierzbicki 2003; Massey and Sánchez R. 2010; Neckerman, Carter, and Lee 1999; Rumbaut and Portes 2001; Schildkraut 2005b). To examine this perspective more closely, *I also test an alternative hypothesis: given the heightened sense of discrimination against Latinos and the contentious political context that emerged as a result of the 2006 protests, respondents interviewed after these events will be more likely to see themselves in pan-ethnic terms compared with similar respondents interviewed before.* Finally, recent scholarship has focused on the question of whether identity choices are a tradeoff, asking whether an increase in self-identification with one group will result in a decrease in self-identification with another (Sidanius, Feshbach, Levin et al. 1997). Reporting on findings from focus group research,

Fraga, Garcia, Hero et al. (2010) point out that Latinos do not appear to view the choice to identify as American, Latino, or with a national origin group as a zero-sum one. These ideas are consistent with my findings in Chapter 6 about incorporationism, which demonstrate that large majorities of Latinos believe it is possible to both maintain a distinct pan-ethnic culture and simultaneously change to blend into the United States. Accordingly, *my third hypothesis anticipates that even as self-identification as American increases, self-identification with national origin will remain constant.* In other words, no tradeoff in identities occurs. Rather, among individuals who strongly identify with their national/ancestral origin, this identity is more stable, or less subject to politicization, than an American identity.

Feeling American

To test the three hypotheses outlined above, I compare Latino self-identification and incorporationist attitudes among individuals interviewed before April 1 (control group) with those interviewed after (treatment group).[1] Using the protests and their patriotic frame as the treatment variable, this approach provides the opportunity to test whether shifts occur in response to questions about self-perception and incorporationism (see Chapter 2 for a full description of the quasi-experimental research design).

For self-identification, I examine responses to the question, "In general, how strongly or not do you think of yourself as _____?" A series of questions was asked in random order, with American, Latino/Hispanic, and a national origin descriptor used separately. Respondents were given four options ranging from not very strongly to very strongly. As in Chapter 6, I also test two additional dependent variables regarding the extent to which an individual thinks it is important for Latinos to change in order to blend into the United States and to maintain a distinct culture, respectively. Both are measured on a three-point scale, from not at all important to very important.

Consistent with the protests' frame, my politics-to-identity theory anticipates that Latinos interviewed after these events were more likely to identify as American than those interviewed before. I begin with a simple bivariate test of this hypothesis using data from Phase 1 of the LNS. Figure 7.1 demonstrates that in the time following the protests, the number of respondents indicating they did "not at all" feel American declined substantially, with a corresponding increase in the number say-ing they "very strongly" felt American. This figure indicates preliminary support for the politics-to-identity hypothesis.

I extend this analysis by testing all three hypotheses about self-identification in a multivariate context. To estimate the effects of the spring 2006 marches on respondents' self-identification, I present three separate ordered logistic regression models. The main independent vari-able of interest in these models is a binary variable indicating whether the respondent is a member of the control group interviewed before the protest or the post-protest treatment group. I also include control vari-ables for gender, self-reported skin color, language dominance, years of education, household income, age, and a series of dummy variables reflecting immigrant generation (for a full description of variables and coding, see Appendix A).[2]

The model in Table 7.1, Column 1 indicates support for my politics-to-identity hypothesis: consistent with the frame of the protests, respon-dents interviewed after these events were more likely to feel American than those interviewed earlier. These findings demonstrate that in con-trast to expectations of existing literature, Latinos did not reactively re-ject an American identity. Rather, despite reporting increased feelings of discrimination, Latinos surveyed after the 2006 events were 4 per-centage points more likely to very strongly identify with the majority.[3]

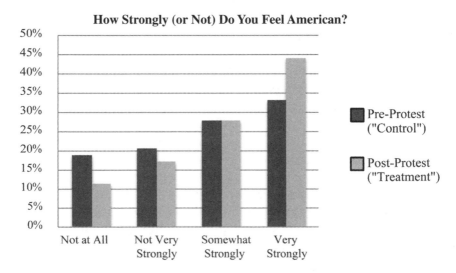

Figure 7.1 Identification as American before and after April 2006 Protests (LNS 2006)

This counterintuitive finding demonstrates the power of protests and frames to influence self-perception. Notably, this predicted probability is calculated using a sample that includes all five national origin groups studied throughout this book, including group members less likely to be influenced by the immigration policy debate. I anticipate that when

Table 7.1 Effects of Spring 2006 Protests on Respondent Self-Identification, Full Sample (LNS 2006)

	American Identity (1)	Pan-Ethnic Identity (2)	Country of Origin (3)	"Blend" into the United States (4)	Maintain Unique Culture (5)
Post-Protests	0.19**	0.03	−0.06	0.29***	−0.14
	(0.07)	(0.66)	(0.04)	(0.08)	(0.09)
Female	−0.40***	0.21**	0.15*	−0.24**	0.33***
	(0.07)	(0.07)	(0.07)	(0.07)	(0.09)
Skin Color	0.19	−0.07	−0.20	0.32*	0.07
	(0.10)	(0.14)	(0.14)	(0.14)	(0.17)
Survey in Spanish	−0.94***	0.37***	−0.01	0.85***	0.50***
	(0.09)	(0.10)	(0.10)	(0.10)	(0.12)
Age	1.86***	−0.57**	−0.48*	1.70***	−0.17
	(0.18)	(0.19)	(0.19)	(0.20)	(0.23)
Years of Education	0.98***	0.23	0.48	−1.07***	−0.21
	(0.23)	(0.24)	(0.26)	(0.25)	(0.32)
Household Income	0.43**	0.23	0.01	0.02	−0.21
	(0.13)	(0.13)	(0.14)	(0.13)	(0.14)
Immigrant Generation					
Newcomer	−0.12	−0.24*	0.08	0.22	−0.19
(in US < 5 years)	(0.10)	(0.12)	(0.13)	(0.12)	(0.15)
Second Generation	0.74***	0.30*	−0.22	−0.13	0.20
	(0.12)	(0.13)	(0.12)	(0.12)	(0.14)
Third Generation	1.64***	−0.29*	−1.07***	−0.46***	−0.08
and Above	(0.13)	(0.12)	(0.11)	(0.11)	(0.13)
Pseudo R-Squared	0.13	0.01	0.03	0.08	0.02
N	5,470	5,489	5,491	5,403	5,480

Note: Ordered logistic regression with robust standard errors. The first three dependent variables are the degree to which a respondent self-identifies as American, with a pan-ethnic identity, and with his or her country of national origin, on a scale of 1 (not at all) to 4 (very strongly). The fourth and fifth dependent variables, opinions about whether Latinos/Hispanics should change to blend into the United States and maintain a distinct culture, are measured on a scale of 1 (not at all important) to 3 (very important). All continuous variables are rescaled from 0 to 1. State-level fixed effects are used, with respondents from DC, Maryland, and Virginia combined as one category representing the DC metropolitan area.

*p < 0.05, **p < 0.01, ***p < 0.001.

looking specifically at national origin groups for whom immigration is most salient, the difference in self-identification after the protests will be even higher.

The alternative hypothesis anticipated that heightened racial profiling and feelings of discrimination would make Latinos feel more pan-ethnic. Column 2 demonstrates no support for this hypothesis, with no statistically significant difference in pan-ethnic identity before and after the protests. This finding counters the conventional wisdom, which assumed that the spring 2006 events would result in greater pan-ethnic sentiment for all Latinos. Importantly, although previous scholarship emphasizes the construction of a pan-ethnic identity as a vehicle for political mobilization, the 2006 immigration events emphasized an *American*—rather than pan-ethnic—identity. These counterintuitive results suggest that social movement mobilization around this patriotic frame matters. Even as feelings of individual-level discrimination increase, the policy feedback process, including a collective response around a frame of belonging, mitigates the reactive rejection of an American identity.

My third hypothesis anticipated that even as an American identity increased, identification with country of origin would remain stable. Column 3 demonstrates support for this hypothesis, indicating that empirically, no tradeoff between identities occurs. Rather, self-identification with a particular group can be "activated" without affecting the level of identification with another group. Indeed, the percentage of respondents who self-identify with a pan-ethnic identifier and with their countries of origin remained consistently high across the treatment and control groups, suggesting a high level of stability with respect to *both* of these two identities across the Latino population. In contrast, for certain subgroups, an American identity is more fluid.[4]

The remaining dependent variables explore incorporationist attitudes, including the maintenance of a distinct Latino culture and whether Latinos should change to blend into greater US society. The results in Columns 4 and 5 mirror the findings in the first two columns. Respondents interviewed after the protests were more likely to say that Latinos should change to blend into US society, whereas no change was evident with respect to maintaining a unique Latino/Hispanic culture.[5] My results demonstrate that after the 2006 protests, Latinos reported both a strong sense of feeling American and a greater desire to change to blend into the United States. In contrast, I did not find any support for the assumption that the protests led Latinos to reactively reject American culture or identity.

Importantly, in contrast to most policy feedback research, which explores the effects of policies already enacted, I look at the effects of a contentious policy *debate* around legislation that never actually became law. In particular, I emphasize the importance of the protests' patriotic frame, which leads to unanticipated shifts in self-identification. This approach is consistent with self-categorization theory, which emphasizes that comparing oneself and one's attributes with those of a prototype group member contributes to self-identification. Self-categorization theory also allows for the formation of temporary prototypes as another influence on self-identification (Huddy 2001). My findings indicate that for some group members, the emphasis placed on Latinos being American in the spring 2006 protests led to the development of such a prototype around an American identity. As Chapter 5 explains, after the protests, Latinos were less likely to define American in terms of birthplace and skin color. Likewise, this shift influenced self-identification among some segments of the Latino population.

What Drives Pan-Ethnic Identification?

Column 2 of Table 7.1 also provides the opportunity to explore other factors associated with the adoption of a pan-ethnic identity. A range of previous research finds that strong identification in pan-ethnic terms was slow to emerge across the Latino community (de la Garza, DeSipio, Garcia et al. 1992; Hero 1992; Jones-Correa and Leal 1996). By 2006, however, an estimated 91 percent of respondents to the LNS indicated that they "very highly" or "somewhat highly" identified in pan-ethnic terms. The adoption of a pan-ethnic identity is treated at length by other scholars and will not be explored in great detail in this book. Below, I briefly outline key findings from Table 7.1.

In Chapter 6 I find that Latinas were less likely to self-identify as American than Latino men were. Here, I demonstrate that Latinas were also more likely than Latino men to identify in both pan-ethnic and national origin terms. These results reaffirm the hypothesis that women are less likely to identify as American because they place greater emphasis on cultural maintenance and community (Dion and Dion 2001;

González, Umaña-Taylor, and Bámaca 2006; Phinney 1990; Phinney, Horenczyk, Liebkind et al. 2001; Vasquez 2011a, 2011b).

Shared language increases feelings of solidarity and community, and language use is commonly associated with both self-identification and policy attitudes (DeSipio 1996a, 1996b; Horowitz 1985; Schmidt 2002; see also Chapter 4 of this volume). Similarly, whereas English speakers were more likely to see themselves as American, Spanish speakers were more likely to identify in pan-ethnic terms. Consistent with existing research, younger individuals were more likely to adopt a pan-ethnic identity (Jones-Correa and Leal 1996; Masuoka 2006), whereas older respondents were more likely to see themselves as American. Older respondents were also less likely to describe themselves in terms of their national origin. As in previous studies, the variables related to socioeconomic status were not associated with a pan-ethnic identifier to any degree of statistical significance (Jones-Correa and Leal 1996; Masuoka 2006).

Using data from the 1999 *Washington Post*/Kaiser/Harvard National Survey on Latinos in America, Masuoka (2006) found that Latinos born in the United States were more likely to demonstrate a sense of group consciousness than were immigrants. Masuoka's results highlight the fact that pan-ethnic identities are also constructions of life in the United States. However, she divides the data into just two categories, immigrants and native-born respondents. My analysis suggests a parabolic relationship between an individual's time in the United States and their preference for a pan-ethnic identity. Because a Latino/Hispanic identity is acquired while living in the United States, respondents who have been in the United States for less than five years were less likely to identify in pan-ethnic terms than those who have been here longer. Compared to first-generation respondents, those in the second generation were significantly more likely to see themselves as Latino or Hispanic. However, this relationship is reversed for respondents who are third generation and above. Later-generation respondents were *less* likely to describe themselves either pan-ethnically or in terms of national origin. My results are consistent with existing scholarship that finds that given the stigma surrounding new arrivals, many established Latinos opt to distance themselves from their coethnics (García Bedolla 2005). Contrary to the fears of anti-immigrant activists, my findings are also consistent with research demonstrating the increased incorporation of Latinos over time and generation (Citrin, Lerman, Murakami et al. 2007; Fraga, Garcia, Hero et al. 2012).

Protests, Identity, and Issue Salience: Examining Intragroup Variation

The analysis above demonstrates support for the first part of my politics-to-identity hypothesis, which emphasizes the importance of the policy feedback process, social movements, and framing in influencing self-identification. Importantly, my theory also argues that any changes in self-identification are contingent upon issue salience. Simply put, for individuals to be affected by the immigration policy debate, this debate must be relevant to them.

Existing research on policy feedback typically focuses only on the target group, consisting of individuals *most affected* by a policy. Indeed, many scholars note that our understanding of policy feedback beyond those in the target group remains limited (Campbell 2012; Mettler and Sorelle 2014; Oberlander 2003; Patashnik and Zelizer 2013; Soss and Schram 2007). My emphasis on the varied salience of immigration policy across the heterogeneous Latino population helps to fill this gap.

Research on framing effects demonstrates that the influence of a frame is contingent upon the salience or relevance of the underlying issue to an individual (Chong and Druckman 2007). Given the significant variation in Latino attitudes on immigration policy, I similarly anticipate that the effects of the 2006 protests and their patriotic frame will be uneven across the Latino population. I additionally contribute to our understanding of framing effects by evaluating them in a real-world setting.

Chapter 4 of this book demonstrates core cleavages in attitudes about immigration policy across different subsets of the Latino population. These cleavages suggest that only some segments of this community should be considered the target group. In particular, I find that compared to English-dominant respondents, Spanish-dominant respondents are much more likely to support liberal policy options such as immediate legalization for undocumented immigrants. With respect to national origin, Puerto Ricans, who are born US citizens, and Cuban exiles, who have preferential immigration status in the United States, support more conservative policy options than do members of other ancestral origin groups. Despite claims that the protests would unite *all* Latinos, I demonstrate that this intragroup variation persists even after these events. I also present evidence from a range of sources that Spanish speakers and individuals of Mexican and Dominican origin were most likely to participate in the 2006 protests, and Cuban exiles were least likely to report participation.

Consistent with these differences, I develop two additional hypotheses: *I expect that the protests and their message will be most likely to influence (1) Spanish-dominant respondents and (2) Mexicans, Dominicans, and Salvadorans.* However, effects are likely to be limited or nonexistent for English-dominant respondents and for respondents of Puerto Rican and Cuban ancestry or origin.

To test these claims, I return to the approach of split samples, which provide the best opportunity to evaluate intragroup differences (Burns, Schlozman, and Verba 2001; Dolan 2014; Masuoka and Junn 2013; Silber Mohamed 2015; Welch 1977). Below, I present a series of models limiting the sample to each of the five national origin groups. I also present separate models for Spanish and English speakers, respectively. The use of split samples allows us to see whether the effects of the protests persist across these different demographic groups, or whether they are limited only to the subset of target groups identified within the Latino population.

National Origin Groups

I begin with national origin, hypothesizing that the effects of the protests will be concentrated among Mexicans, Dominicans, and Salvadorans, for whom the issue of immigration reform is most salient. As established in Chapter 3, the Mexican and Salvadoran communities encompass the highest proportion of undocumented immigrants. Although Dominicans have a lower percentage of group members in the United States without legal status, as a result of legal changes from the 1996 Illegal Immigration Reform and Immigrant Responsibility Act (IIRIRA), deportations have risen dramatically, and this community has been disproportionately affected by the increase. Chapter 3 documents the strong Dominican presence at the 2006 protests, in which group members were motivated by the goal of reforming deportation policies (Northern Manhattan Coalition for Immigrant Rights 2009; Zepeda-Millán 2014). In contrast to these target populations, I anticipate little or no change in self-identification among Puerto Ricans, who are US citizens, and Cuban exiles, who receive special legal protections with respect to immigration status.

Table 7.2 presents the results of multivariate analysis for the split sample by national origin, and Figure 7.2 presents predicted probabilities for the different national origin groups. In the figure, the bullet represents the change in predicted probability that a respondent from a given subgroup will very strongly self-identify as American if interviewed after the protests, compared with a similar respondent interviewed before. The line on either side of the bullet represents the 95 percent confidence interval.

As anticipated, respondents of Dominican and Mexican origin or ancestry were more likely to indicate feeling very strongly American following the spring 2006 protests. Indeed, group members interviewed

Table 7.2   Effects of Spring 2006 Protests on American Self-Identification by National Origin (LNS 2006)

	Cuban (1)	Dominican (2)	Mexican (3)	Puerto Rican (4)	Salvadoran (5)
Post-Protests	0.26	**0.61****	**0.21****	−0.21	−0.21
	(0.36)	**(0.21)**	**(0.06)**	(0.19)	(0.24)
Female	0.17	0.14	**−0.47*****	**−0.40***	−0.52
	(0.23)	(0.30)	**(0.07)**	**(0.16)**	(0.37)
Skin Color	0.06	0.15	0.15	0.14	0.28
	(0.35)	(0.28)	(0.14)	(0.33)	(0.51)
Survey in Spanish	**−0.96*****	**−0.99****	**−0.88*****	**−0.50***	**−0.80*****
	(0.20)	**(0.34)**	**(0.10)**	**(0.02)**	**(0.18)**
Age	**1.99*****	**0.39*****	**1.6*****	**1.95*****	0.85
	(0.35)	**(0.10)**	**(0.22)**	**(0.41)**	(0.90)
Years of Education	**−0.96*****	0.04	**0.95*****	**1.83*****	1.21
	(0.20)	(0.49)	**(0.23)**	**(0.42)**	(0.75)
Household Income	**1.36*****	0.30	**0.48****	−0.08	−0.19
	(0.21)	(0.55)	**(0.08)**	(0.27)	(0.37)
Immigrant Generation					
Newcomer	−0.11	**−1.15*****	−0.05	**−0.81****	−0.38
(in US < 5 years)	(0.26)	**(0.27)**	(0.14)	**(0.27)**	(0.36)
Second Generation	0.12	−0.15	**0.79*****	**0.90*****	**0.91***
	(0.53)	(0.45)	**(0.11)**	**(0.15)**	**(0.45)**
Third Generation	0.18	**−1.69*****	**1.89*****	**0.86****	1.18
and Above	(0.64)	**(0.64)**	**(0.12)**	**(0.27)**	(1.07)
Pseudo R-Squared	0.07	0.06	0.15	0.06	0.06
N	298	234	4,050	620	268

Note: Ordered logistic regression with robust standard errors, clustered by state. The dependent variable in both models is the extent to which a respondent self-identifies as American. All continuous variables are rescaled from 0 to 1.

*p < 0.05, **p < 0.01, ***p < 0.001.

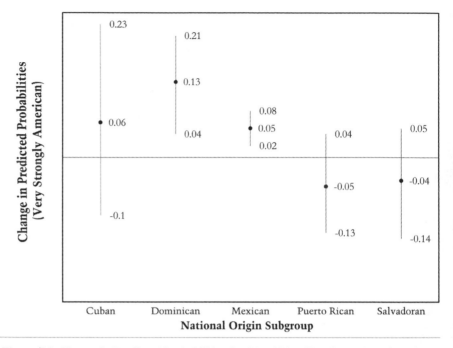

Figure 7.2 Change in Predicted Probabilities for Identifying Very Strongly as American, Pre- and Post-2006 Protests, by National Origin Subgroup (LNS 2006)

Note: Predicted probabilities are calculated with all continuous variables held at their mean and dummy variables set as follows: male, Spanish-speaking respondent, born outside of the United States but arrived more than five years ago.

after the protests were 13 percentage points and 5 percentage points more likely to identify as American, respectively. In particular, the findings about Dominicans serve as an important robustness check of this analysis, as no demographic differences exist between the control and treatment groups within this population, yet a significant shift in self-identification persists.

In contrast, as Figure 7.2 reflects, the confidence intervals for Cubans, Puerto Ricans, and Salvadorans all cross 0, indicating that no statistically significant shift in identities occurred for these group members. Because immigration issues are less salient for Cubans and Puerto Ricans, respondents from these subgroups were less likely to identify with the protest movement, and consequently, less likely to experience shifts in identification.

The Salvadoran case is more puzzling. This community has the second-largest number of undocumented individuals living in the United States, and group members also have the highest level of support for liberal immigration policies. If anything, the immigration debate should be especially salient for this community, composed of relatively new arrivals to the United States. To better understand this result, I return to the findings of Chapter 5, which show that Salvadorans were significantly more likely than respondents from other subgroups to define American in terms of ascriptive characteristics such as birthplace, language skills, and religion. Given the high emphasis placed by Salvadoran respondents on ascriptive categories, I speculate that group members are less likely to perceive American as an accessible category that they are able to join. Thus, despite the high salience of the immigration debate to this community, group members were less open to the protests' identity-based message because they were less likely to view American as a category to which they are eligible for admission.

Language Preference

In addition to national origin, Chapter 4 demonstrates that the immigration policy debate is far more salient for Spanish-dominant respondents than for English-dominant Latinos. Similarly, I find that the shift in self-identification after the protests is concentrated among Spanish-dominant individuals. As Table 7.3 reflects, limiting the analysis to English speakers, the protests had no effect on the extent to which a respondent self-identifies as American. In contrast, Spanish speakers in the treatment group were 6 percentage points more likely to very strongly identify as American than those in the pre-protest group. These findings are also consistent with research demonstrating that Spanish-speaking Latinos and less incorporated group members are more influenced by ethnic appeals and identity-based messages (Abrajano 2010; Valenzuela and Michelson, forthcoming), leaving these groups more open to the patriotic frame of the 2006 protests.

Comparing the two models, in both groups there was a relationship between a higher level of education and identifying as American. However, the income variable was significant only for Spanish speakers, suggesting that for this population, a combination of socioeconomic factors contributes to self-identification choices.

Collectively, the findings in this section demonstrate that the effects of the spring 2006 protests on respondents' self-identification are

Table 7.3 Effects of Spring 2006 Protests on American Self-Identification by Language Preference (LNS 2006)

	English Speakers (Standard Error)	Change in Predicted Probability (95% CI)	Spanish Speakers (Standard Error)	Change in Predicted Probability (95% CI)
Post-Protests	-0.06	-0.01	0.33***	0.06
	(0.14)	[-0.08, 0.05]	(0.08)	[0.03, 0.09]
Female	-0.35**	-0.09	-0.41***	-0.08
	(0.12)	[-0.15, -0.03]	(0.08)	[-0.11, -0.04]
Skin Color	-0.02	-0.00	0.33*	0.07
	(0.23)	[-0.12, 0.11]	(0.16)	[0.00, 0.13]
Age	2.50***	0.50	1.58***	0.35
	(0.32)	[0.40, 0.60]	(0.23)	[0.25, 0.45]
Years of Education	1.68***	0.40	0.65**	0.13
	(0.48)	[0.20, 0.59]	(0.26)	[0.02, 0.23]
Household Income	0.37	0.09	0.46**	0.10
	(0.21)	[-0.01, 0.19]	(0.16)	[0.03, 0.17]
Immigrant Generation				
Newcomer	-0.37	-0.09	-0.15	-0.03
(in US < 5 years)	(0.31)	[-0.24, 0.06]	(0.11)	[-0.07, 0.01]
Second Generation	0.66***	0.15	1.02***	0.24
	(0.15)	[0.09, 0.22]	(0.21)	[0.14, 0.34]
Third Generation	1.71***	0.32	1.03***	0.24
and Above	(0.16)	[0.26, 0.37]	(0.23)	[0.13, 0.35]
Pseudo R-Squared	0.11		0.04	
N	2,352		3,118	

Note: Ordered logistic regression with robust standard errors and state-level fixed effects. The dependent variable in both models is the extent to which a respondent self-identifies as American. All continuous variables are rescaled from 0 to 1. The change in predicted probabilities reflects the increase or decrease in identifying "very strongly" as American, with independent variables moving from their lowest to highest value. To calculate changes in predicted probabilities, all continuous variables are set at their mean, with dummy variables set as follows: male respondents interviewed after the protests, born outside the United States, living here more than five years.

*p < 0.05, **p < 0.01, ***p < 0.001.

concentrated primarily among groups most affected by the immigration debate, highlighting the importance of issue salience in the policy feedback process. More broadly, they also illustrate the vast diversity of the Latino community as well as the importance of developing a fine-grained understanding of intragroup differences based on characteristics such as language and national origin.

Discussion

This chapter employs a natural experiment to investigate the politics-to-identity link, studying the effects of the 2006 protests and their distinct patriotic frame on self-identification across the Latino population. Consistent with the protests' "We Are America" frame, Latinos interviewed after these events were more likely to self-identify as American than were comparable respondents interviewed before. Individuals interviewed after the protests were also more likely to say that Latinos should change to blend into the United States. In contrast to conventional wisdom, which holds that Latinos will be more likely to identify in pan-ethnic terms after the protests, I find no support for this alternative hypothesis. Both pan-ethnic identity and identification with a national origin group remained constant before and after the protests. Whereas a range of existing research demonstrates framing effects in a laboratory setting, my results demonstrate that frames can also influence individuals' attitudes and perceptions in a real-world setting in seemingly counterintuitive ways.

My analysis also extends our understanding of policy feedback by examining whether and how political debate influences a heterogeneous group. I hypothesized that within the Latino population, only target groups for whom the immigration debate is most salient would be influenced by the protests and their frame. Limiting the analysis to different subgroups, I find support for this hypothesis. The shift in self-identification was limited to Spanish-dominant respondents, with no effects among English-speakers. Among national origin groups, a change in self-identification is evident only among Mexicans and Dominicans. Despite the high salience of immigration reform to Salvadorans, I find no effects within this population. I speculate that this null finding is the result of the distinct background and experiences of this community as well as group members' restrictive understanding of what it means to be American.

Importantly, in my model, the treatment variable refers to the protests as well as their patriotic frame. Because the protests were completely exogenous from the LNS, unfortunately, no information is available regarding whether respondents actually participated in these events. Given the dramatic increase in immigration-related media coverage between April and June 2006 (Dunaway, Branton, and Abrajano 2010), however, the contentious political atmosphere during that time is likely a sufficient condition for treatment; even if respondents did not actually attend the protests, they were very likely exposed to their message.[6] This assumption is consistent with a wide range of research emphasizing the consequences of media effects and framing (Ansolabehere and Iyengar 1995; Berelson, Lazarsfeld, and McPhee 1956; Iyengar 1991; Zaller 1992) as well as my theory that both the protests and their patriotic frame led to shifts in self-identification.

Conclusion

As the opening quote of this chapter demonstrates, in the spring of 2006, Latino leaders strategically advanced a patriotic frame as they protested the immigration reform proposal embodied in H.R. 4437. As they encouraged their widespread base of listeners to participate in the protests, popular Spanish-language deejays reiterated that Latinos represent America. Event organizers distributed US flags and instructed participants to leave their Mexican flags at home. This approach represented a stark departure from Latino social movements of the late twentieth century, which emphasized differences with the Anglo majority. Rather, the 2006 protests returned to the pro-American frame advanced by the earliest Latino social movements of a century prior. Yet, those early movements generally represented a small segment of the Mexican American community: middle-class US citizens. In contrast, in 2006, a far more diverse group of activists embraced this message, including citizens and noncitizens alike.

This chapter demonstrates that the protests and their frame shaped self-identification among certain segments of the Latino population in a seemingly counterintuitive way. Existing research anticipates that in the face of heightened discrimination, group members would reactively reject an American identity and increasingly adopt a pan-ethnic identity. *In contrast to these expectations, my politics-to-identity theory emphasizes that the policy feedback process, social movements, and framing can influence self-identification in varied ways.* Specifically, I hypothesized that changes in Latino self-identification would be consistent with the "We Are America" frame advanced at the protests.

Counter to the widespread expectation that the immigration protests would result in greater feelings of pan-ethnicity across the Latino population, my findings demonstrate support for my politics-to-identity theory, which argues that contentious policy debate can result in *varied* outcomes contingent upon both framing and issue salience. Employing evidence from a natural experiment that occurred during data collection for the LNS, I demonstrate that many individuals did indeed internalize the messages of the 2006 protests. Consistent with the framing of these events, I find strong statistically significant evidence that Latinos interviewed after the protests were more likely to identify as American and more likely to express a desire to change to blend into the United States. Given the widespread press coverage of these events and the documented role of Latino deejays in building support for the protests, I contend that actual participation is not a prerequisite for treatment. This shift suggests the power of social movements and their frames to transform identities in a complex fashion.

In contrast, I found no change in identification with either a Latino/Hispanic or national origin identity. Likewise, there was no change in attitudes about maintaining a distinct Hispanic/Latino culture. Overall, I demonstrate that even as some identities remain stable, others can be "activated" in a seemingly counterintuitive way as part of the policy feedback process (Chandra 2009).

Importantly, my argument expands upon our existing understanding of policy feedback by focusing on contentious political *debate* rather than an existing policy or program. Additionally, my analysis seeks to understand the effects of policy debate on a heterogeneous group, looking beyond the target groups most directly affected by a policy change. Highlighting the diversity of the Latino population, I demonstrate that these events have differential effects across the Latino community based largely on the salience of immigration reform.

My findings demonstrate that efforts to frame social movements around a particular identity-based message can influence the self-perception of individuals under certain conditions. These findings have significant implications for the process of immigrant incorporation, citizenship, and our understanding of the malleability of identity within a participatory democracy. Yet, self-identification is not only a one-sided process, and my results also raise important questions about whether these new Americans will be accepted by the Anglo majority as well as the constraints that other groups place on an individual's self-identification. In Chapter 8, I reflect on these questions as well as my broader findings, connecting them to the 2016 presidential election and the ongoing debate over immigration policy.

8 | Epilogue

Ten years after the 2006 policy debate over H.R. 4437 and the unprecedented wave of Latino protests discussed throughout this book, the debate over comprehensive immigration reform remains unresolved, and the political landscape surrounding the immigration debate has shifted dramatically. At the time of this writing, the 2016 presidential election cycle was well under way, with the rhetoric about immigration and immigrants becoming ever more polarizing.

In the announcement of his candidacy for the Republican nomination for president, Donald J. Trump inveighed against Latino immigrants, accusing Mexico of sending criminals, rapists, and drug dealers north to the United States ("Full Text" 2015). This language, along with repeated calls for the federal government to actively track and deport all undocumented immigrants in the United States and to build a wall along the entirety of the US-Mexico border, pushed immigration back into the forefront of US politics with a new, vitriolic tone. Indeed, the campaign of Republican nominee Donald J. Trump is thought to be fueled by racial resentments, with the implicit racial appeals of previous elections replaced by "explicitly hostile" statements (Tesler 2016b). These statements appeared at both the elite and the mass level, with attendees at Trump's rallies frequently chanted "Build the Wall," as well as other harsh language against immigrants and minorities (Parker, Corasaniti, and Berenstein 2016).

Throughout this book, I explore some of the varying ways in which the debate over immigration reform can influence the broader process of Latino political incorporation. Although it is too soon to systematically evaluate the effects of this increasingly polarized debate on the Latino electorate, in this chapter, I review the book's key findings and speculate about the implications of the current political context. Will the heightened polarization around the immigration debate alienate Latinos, or will it encourage them to participate in the political process? Within this context, what cleavages can we expect to see within this population? More generally, what are some of the implications for Latino political incorporation and for partisan politics in the United States?

The Politics-to-Identity Link Revisited

My politics-to-identity theory argues that in a context of threat, Latino mobilization can have varied outcomes for political incorporation. Existing research anticipates that a contentious political environment will lead marginalized group members to embrace identities different from that of the majority group. Focusing on the 2006 national debate over immigration reform and the unprecedented protests that occurred in response, I contend that mobilization around a patriotic frame can mitigate the reactive rejection of an American identity. Instead, under certain circumstances, Latinos will embrace this identity, promoting political incorporation that emphasizes inclusion rather than difference.

Chapter 3 describes the ways in which Latino organizations of the late twentieth century politicized identities to promote cultural difference. In contrast to these approaches, during the 2006 protests, Latino leaders and Spanish-language media personalities emphasized that Latinos are part of America. At events across the country, participants, regardless of immigrant generation and even legal status, vocally claimed membership and belonging in the United States.

The second half of this book evaluates the varying ways in which these protests influenced Latinos' attitudes and sense of belonging in the United States. Taking advantage of the rare coincidence between data collection for the Latino National Survey (LNS 2006) and the unprecedented waves of protests that occurred in the spring of 2006, I treat this dataset as a natural experiment. Accordingly, I divide the data into two groups, comparing the attitudes of those surveyed before these events (control group) and those interviewed after (treatment group) to analyze the effects of these protests and their patriotic theme. Using this research design, I show that in comparison to similar respondents interviewed before the protests, Latinos interviewed after these events were more likely to support liberal immigration policies (Chapter 4), less likely to define what it means to be American in closed, ascriptive terms (Chapter 5), and more likely to self-identify as American (Chapter 7). Respondents interviewed after the protests were also more likely to say Latinos should change to blend into the United States. In line with my politics-to-identity theory, my results demonstrate the ability of contentious political debates to transform an individual's very sense of belonging.

Importantly, my theory emphasizes that the link between politics and self-identification is contingent upon both the frame used to mobilize a marginalized group and the salience of the policy debate. Drawing on intersectionality theory, I examine cleavages that influence the extent to which the immigration debate is salient for different Latino subgroups. In particular, I focus on national origin, gender, and level of acculturation, testing whether each of these variables have a relationship with attitudes toward immigration policy (Chapter 4), definitions of what it means to be American (Chapter 5), and individual self-perception (Chapters 6 and 7). I find that although Latino public opinion and self-identification change after the protests, these shifts do not affect all group members equally. Rather, significant variation in policy preferences persist within this population even after the 2006 protests. Likewise, the post-protest shift in self-identification is concentrated among subgroups for whom the immigration debate is more salient. In the pages that follow, I review major developments in the immigration policy debate since the 2006 protests and discuss some of the implications of my theory.

Immigration Policy and Latino Attitudes, 2006–2016

In Chapter 4, I develop the concept of the immigration paradox: although Latinos have not traditionally emphasized immigration as a priority policy issue, the ongoing debate over comprehensive immigration reform remains uniquely positioned to influence the political behavior of certain parts of the Latino community. More recent polling data further supports the idea that the highly polarized immigration policy debate is poised, as I argue, to shape the political attitudes of a growing number of Latinos.

In the short term, the millions of protesters who mobilized in the spring of 2006 achieved their immediate goal of defeating H.R. 4437. Three weeks after the May protests, the Senate passed a more moderate, comprehensive immigration reform bill (S. 2611), omitting the most contentious provisions of the House proposal.[1] In the long run, however, protesters failed to attain their ultimate goal of bipartisan comprehensive immigration reform. The House of Representatives and the Senate were unable to reconcile the differences between their bills, and national efforts for immigration reform were effectively stymied. Renewed efforts by President George W. Bush and bipartisan allies in the Senate to enact comprehensive immigration reform failed to advance again in 2007 (Pear and Hulse 2007).

On the campaign trail in 2008, then-Democratic candidate Barack Obama repeatedly declared his commitment to passing comprehensive immigration reform during the first year of his presidency. In the Latino community, this pledge became known as *la Promesa de Obama* (Obama's promise). After he was in office, however, immigration quickly slipped on the president's policy agenda, superseded by initiatives on the economy and health care. For the remainder of his term, Obama's failure to fulfill his "promise" was a significant source of criticism by Latino activists. This broken promise, coupled with record-high levels of deportations and other policies thought to be tough on immigrants, led to a significant decline in Latino approval for Obama's administration (for details, see Wallace 2012).[2]

In Congress, even efforts to pass the widely popular, bipartisan Development, Relief, and Education for Alien Minors (DREAM) Act floundered. This legislation would have provided a path to citizenship for certain undocumented youth pursuing higher education or military service.[3] As the 2012 presidential election approached, critiques over Obama's lack of progress on immigration reform mounted. On June 15, 2012, the president announced an executive order to stop the deportation of certain immigrant youth living in the United States. The new program, known as Deferred Action for Childhood Arrivals (DACA), targeted those who would have benefitted from the DREAM Act.[4] The Latino community greeted this announcement with enthusiasm as well as immediate speculation that the program would increase support for Obama in the 2012 election (Dade and Halloran 2012). Polls conducted the week after Obama's announcement supported these claims: on June 17, two days after the initial announcement, 49 percent of Latino voters said they were more enthusiastic about Obama. By the end of the week, as news of the plan spread, that figure rose to 58 percent (Latino Decisions 2012a).

Analysis of 2012 exit polls conducted by Latino Decisions demonstrates that group outreach about immigration reform was the single biggest factor in determining Latino vote choice in that year's presidential election (Barreto and Collingwood 2015). Indeed, 58 percent of Latinos indicated that Obama's DACA policy made them more enthusiastic about his candidacy. In contrast to Obama, Republican nominee

Mitt Romney advocated the passage of policies designed to make undocumented immigrants' lives so difficult that they opted to leave the United States voluntarily ("self-deportation"). An estimated 57 percent of Latinos said Romney's position made them less enthusiastic about his candidacy (Latino Decisions 2012b). Consistent with the variation described throughout this book, nearly one-third of voters in both cases indicated these policies did not change their opinions of the candidates (Latino Decisions 2012b).

On the Republican side, after Romney's loss in the 2012 presidential election and the low level of support he received from the Latino community, the Republican Party commissioned an extensive report outlining ways in which the party could appeal to a broader audience. The Growth and Opportunity Project, also referred to as "the Republican Autopsy Report," concluded that previous Republican language about immigration, including calls for self-deportation, prevented Latinos from listening to the party's broader policy message (Edsall 2013). The report urged Republicans to embrace a more inclusive strategy, with more welcoming rhetoric on immigration reform, in order to regain support from the Latino community.

Consistent with these recommendations, in early 2013, politicians on both sides of the aisle once again expressed enthusiasm for enacting comprehensive immigration reform. In the months that followed, a bipartisan group of senators worked together to craft new legislation. Their bill, S. 744, passed the Senate by a vote of 68–23 in June of 2013.[5] Yet, deep divisions persisted within the Republican Party. The question of whether to offer an eventual path to citizenship to the estimated 11 million undocumented immigrants in the United States remained the most contentious topic, with conservative critics equating any path to citizenship to "amnesty" for those who had broken the law (Leal 2014). Reflecting these tensions, the Republican leadership in the House of Representatives refused to vote on the Senate's bipartisan proposal, ultimately killing the bill by inaction.

With midterm elections again approaching, in June 2014, President Obama announced his intention to enact another executive order on immigration policy prior to the November contest (Davis and Preston 2014). Following the president's announcement, a number of conservative Democratic senators facing difficult reelection contests publicly urged the president not to undertake new unilateral action on immigration policy (Silber Mohamed forthcoming). In the weeks that followed, the United States also experienced a dramatic influx of unaccompanied minors from Central America, with an estimated 57,000 children arriving that summer (Archibold 2014). Within months, Obama changed course, announcing he would postpone new executive action until after the 2014 election.

Latinos expressed significant disappointment with the president's delay, leading pundits and scholars alike to ask not *which* party group members would support, but whether inaction on immigration reform would lead them to abstain from voting altogether (Bergman, Segura, and Barreto 2014). Indeed, in a poll of registered *non*voters conducted by Latino Decisions, 60 percent reported that Obama's postponement made them less enthusiastic about both Obama and the Democratic Party (Latino Decisions 2014).

The range of surveys cited above demonstrates the powerful influence that the immigration debate has on a majority of Latinos. Yet, as established throughout this book, significant differences exist in Latino attitudes toward immigration policy. Consistent with this variation, although a majority of Latinos indicated the primacy of immigration policy in their political decisions, the numbers suggest a ceiling of around 60 percent of group members reporting that their electoral decisions were affected by the ongoing immigration policy debate.

Immigration and the 2016 Election: Incorporation, Disengagement, Partisan Realignment?

Following the 2014 midterm election, President Obama enacted a series of executive orders on immigration reform designed to expand eligibility for his earlier DACA program. During the summer of 2016, a deadlocked Supreme Court upheld a lower court's injunction against these expansions, which would have helped an estimated 5 million undocumented immigrants (Liptak and Shear 2016).

As the start of this chapter describes, the rhetoric surrounding the immigration debate during the 2016 presidential election cycle also became significantly more hostile. Four years after Romney ran on a platform of self-deportation, Trump called for the federal government to find and deport all undocumented immigrants, with the construction of a wall on the US-Mexico border a centerpiece of his campaign. Trump's assertions that Mexican immigrants are criminals and rapists and his comment that a US-born judge of Mexican descent would be unable to rule fairly on a case against him because "I'm building a wall" along the US-Mexican border extended the national conversation far beyond the realm of government policy (Rappeport 2016), with his harsh language and racist overtones making the debate personal for an even wider range of Latinos.

Surveys of the Latino population demonstrated the broad reach of Trump's rhetoric. A November 2015 poll found that 80 percent of Latinos gave Trump either a "somewhat" or "very" unfavorable rating (Latino Decisions 2015). Similarly, in a Gallup poll conducted between January and March 2016, 77 percent of Latinos viewed Trump unfavorably (Newport 2016). These numbers are far higher than the 60 percent ceiling described above, suggesting Trump's capacity to influence Latino attitudes extends far beyond the share of this population who typically responds to the immigration debate. At the elite level, several Latino celebrities also voiced their opposition to Trump, including Cuban American rapper Armando Perez, also known as "Pitbull" (Kurtz 2015) and Puerto Rican singer Ricky Martin (Martin 2015). Producer and musician Emilio Estefan, who was born in Cuba, brought together more than a half-dozen Latino musicians from different countries to record the song, "We're All Mexican," as a demonstration of unity in the face of Trump's critical remarks against Mexicans (Puente 2015).

Returning to the questions posed at the start of this book: Will these efforts lead to heightened feelings of similarity or difference across the Latino population? And, what are the implications for Latinos as new Americans? My politics-to-identity theory argues that under certain circumstances, contentious policy *debate* has the power to increase feelings of belonging among marginalized group members. This focus on policy debate, rather than enacted policies, distinguishes my research from much existing scholarship on policy feedback. I return to this important distinction as I speculate on the implications of the ongoing immigration policy debate and the 2016 election.

Latinos have consistently voted at rates lower than whites and African Americans, with this population frequently referred to as the "sleeping giant" (Leighley 2001; Ramakrishnan and Espenshade 2001). Within this community, responses to immigration reform are often the result of the work of political entrepreneurs who actively promote participation (Leighley 2001). For instance, in 2006, a range of organizations united to spearhead the reactive mobilization of Latinos (Ramírez 2013).

Under the umbrella of the *ya es hora* (the time is now) campaign, more than 400 groups joined with Spanish-language media partners including Univision, Entravision, and impreMedia to promote naturalization efforts and electoral participation among Latinos.

In the months before the 2016 election, extensive efforts were again under way to develop new Latino identities as citizens and voters, with Univision announcing a goal of registering 3 million new voters before the November vote (Corasaniti 2016). Record-breaking efforts were also undertaken by partisan organizations on both sides of the aisle to register and mobilize Latino voters for the 2016 contest. By the spring before the general election, a network of right-leaning donors committed $10 million to reach out to conservative Latinos through the *Libre* Initiative (Freedom Initiative), whereas liberal donors planned to contribute $15 million to a Democratic-leaning superPAC, the Immigrant Voters Win PAC, to support voter mobilization including get-out-the-vote efforts (GOTV) (Confessore and Preston 2016).

Although it is too soon to say whether these efforts will significantly increase turnout, face-to-face GOTV canvassing within the Latino community can produce double-digit increases at the ballot box. Moreover, as individuals take on the identity of voters, political engagement and participation becomes self-reinforcing (García Bedolla and Michelson 2012). In other words, if efforts to mobilize Latino voters are successful in 2016, they are likely to create repeat voters, resulting in enduring changes to the US political system.

On the other end of the political spectrum, Democratic nominee Hillary Rodham Clinton promised quick action on comprehensive immigration reform, vowing that she would send a proposal to Congress in the first 100 days of her presidency (Merica 2015). As noted above, the Latino community expressed significant disappointment in President Obama's failure to uphold a similar campaign commitment to prioritize immigration reform during his first term in office. If Clinton is elected but does not succeed in enacting comprehensive immigration reform, Latino frustrations over inaction could also work to demobilize this community in future electoral contests.

The tenor of the contemporary immigration debate also has significant implications for Latino partisanship. Historically, Latinos have had weak levels of partisan identification compared with whites and African Americans (Hajnal and Rivera 2014). One question to emerge from the 2016 election is whether this debate will transform group members into not just American voters but also *partisan* Americans. During California's 1994 referendum on Proposition 187, which sought to deny immigrants access to a range of social welfare benefits, the state's Republican governor forcefully advocated for the proposal, and the immigration debate took on an unprecedented partisan tone. In the aftermath of this debate, California's Latino population solidified into a reliably Democratic voting bloc (Bowler, Nicholson, and Segura 2006). Candidate Trump's hostile rhetoric toward Latinos and other minority groups extends well beyond the language used in California two decades ago, and national data suggest Trump's candidacy could transform previously nonpartisan Latinos into Democrats. Indeed, the percentage of Latinos who perceive the Republican Party as hostile toward their community increased from just 18 percent in 2012 to 45 percent in November 2015 (Latino Decisions 2015). In a July 2016 poll of Latino voters in battleground states, three-quarters of those surveyed believed Trump's campaign had encouraged people and audiences to be more hostile toward Latinos and other minorities (Manzano 2016). These numbers suggest that Trump's campaign could be activating partisan identities within this community. As the number of Latinos in the United States continues to grow, and members of this very young population increasingly reach voting age, the potential solidification of Latinos as a Democratic voting bloc could have a major impact on the US political system.

Importantly, the ongoing immigration debate also has significant partisan implications for other voters. In recent years, the debate over immigration reform has worked as a wedge issue, pushing white Democrats toward the Republican Party (Abrajano and Hajnal 2015). Indeed, evidence suggests that as the number of noncitizen migrants increases, Republican candidates' vote share increases at both the county level and by congressional district (Baerg, Hotchkiss, and Quispe-Agnoli unpublished; Baerg and Voeten 2016; Mayda, Peri, and Steingrass 2016). Similarly, polling data demonstrate that racial resentment has fueled support for Trump's candidacy (Tesler 2016a, 2016b).

As these different scenarios demonstrate, policy feedback, whether in response to political debates or existing policies, can lead to varied outcomes; whereas some policies promote a greater sense of citizenship, others lead to heightened feelings of alienation. For instance, African Americans who have had negative experiences with law enforcement are more likely to distrust the government and less likely to participate politically (Weaver and Lerman 2010). Likewise, high levels of deportations and hostile political contexts also increase mistrust and feelings of alienation within the Latino community (Rieser-Murphy and DeMarco 2012; Rocha, Knoll, and Wrinkle 2015).

Similarly, the long-term impact of the 2006 events as well as the renewed debate over immigration reform ultimately depends on the broader political context, including the implementation of policies poised to incorporate or alienate Latinos. My research demonstrates the power of protest politics to shape the identity of marginalized group members in multiple ways, with protests serving as a tool for empowerment in which even those in the far-periphery can advance claims of membership and belonging. Yet, these subjective interpretations of identities can also be limited or reversed by other political actions.

The heightened focus on racial animus in the United States today also leads to another important question: What does it mean if Latinos feel more American, but white Americans do not accept these claims? Among earlier generations of European immigrants, a new understanding of what it means to be "white" eventually emerged to accommodate these groups (Roediger 2005; Waters 1990). In the contemporary political climate, however, it is far less clear whether and when this shift will happen, or among whom. Experimental research demonstrates that members of the majority population become more accepting of Latinos after viewing images of a pro-US frame such as that featured in the 2006 protests (Wright and Citrin 2010). Future research should focus on this phenomenon, including efforts to understand the variation that underlies these effects as well as the limitations of these identity claims.

Although identity is clearly an interactive process, the extent to which the claims of a minority are constrained by the opinions of the majority remains unclear. Chapter 6 describes survey data demonstrating that a majority of Americans embrace incorporationism, which suggests it is possible for newcomers to incorporate while also maintaining their own culture. Yet, campaign rhetoric during the 2016 elections about "taking our country back" and increased evidence that racial hostility contributes to support for Republican front-runner Donald Trump (Tesler 2016a, 2016b) cast doubt on whether *some* Americans will ever take seriously the membership claims of "outsiders" to this category. Moreover, reports of increased hate crimes and the emboldening of white nationalist figures during the campaign underscore the limits of identity claims advanced by minority groups. Indeed, the 2016 presidential election indicates that many Americans continue to define this membership category in closed, ascriptive terms such as race, religion, and birthplace. Although the election highlights many uncertainties in the US political system, one clear implication of these events is that the contestation over what it means to be American—and who is included in that category—will remain central to the country's political debate in the months and years ahead.

Appendix A
Question Wording and Variable Coding for Latino National Survey (2006)

Dependent Variables

What is your preferred policy on undocumented or illegal immigration? Should there be (Read List): 1 = Immediate legalization of current undocumented immigrants; 2 = A guest worker program leading to legalization eventually; 3 = A guest worker program that permits immigrants to be in the country, but only temporarily; 4= An effort to seal or close off the border to stop illegal immigration

When you think of what it means to be fully American in the eyes of most Americans, do you think it is very important, somewhat important, or not important to: Have been born in the United States? To speak English well? To be White? To be Christian? 1 = Not important; 2 = Somewhat important; 3 = Very important

In general, how strongly or not do you think of yourself as _____? (American; Hispanic/Latino; Cuban/Dominican/Mexican/Puerto Rican/Salvadoran). 1 = Not at all; 2 = Not very strongly; 3 = Somewhat strongly; 4 = Very strongly

How important is it for (Hispanics/Latinos) to change so that they blend into the larger American society? Is this very important, somewhat important, or not at all important? 1 = Not at all important; 2 = Somewhat important; 3 = Very important

How important is it for (Hispanics/Latinos) to maintain their distinct cultures? Is this very important, somewhat important, or not at all important? 1 = Not at all important; 2 = Somewhat important; 3 = Very important

Independent Variables

POST-PROTESTS: 1 = Respondent interviewed on or after April 1, 2006; 0 = Respondent interviewed prior to April 1, 2006

FEMALE: 1 = Yes; 0 = No

SKIN COLOR: (Latinos/Hispanics) can be described based on skin tone or complexion shades. Using a scale from 1 to 5 where 1 represents very dark and 5 represents being very light, where would you place yourself on that scale?

PREFER SPANISH: Language of interview. 1 = Spanish; 0 = English

AGE: What year were you born? Responses are coded continuously by decade: 1 = less than 20 years old; 2 = 20–29; 3 = 30–39; 4 = 40–49; 5 = 50–59; 6 = 60–69; 7 = 70–79; 8 = 80–89; 9 = 90–97

SUBNATIONAL GROUPS: Families of Latino/Hispanic origin or background in the United States come from many different countries. From which country do you trace your Latino heritage? IF MORE THAN ONE RESPONSE GIVEN READ: Which country does most of your family come from? Dummy variables are assigned for each subnational group such that 1 = yes and 0 = no. Analysis is limited to 5 main demographic groups: Mexicans, Cubans, Dominicans, Puerto Ricans, and Salvadorans.

INCOME: Which of the following best describes the total income earned by all members of your household during 2004? Coded continuously such that 12 = below $15,000; 20 = $15,000–24,999; 30 = $35,000–44,999; 40 = $45,000–54,999; 50 = $55,000–64,999; 80 = Above $65,000

YEARS OF EDUCATION: What is your highest level of formal education completed? Coded continuously such that 0 = None; 8 = Eighth grade or below; 10 = Some high school/GED; 12 = High school graduate; 14 = Some college; 16 = 4-year college degree; 19 = Graduate or professional degree

NEW ARRIVAL: When did you first arrive to live in the United States [mainland]? 1 = 2000 and above; 0 = prior to 2000

NON-NATIVE: 1 = Respondents born elsewhere; 0 = respondents born in mainland United States/Puerto Rico

FIRST GENERATION: 1 = Respondents born in the United States with both parents born outside the U.S.; 0 = all others

SECOND GENERATION: 1 = Respondents born in the United States with at least 1 parent born in the United States; 0 = all others

LINKED FATE: How much does your "doing well" depend on other Latinos/Hispanics also doing well? A lot, some, a little, or not at all? 1 = Nothing; 2 = A little; 3 = Some; 4 = A lot

RELIGIOSITY: How often do you attend religious services? Do you attend . . . ? 1 = More than once a week; 2 = Once a week; 3 = Once a month; 4 = Only major religious holidays; 5 = Never

PARENTAL EDUCATION: Which of the following best describes your parents' educational attainment? Did Coded continuously such that 9 = neither of them finished high school; 12 = at least one of them finished high school; 14 = at least one of them went to college; 16 = at least one of them got a college degree; 19 = at least one or both of them received an advanced degree

LATINO FRIENDS: How would you describe your friends? 1 = Mostly Latino/Hispanic; 0 = all others

MIXED FRIENDS: How would you describe your friends? 1 = Mostly Latino/Hispanic and white; Mostly Latino/Hispanic and black; Mostly Latino/Hispanic and Asian; 0 = all others

LATINO COWORKERS: How would you describe your coworkers? Stop me when I get to your answer. Are they: 1 = Mostly Latino/Hispanic; 0 = Mostly white; Mixed Latino/Hispanic and white; Mostly black; Mostly Latino/Hispanic and black

MIXED COWORKERS: How would you describe your coworkers? Stop me when I get to your answer. Are they: 1 = Mostly Latino/Hispanic and white; Mostly Latino/Hispanic and black; Mostly Latino/Hispanic and Asian; 0 = all others

KIDS IN SCHOOL: Did you have children enrolled in elementary or secondary/high school last year? 1 = Yes; 0 = No

NO JOB OUTSIDE THE HOME: What is your employment status? Stop me when I describe your situation. Are you: 1 = Not working outside the home; 0 = all other categories (employed full time; working more than one job; employed part time; engaged in occasional or day labor; currently unemployed; full-time student; retired or permanently disabled)

Appendix B
Supplemental Tables for Chapter 2

Table B.1　**Mean Characteristics of Respondents in Treatment and Control Groups, Full Sample (LNS 2006)**

	Control (1)	Treatment (2)	P-Value	P-Value with State-Level Fixed Effects
Female	0.52	0.53	0.37	0.54
Skin Color	0.63	0.62	**0.01**	**0.00**
Survey in Spanish	0.74	0.49	**0.00**	**0.00**
Years of Education	0.59	0.63	**0.00**	**0.01**
Income	0.29	0.37	**0.00**	**0.00**
Age	0.20	0.20	0.59	**0.05**
Immigrant Generation+				
Newcomer (in US < 5 years)	0.20	0.14	**0.00**	**0.00**
First Generation	0.10	0.15	**0.00**	**0.00**
Second Generation and Above	0.13	0.23	**0.00**	**0.00**
Country of Origin/Ancestry				
Cuban	0.04	0.05	**0.03**	0.09
Dominican	0.04	0.04	0.33	0.26
Mexican	0.80	0.77	**0.02**	0.74
Puerto Rican	0.05	0.11	**0.00**	**0.00**
Salvadoran	0.08	0.04	**0.00**	**0.00**

Note: Boldface entries are significant at the p < .05 level. All continuous independent variables have been scaled from 0 to 1. Analysis uses the revised national weights and is limited to respondents of Cuban, Dominican, Mexican, Puerto Rican, and Salvadoran origin or ancestry.

Table B.2   Mean Characteristics of Respondents in Treatment and Control Groups, Spanish Speakers Only (LNS 2006)

	Control (1)	Treatment (2)	P-Value	P-Value with State-Level Fixed Effects
Female	0.53	0.55	0.15	0.24
Skin Color	0.64	0.62	**0.02**	**0.00**
Years of Education	0.55	0.57	**0.00**	0.49
Income	0.21	0.23	0.07	0.78
Age	0.21	0.22	**0.00**	0.98
Immigrant Generation				
Newcomer (in US < 5 years)	0.26	0.25	0.44	0.70
First Generation	0.05	0.06	0.50	0.69
Second Generation and Above	0.02	0.03	0.75	0.88
Country of Origin/Ancestry				
Cuban	0.03	0.06	**0.00**	0.29
Dominican	0.03	0.06	**0.00**	0.56
Mexican	0.82	0.75	**0.00**	0.55
Puerto Rican	0.02	0.08	**0.00**	**0.00**
Salvadoran	0.09	0.05	**0.00**	**0.00**

Note: Boldface entries are significant at the p < .05 level. All continuous independent variables have been rescaled from 0 to 1. Analysis uses the revised national weights and is limited to respondents of Cuban, Dominican, Mexican, Puerto Rican, and Salvadoran origin or ancestry.

Table B.3   External Validity of the Latino National Survey (2006), by National Origin

	Population	Percent Foreign Born*++	US Citizens++	Bachelor's Degree and Above**	Median Household Income
Cubans	**1,631,000**	**60.1%**	**74.9%**	**25.1%**	**$43,587**
LNS—Cubans	*522*	*84.1%*	*66.5%*	*30.3%*	*$35,000–44,999*
Dominicans	**1,334,000**	**57.3%**	**69.9%**	**15.6%**	**$35,644**
LNS—Dominicans	*413*	*87.7%*	*54.2%*	*20.8%*	*$25,000–34,999*
Mexicans	**30,746,000**	**37.0%**	**71.1%**	**9.1%**	**$40,736**
LNS—Mexicans	*5,903*	*68.8%*	*50.7%*	*13.3%*	*$35,000–44,999*
Puerto Ricans	**4,151,000**	**1.1%**	**99.4%**	**16.0%**	**$40,736**
LNS—Puerto Ricans	*848*	*11.0%**	*90.1%*	*26.3%*	*$45,000–54,999*
Salvadorans	**1,560,000**	**64.7%**	**54.2%**	**8.4%**	**$43,791**
LNS—Salvadorans	*477*	*92.7%*	*37.3%*	*9.9%*	*$25,000–34,999*

Notes: * Foreign born = Born outside the fifty states and Puerto Rico.
** Because education figures in the US Census include only those aged twenty-five or over, LNS education figures are also limited to this age group.
++ For US Census data, percent foreign born and percentage of respondents with citizenship status refer to the general Latino population.

Sources: Pew Hispanic Center/American Community Survey data (2008), Latino National Survey (2006) raw data.

Table B.4   Distribution of Respondents by State, before and after April 1, 2006 (LNS 2006)

State	Pre-Protest N	Post-Protest N	Total N
Arizona	108	292	400
Arkansas	208	193	401
California	599	605	1,204
Colorado	121	283	404
DC Area	205	199	404
Florida	301	499	800
Georgia	219	181	400
Illinois	175	425	600
Iowa	209	191	400
Nevada	205	198	403
New Jersey	173	230	403
New York	288	512	800
North Carolina	203	198	401
Texas	312	499	811
Washington	218	185	403

Appendix C
Supplemental Tables for Chapter 3

Table C.1   Major Legal Milestones in Immigration Law, 1790–2006

1790	Establishment of the Naturalization Rule.
1848	Treaty of Guadalupe Hidalgo annexes significant amount of Mexican territory, adding an estimated 75,000 new citizens.
1870s	Supreme Court ended state control over immigration policy, asserted federal supremacy.
1880s	Immigration quotas/preferences first imposed in wake of national economic recession.
1892	Ellis Island opens. By 1953, more than 12 million immigrants will be processed there.
1917	Literacy test introduced for all immigrants sixteen or older. Virtually all Asian immigrants banned from entering the United States.
1921	Quota Act. Annual immigration ceiling set at 350,000. New nationality quota instituted, limiting admissions to 3 percent of each nationality group's representation in 1910 US Census (designed to restrict flow of immigrants from eastern and southern Europe).
1924	Congress passed Immigration Act of 1924, limiting the number of people who could enter the country to 2 percent of the number of people from that country in the 1890 census, and the ceiling is lowered to 165,000.
1927	Immigration ceiling further reduced to 150,000, with quotas revised to 2 percent of each nationality based on the 1920 census. This system essentially lasted until 1965.
1929	National Origins Act. Annual immigration ceiling of 150,000 is made permanent, with 70 percent of admissions slated for those from northern and western Europe, and the other 30 percent reserved for southern and eastern Europeans.
1930s	Mexican Repatriation, during which time hundreds of thousands of Mexicans and Mexican Americans were forced to return to Mexico.
1940s	Start of controversial Mexican *bracero* program, providing temporary US work permits to Mexican nationals, primarily in agriculture and construction.
1952	Truman administration first took note of "wetbacks" (unauthorized Mexican immigrants) and proposed sanctions to impose upon those harboring them.
1964	LBJ allows *bracero* program to expire; more employers turned to hiring workers without employment authorization.

Table C.1 *continued*

1965	Immigration Act of 1965 repeals national origin quotas, emphasizes family reunification and employment skills needed in the United States. Effective in 1968, the law contains a 170,000 annual cap on Eastern Hemisphere immigration, with a 20,000 per country subcap, and a 120,000 cap on Western Hemisphere immigration without per country subcap. These changes, which were enacted with strong bipartisan consensus, led to increases in Hispanic and Asian immigrant populations; vast majority of immigrant visas granted on basis of family preference categories.
1980	Refugee Act. New system developed to handle refugees as a class separate from other immigrants. President and Congress can establish annual ceiling on refugees, though president is allowed to admit any group of refugees in an emergency.
1980s	Sanctuary Movement in the United States fights to protect Central American refugees.
1981	Select Commission on Immigration and Refugee Policy (headed by Father Theodore Hesburgh, president of Notre Dame University) releases recommendations centering around four themes: employer sanctions, enhanced border enforcement, humane solutions for undocumented immigrants already in the United States, and stopping illegal immigration as a means to legal immigration. These recommendations form the foundation of Simpson-Mazzoli legislation (1986).
1981– 1985	Congress repeatedly tries to pass immigration reform, without success.
1982	*Plyer v. Doe* (457 U.S. 202). Supreme Court rules states do not have the right to deny undocumented immigrants the benefit of a free public education because Congress has not passed a law granting them this power.
1984	Congress considered immigration legislation similar to the Simpson-Mazzoli Act (1986). Legislation passed HR and Senate but died in conference committee three weeks before presidential election.
1986	Simpson (R-WY) and Mazzoli (D-KY) finally pass the Immigration Reform and Control Act (PL 99-603), granting amnesty and permanent legal status to more than two million people living in the United States without authorization (Final passage: 63–24 Senate, 238–173 House). The legislation authorizes "amnesty" for undocumented workers in the United States since January 1, 1982, provides $1 billion per year to states to cover any related costs, and establishes sanctions and penalties against employers who knowingly hired undocumented immigrants. This legislation had the most sweeping impact on immigration policy since the repeal of national origins quotas in 1965.
1990	Immigration Act of 1990 (PL 101-649). Provisions include: substantial increase to the nation's annual immigration quotas (700,000 for 1992, 1993, and 1994; thereafter down to 675,000); attorney general authorized to grant Temporary Protected Status (TPS) to undocumented alien nationals of designated countries with armed conflict/natural disaster. Revises/establishes new nonimmigrant admissions categories and creates new temporary worker categories, including the Diversity Visa Lottery Program. Transfers exclusive jurisdiction of naturalization from federal/state courts to the attorney general.

Table C.1 *continued*

1994	California's Proposition 187 seeks to prohibit undocumented immigrants from accessing public services, including healthcare and education. The referenda was approved by voters in November 1994 but ultimately ruled unconstitutional in 1997.
1996	Personal Responsibility and Work Opportunity Reconciliation Act of August 22, 1996 (110 Statutes-at-Large 2105) establishes restrictions on eligibility of legal immigrants for means-tested public assistance (food stamps, SSI), barring most from receiving such assistance for five years; broadens restrictions on public benefits for illegal aliens and nonimmigrants. Undocumented immigrants become ineligible for virtually all areas of federal and state benefits except emergency medical care, immunization programs, and disaster relief. Illegal Immigration Reform and Immigrant Responsibility Act of September 30, 1996 (110 Statutes-at-Large 3009). Increases border-control measures, workplace enforcement, and removal of criminal aliens. Also adds additional restrictions on benefits for aliens (e.g., pilot program limiting issuance of driver's licenses).
2002	USA Patriot Act amended Immigration and Nationality Act to broaden the scope of aliens not eligible for admission or deportable, due to affiliation with terrorist activities, groups, or organizations.
2005	H.R. 4437 (Sensenbrenner Bill) passes the US House of Representatives.
2006	Massive protests occur across the United States in opposition to the Sensenbrenner Bill. Senate passes S. 2611, the Comprehensive Immigration and Reform Act. House and Senate fail to reach agreement on immigration reform legislation.

Sources: Gimpel and Edwards (1999); U.S. Citizenship and Immigration Services, Department of Homeland Security (2009); PBS (2012).

Table C.2   Database of Immigrants' Rights Protests, Spring 2006

City	State	Date of Event	Estimate of Participants
Georgetown	DE	2/14/06	1,500
Philadelphia	PA	2/14/06	5,000
Fort Myers	FL	2/22/06	1,000
Portland	OR	3/4/06	2,000
Washington	DC	3/6/06	30,000
Chicago	IL	3/10/06	100,000–300,000
Monterey	CA	3/15/06	100
Santa Cruz	CA	3/17/06	500
Knoxville	TN	3/18/06	600
Milwaukee	WI	3/23/06	10,000–30,000
Phoenix	AZ	3/24/06	20,000–25,000
Los Angeles	CA	3/24/06	2,700
Atlanta	GA	3/24/06	80,000
Kansas City	KS	3/24/06	2,000

City	State	Date of Event	Estimate of Participants
Los Angeles	CA	3/25/06	200,000–500,000
Sacramento	CA	3/25/06	4,000
Watsonville	CA	3/25/06	2,000
Denver	CO	3/25/06	50,000
Charlotte	NC	3/25/06	3,000–7,000
New York City	NY	3/25/06	200
Cleveland	OH	3/25/06	1,800
Dallas	TX	3/25/06	1,500
Houston	TX	3/25/06	6,000
Los Angeles	CA	3/26/06	3,500
San Francisco	CA	3/26/06	5,000
New York City	NY	3/26/06	1,000
Columbus	OH	3/26/06	3,000
Dallas	TX	3/26/06	1,500
Phoenix	AZ	3/27/06	400
Los Angeles	CA	3/27/06	8,500–36,500
Riverside	CA	3/27/06	1,000
San Diego	CA	3/27/06	1,500–2,000
Watsonville	CA	3/27/06	1,000
Washington	DC	3/27/06	1,000
Wilmington	DE	3/27/06	12
Boston	MA	3/27/06	2,500
Detroit	MI	3/27/06	50,000
Grand Rapids	MI	3/27/06	7,000
Dallas	TX	3/27/06	1,500–4,000
El Paso	TX	3/27/06	6,000
Houston	TX	3/27/06	1,000
Phoenix	AZ	3/28/06	2,000
Farmersville	CA	3/28/06	200
Los Angeles	CA	3/28/06	6,000
San Diego	CA	3/28/06	1,500–2,000
Watsonville	CA	3/28/06	350
Dallas	TX	3/28/06	3,000–4,000
Tucson	AZ	3/29/06	1,300
Bakersfield	CA	3/29/06	1,800
Kern County	CA	3/29/06	3,000
San Diego	CA	3/29/06	1,500–2,000
Watsonville	CA	3/29/06	150
Nashville	TN	3/29/06	9,000–15,000
Birdville	TX	3/29/06	100
El Paso	TX	3/29/06	700
Tucson	AZ	3/30/06	1,500
San Diego	CA	3/30/06	1,500–2,000
Kensington	MD	3/30/06	300

City	State	Date of Event	Estimate of Participants
Trenton	NJ	3/30/06	200–1,200
El Paso	TX	3/30/06	2,000
Northern Virginia (Arlington)	VA	3/30/06	1,500
Kennewick and Pasco	WA	3/30/06	300
Tucson	AZ	3/31/06	1,000
Bakersfield	CA	3/31/06	1,000
Fresno	CA	3/31/06	50
Los Angeles	CA	3/31/06	100
San Diego	CA	3/31/06	1,500–2,000
Las Vegas	NV	3/31/06	4,000
El Paso	TX	3/31/06	6,000
Walla Walla	WA	3/31/06	400
Costa Mesa	CA	4/1/06	1,500
Las Vegas	NV	4/1/06	150
New York City	NY	4/1/06	4,000–10,000
Arlington	TX	4/1/06	100
Haltom City	TX	4/1/06	150
Fort Wayne	IN	4/2/06	1,000
Yakima	WA	4/2/06	2,000
Louisville	KY	4/4/06	450
Fresno	CA	4/5/06	150
Los Angeles	CA	4/6/06	100–900
Aurora	IL	4/6/06	1,000
Costa Mesa	CA	4/8/06	100
Goshen	IN	4/8/06	1,700–2,000
Birmingham	AL	4/9/06	4,000
San Diego	CA	4/9/06	50,000
Miami	FL	4/9/06	7,000
Orlando	FL	4/9/06	2,000
Pensacola	FL	4/9/06	1,000
Des Moines	IA	4/9/06	5,000–6,000
Boise	ID	4/9/06	4,000
Portland	ME	4/9/06	150
Detroit	MI	4/9/06	100
St. Paul	MN	4/9/06	30,000–40,000
St. Louis	MO	4/9/06	5,000
Lenoir/Hickory	NC	4/9/06	200
Wilmington	NC	4/9/06	100
Albuquerque	NM	4/9/06	1,000
Santa Fe	NM	4/9/06	2,000
Salem	OR	4/9/06	5,000–10,000
Dallas	TX	4/9/06	350,000–500,000

City	State	Date of Event	Estimate of Participants
Fort Worth	TX	4/9/06	7,000
Salt Lake City	UT	4/9/06	20,000
Anchorage	AK	4/10/06	24
Albertville	AL	4/10/06	5,000
Birmingham	AL	4/10/06	3,000
Little Rock	AR	4/10/06	3,000
Phoenix	AZ	4/10/06	100,000–300,000
Tucson	AZ	4/10/06	15,000
Bakersfield	CA	4/10/06	10,000
Berkeley	CA	4/10/06	200
Concord	CA	4/10/06	400
Farmersville	CA	4/10/06	100
Fresno	CA	4/10/06	12,000
Los Angeles	CA	4/10/06	10,000
Madera	CA	4/10/06	150
Oakland	CA	4/10/06	5,000
Richmond	CA	4/10/06	250–300
Sacramento	CA	4/10/06	1,000–10,000
San Jose	CA	4/10/06	25,000
Boulder	CO	4/10/06	150
Colorado Springs	CO	4/10/06	1,000
Denver	CO	4/10/06	7,000–10,000
Grand Junction	CO	4/10/06	3,500–4,000
Hartford	CT	4/10/06	1,000
New Haven	CT	4/10/06	1,000–2,500
Washington	DC	4/10/06	180,000
Belle Glade	FL	4/10/06	500–800
Fort Lauderdale	FL	4/10/06	150
Fort Myers	FL	4/10/06	75,000
Lake Worth	FL	4/10/06	4,500
Miami	FL	4/10/06	3,000–5,000
Plant City	FL	4/10/06	200
Sarasota	FL	4/10/06	100
Tampa	FL	4/10/06	3,000
West Palm Beach	FL	4/10/06	5,000
Atlanta	GA	4/10/06	40,000–50,000
Chicago	IL	4/10/06	1,000
Urbana-Champaign	IL	4/10/06	1,000
Indianapolis	IN	4/10/06	10,000
South Bend	IN	4/10/06	3,000
Garden City	KS	4/10/06	3,000
Kansas City	KS	4/10/06	2,000
Wichita	KS	4/10/06	4,000
Lexington	KY	4/10/06	7,000

City	State	Date of Event	Estimate of Participants
Boston	MA	4/10/06	10,000
Salisbury	MD	4/10/06	200
Detroit	MI	4/10/06	20,000
Jackson	MS	4/10/06	400–500
Chapel Hill	NC	4/10/06	100
Columbia	NC	4/10/06	3,000
Durham	NC	4/10/06	50
Raleigh	NC	4/10/06	200
Siler City	NC	4/10/06	4,000
Smithfield	NC	4/10/06	200
Wilmington	NC	4/10/06	100
Winston-Salem	NC	4/10/06	1,500
Lincoln	NE	4/10/06	4,000
Norfolk	NE	4/10/06	1,000
Omaha	NE	4/10/06	8,000–10,000
South Sioux City	NE	4/10/06	5,000
Santa Fe	NM	4/10/06	2,000
Las Vegas	NV	4/10/06	3,500
New York City	NY	4/10/06	100,000
Rochester	NY	4/10/06	250
Toledo	OH	4/10/06	300
Eugene	OR	4/10/06	300
Salem	OR	4/10/06	10,000
Harrisburg	PA	4/10/06	200
Philadelphia	PA	4/10/06	7,000
Pittsburgh	PA	4/10/06	100
Providence	RI	4/10/06	2,000
Charleston	SC	4/10/06	4,000
Columbia	SC	4/10/06	3,000–5,000
Greenville	SC	4/10/06	2,500
Sioux Falls	SD	4/10/06	300
Chattanooga	TN	4/10/06	200
Jonesborough	TN	4/10/06	300
Knoxville	TN	4/10/06	2,500
Memphis	TN	4/10/06	10,000
Austin	TX	4/10/06	10,000
El Paso	TX	4/10/06	300
Harlington	TX	4/10/06	100
Houston	TX	4/10/06	50,000
San Antonio	TX	4/10/06	18,000
Tyler	TX	4/10/06	2,000
Blacksburg	VA	4/10/06	25
Richmond	VA	4/10/06	4,000
Seattle	WA	4/10/06	25,000

City	State	Date of Event	Estimate of Participants
Madison	WI	4/10/06	10,000
Los Fresnos	TX	4/12/06	80
Huntersville	NC	4/13/06	50
Charlotte	NC	4/18/06	50
Denver	CO	4/19/06	1,000
San Francisco	CA	4/23/06	2,000
Anchorage	AK	5/1/06	1,000
Phoenix	AZ	5/1/06	2,400
Tucson	AZ	5/1/06	700
Bakersfield	CA	5/1/06	3,000
Concord	CA	5/1/06	1,000–2,500
Fresno	CA	5/1/06	15,000
Hemet	CA	5/1/06	300
Huntington Park	CA	5/1/06	8,000
Los Angeles	CA	5/1/06	650,000–700,000
Moreno Valley	CA	5/1/06	500
Oakland	CA	5/1/06	15,000–17,000
Pajaro	CA	5/1/06	6,000–10,000
Palm Springs	CA	5/1/06	2,000
Petaluma	CA	5/1/06	200
Riverside	CA	5/1/06	3,000
Sacramento	CA	5/1/06	15,000–18,000
Salinas	CA	5/1/06	13,000
San Bernardino	CA	5/1/06	1,200
San Diego region	CA	5/1/06	2,500
San Francisco	CA	5/1/06	30,000
San Jose	CA	5/1/06	100,000
San Ysidro	CA	5/1/06	1,000–1,100
Santa Ana	CA	5/1/06	5,000–10,000
Santa Barbara	CA	5/1/06	15,000
Santa Cruz	CA	5/1/06	3,000
Santa Rosa	CA	5/1/06	5,000–7,500
Stockton	CA	5/1/06	6,000
Tracy	CA	5/1/06	75
Union City	CA	5/1/06	400–1,000
Denver	CO	5/1/06	50,000–75,000
Hartford	CT	5/1/06	1,000
New Haven	CT	5/1/06	2,000–4,000
Stamford	CT	5/1/06	3,000
Fort Lauderdale	FL	5/1/06	500
Homestead	FL	5/1/06	1,200–5,000
Miami	FL	5/1/06	5,000
Orlando	FL	5/1/06	20,000
Atlanta	GA	5/1/06	4,500

City	State	Date of Event	Estimate of Participants
Storm Lake	IA	5/1/06	400–500
Aurora	IL	5/1/06	9,000
Chicago	IL	5/1/06	400,000–750,000
Cicero	IL	5/1/06	200
DeKalb	IL	5/1/06	500
Elgin	IL	5/1/06	1,000
Joliet	IL	5/1/06	600
Louisville	KY	5/1/06	550
Morehead	KY	5/1/06	60
New Orleans	LA	5/1/06	3,000
Boston	MA	5/1/06	5,000–8,000
Fitchburg	MA	5/1/06	500
Detroit	MI	5/1/06	1,000
Burlington	NC	5/1/06	1,000
Chapel Hill-Carrboro	NC	5/1/06	40
Lumberton	NC	5/1/06	5,000
Trenton	NJ	5/1/06	1,500
Albuquerque	NM	5/1/06	1,500
Las Vegas	NV	5/1/06	1,500
New York City	NY	5/1/06	3,000
Tulsa	OK	5/1/06	2,000–4,000
Eugene	OR	5/1/06	400
Hood River	OR	5/1/06	1,300
Medford/Rogue Valley	OR	5/1/06	500
Portland	OR	5/1/06	8,000–10,000
Salem	OR	5/1/06	8,000
Allentown	PA	5/1/06	500
Philadelphia	PA	5/1/06	1,000
Chattanooga	TN	5/1/06	700
Houston	TX	5/1/06	10,000–15,000
San Antonio	TX	5/1/06	18,000
Seattle	WA	5/1/06	20,000–65,000
Yakima	WA	5/1/06	5,000-8,000
Madison	WI	5/1/06	3,000
Milwaukee	WI	5/1/06	10,000–70,000

Source: Xóchitl Bada, Jonathan Fox, Elvia Zazueta, and Ingrid García Protest Database, 2006.

Appendix D
Supplemental Table for Chapter 5

Table D.1   Post-Protest Change in Importance of Ascriptive Categories by Language Preference (LNS 2006)

| | Born in the United States | | White | |
	Spanish Speakers	English Speakers	Spanish Speakers	English Speakers
Post-Protests	−0.08	**−0.27***	**−0.28****	−0.16
	(0.09)	**(0.11)**	**(0.10)**	(0.12)
Female	−0.05	0.03	−0.12	0.03
	(0.09)	(0.10)	(0.09)	(0.11)
Skin Color	**−0.36***	0.18	−0.25	0.03
	(0.17)	(0.20)	(0.18)	(0.21)
Age	0.14	**0.60***	**0.69****	0.21
	(0.26)	**(0.25)**	**(0.27)**	(0.26)
Incorporation				
Income	−0.16	**0.60***	0.26	−0.04
	(0.17)	**(0.25)**	(0.19)	(0.18)
Years of Education	**−0.76****	−0.65	−0.33	−0.35
	(0.26)	(0.39)	(0.26)	(0.40)
New Arrival	−0.08	0.47	−0.19	0.16
(in US < 5 years)	(0.12)	−0.35	(0.13)	(0.39)
First Generation	**0.69****	**0.87*****	0.14	0.04
	(0.21)	**(0.14)**	(0.15)	(0.15)
Second Generation	**0.57***	**0.74*****	−0.36	−0.27
and Above	**(0.28)**	**(0.12)**	(0.26)	(0.14)
Linked Fate	**0.34***	0.26	0.14	**0.37***
	(0.13)	(0.14)	(0.15)	**(0.15)**
Religiosity	−0.20	0.16	−0.11	0.07
	(0.15)	(0.16)	(0.16)	(0.17)
N	3,028	2,279	3,028	2,279
Pseudo R2	0.01	0.03	0.02	0.01

Note: The unit of observation in an individual respondent. Standard errors in parentheses. Estimation is done using ordered logistic regression using weighted data from Phase I of the Latino National Survey. Analysis is limited to Cubans, Dominicans, Mexicans, Puerto Ricans, and Salvadorans.

Two-tailed tests, significance levels: *p < 0.05, **p < 0.01, ***p < 0.001.

Appendix E
Supplemental Table for Chapter 6

Table E.1   Predictors of Strong American Identity without Gender (LNS 2006)

	American
Skin Color	0.04
	[−0.22, 0.31]
Survey in Spanish	**0.77***
	[−0.97, −0.57]
Age	**1.35***
	[0.96, 1.75]
Years of Education	**0.54***
	[0.07, 1.01]
Household Income	**0.36****
	[0.10, 0.62]
US Citizen	**0.57***
	[0.38, 0.75]
First Generation	**0.46***
	[0.21, 0.70]
Second Generation	**1.35***
and Above	**[1.08, 1.63]**
Cuban	**0.44***
	[0.03. 0.84]
Dominican	0.13
	[−0.23, 0.49]
Puerto Rican	**0.32***
	[0.00, 0.64]
Salvadoran	0.13
	[−0.20, 0.46]
Parental Education	0.11
	[−0.18, 0.40]
Latino Friends	**−0.75***
	[−1.09, −0.41]
Mixed Friends	**−0.41***
	[−0.74, −0.09]
Latino Coworkers	−0.04
	[−0.23, 0.16]
Mixed Coworkers	0.12
	[−0.06, 0.29]

Table E.1 *continued*

	American
Kids in School	0
	[−0.13, 0.13]
No Job Outside the Home	**−0.40****
	[−0.67, −0.12]
Pseudo R-Squared	0.15
N	5,168

Note: The unit of observation in an individual respondent. Standard errors in parentheses. Estimation is done using ordered logistic regression using weighted data from Phase I of the Latino National Survey. Analysis is limited to Cubans, Dominicans, Mexicans, Puerto Ricans, and Salvadorans.

Two-tailed tests, significance levels: *p < 0.05, **p < 0.01, ***p < 0.001.

Appendix F
Supplemental Tables for Chapter 7

Table F.1   Effects of Spring 2006 Protests on Self-Identification, Month-by-Month Analysis (LNS 2006)

	American Identity	Pan-Ethnic Identity	Country of Origin	"Blend" into the United States	Maintain Unique Culture
November 2005	0.04	0.38	−0.51	−0.02	0.30
	(0.28)	(0.30)	(0.28)	(0.28)	(0.37)
December 2005	0.14	−0.05	0.04	0.10	0.04
	(0.23)	(0.26)	(0.29)	(0.26)	(0.33)
January 2006	−0.19	−0.07	−0.40	−0.20	−0.12
	(0.19)	(0.21)	(0.21)	(0.20)	(0.24)
February 2006	0.25	0.04	−0.14	−0.21	0.06
	(0.17)	(0.18)	(0.18)	(0.18)	(0.21)
March 2006	0.18	0.20	−0.09	−0.10	−0.01
	(0.32)	(0.19)	(0.20)	(0.18)	(0.22)
May 2006	**0.40***	0.02	−0.33	0.23	−0.16
	(0.18)	(0.19)	(0.19)	(0.18)	(0.21)
June 2006	**0.35***	0.18	−0.15	0.19	−0.02
	(0.17)	(0.19)	(0.19)	(0.19)	(0.21)
July 2006	**0.36***	0.22	−0.28	0.05	−0.11
	(0.16)	(0.17)	(0.17)	(0.17)	(0.19)
August 2006	0.13	0.26	0.24	−0.46	−0.18
	(0.39)	(0.39)	(0.39)	(0.32)	(0.40)
Female	**−0.40********	**0.21*****	**0.16***	**−0.24*****	**0.34********
	(0.07)	**(0.07)**	**(0.72)**	**(0.07)**	**(0.09)**
Skin Color	0.21	−0.04	−0.17	**0.32***	0.10
	(0.13)	(0.14)	(0.14)	**(0.14)**	(0.16)
Survey in Spanish	**−0.93********	**0.39********	0.05	**0.81********	**0.49********
	(0.10)	**(0.11)**	(0.10)	**(0.10)**	**(0.12)**
Years of Education	**1.08********	0.22	**0.55***	**−1.12********	−0.12
	(0.22)	(0.24)	(0.26)	**(0.25)**	(0.31)
Income	**0.47********	0.22	0.05	0.05	−0.23
	(0.12)	(0.13)	(0.14)	(0.12)	(0.15)
Age	**1.99********	**−0.52*****	**−0.42***	**1.75********	−0.10
	(0.18)	**(0.19)**	**(0.19)**	**(0.20)**	(0.23)

Table F.1 *continued*

	American Identity	Pan-Ethnic Identity	Country of Origin	"Blend" into the United States	Maintain Unique Culture
Newcomer	−0.11	**.05***	0.05	0.20	−0.18
(in US < 5 years)	(0.10)	**(0.12)**	(0.13)	(0.12)	(0.15)
First Generation	**0.75***	**0.33***	−0.22	−1.33	0.22
	(0.12)	**(0.13)**	(0.12)	(0.12)	(0.14)
Second Generation	**1.61***	**−0.26***	**−1.15***	**−0.47***	−0.09
and Above	(0.12)	(0.11)	(0.11)	(0.11)	(0.12)
Pseudo-R Squared	0.13	0.01	0.03	0.07	0.02
N	5,470	5,489	5,491	5,403	5,480

Note: Ordered logistic regression with robust standard errors. Month of interview is included as a series of dummy variables, with April excluded. The first three dependent variables are the degree to which a respondent self-identifies as American, with a pan-ethnic identity, and with his or her country of national origin, on a scale of 1 (not at all) to 4 (very strongly). The fourth and fifth dependent variables, opinions about whether Latinos/Hispanics should change to blend into the United States and maintain a distinct culture, are measured on a scale of 1 (not at all important) to 3 (very important). All continuous variables are rescaled from 0 to 1. *p < 0.5, **p < 0.01, ***p < 0.001.

Table F.2 Effect of Spring 2006 Protests on Self-Identification, without State Fixed Effects (LNS 2006)

	American Identity (1)	Pan-Ethnic Identity (2)	Country of Origin (3)	"Blend" into the United States (4)	Maintain Unique Culture (5)
Post-Protests	0.21**	0.08	−0.04	0.26**	−0.10
	(0.07)	(0.07)	(0.08)	(0.07)	(0.09)
Female	−0.4***	0.22*	0.16*	−0.24**	0.34***
	(0.07)	(0.07)	(0.07)	(0.07)	(0.09)
Skin Color	0.21	−0.04	−0.17	0.30*	0.10
	(0.13)	(0.14)	(0.14)	(0.14)	(0.16)
Survey in Spanish	−0.89***	0.39***	0.03	0.85***	0.51***
	(0.18)	(0.10)	(0.10)	(0.10)	(0.11)
Age	1.98***	−0.50*	−0.41*	1.74***	−0.11
	(0.18)	(0.19)	(0.19)	(0.19)	(0.31)
Years of Education	1.1***	0.27	0.55*	−1.11***	−0.09
	(0.22)	(0.23)	(0.26)	(0.25)	(0.23)
Household Income	0.45***	0.22	0.06	0.04	−0.23
	(0.13)	(0.13)	(0.14)	(0.12	(0.15)
Immigrant Generation					
Newcomer	−0.11	−0.25*	0.05	0.21	−0.19
(in US < 5 years)	(0.26)	(0.12)	(0.13)	0.12	(0.15)
First Generation	0.74***	0.32*	−0.21	−0.14	0.22
	(0.12)	(0.13)	(0.12)	0.12	(0.14)
Second Generation	1.60***	−0.26*	−1.15***	−0.47***	−0.09
and Above	(0.13)	(0.11)	(0.11)	(0.11)	(0.12)
Pseudo R-Squared	0.13	0.01	0.03	0.07	0.02
N	5470	5489	5491	5403	5480

Note: Ordered logistic regression with robust standard errors. The first three dependent variables are the degree to which a respondent self-identifies as American, with a pan-ethnic identity, and with his or her country of national origin, on a scale of 1 (not at all) to 4 (very strongly). The fourth and fifth dependent variables, opinions about whether Latinos/Hispanics should change to blend into the United States and maintain a distinct culture, are measured on a scale of 1 (not at all important) to 3 (very important). All continuous variables are rescaled from 0 to 1. *p < 0.05, **p < 0.01, ***p < 0.001.

Table F.3 Effects of Spring 2006 Marches on American Self-Identification, by National Origin (LNS 2006)

	Cuban	Dominican	Mexican	Puerto Rican	Salvadoran
Post-Protests	0.26	**0.61****	**0.21*****	−0.21	−0.21
	(0.36)	**(0.21)**	**(0.06)**	(0.19)	(0.24)
Female	0.17	0.14	**−0.47*****	**−0.40***	−0.52
	(0.23)	(0.30)	**(0.07)**	**(0.16)**	(0.37)
Skin Color	0.06	0.15	0.15	0.14	0.28
	(0.35)	(0.28)	(0.14)	(0.33)	(0.51)
Survey in Spanish	**−0.96*****	**−0.99****	**−0.88*****	**−0.50***	**−0.80*****
	(0.20)	**(0.34)**	**(0.10)**	**(0.02)**	**(0.18)**
Age	**1.99*****	**0.39*****	**1.6*****	**1.95*****	0.85
	(0.35)	**(0.10)**	**(0.22)**	**(0.41)**	(0.90)
Years of Education	**−0.96*****	0.04	**0.95*****	**1.83*****	1.21
	(0.20)	(0.49)	**(0.23)**	**(0.42)**	(0.75)
Household Income	**1.36*****	0.30	**0.48*****	−0.08	−0.19
	(0.21)	(0.55)	**(0.08)**	(0.27)	(0.37)
Immigrant Generation					
Newcomer	−0.11	**−1.15*****	−0.05	**−0.81****	−0.38
(in US < 5 years)	(0.26)	**(0.27)**	(0.14)	**(0.27)**	(0.36)
First Generation	0.12	−0.15	**0.79*****	**0.90*****	**0.91***
	(0.53)	(0.45)	**(0.11)**	**(0.15)**	**(0.45)**
Second Generation	0.18	**−1.69****	**1.89*****	**0.86****	1.18
and Above	(0.64)	**(0.64)**	**(0.12)**	**(0.27)**	(1.07)
Pseudo R-Squared	0.07	0.06	0.15	0.06	0.06
N	298	234	4050	620	268

Note: Ordered logistic regression with robust standard errors, clustered by state. The dependent variable in all models is the extent to which a respondent self-identifies as American. All continuous variables are rescaled from 0 to 1. *$p < 0.05$, **$p < 0.01$, ***$p < 0.001$.

Notes

Chapter 1. "We Are America"

1. Beginning in the fall of 2012, a number of major news organizations, including the Associated Press, eliminated the term "illegal immigrant" as a way of describing individuals residing in the United States without legal status. Instead, these organizations replaced the term with "undocumented" or "unauthorized" immigrant, arguing that although actions can be illegal, human beings are not (Weiner 2013). This book will follow the AP protocol for describing individuals who fall into this category, including those who overstayed their visas in the United States, those who entered the country illegally, and those who entered the country using fraudulent or fake documents (Wasem 2013a).

2. Although Proposition 187 passed by popular vote, it was later declared unconstitutional by the courts.

3. According to analysis by the Pew Hispanic Center, the difference in these numbers is statistically indistinguishable.

4. Scholars point to a number of states across the country in which the Latino population has doubled or nearly tripled. Within this body of literature, the specific number of states considered "new destinations" varies. By one measure, Marrow (2005) points to eight "new Hispanic settlement states"—Arizona, Nevada, Georgia, North Carolina, Oregon, Virginia, Washington, and Massachusetts.

5. Principal investigators for Phase 1 of the survey include Luis Fraga, John García, Rodney Hero, Michael Jones-Correa, Valerie Martinez-Ebers, and Gary Segura. All data are publicly available through the Inter-university Consortium for Political and Social Research (ICPSR).

Chapter 2. Becoming American

1. Prior to 1970, last name, birthplace, and language proficiency were the only US Census indicators of Hispanic origin or ancestry (Ennis, Rios-Vargas, and Albert 2011). For more on the relationship between census measures and race and ethnicity, see Rodríguez (2000) and Skerry (2000).

2. For instance, in 2009, some Latino clergy called on undocumented immigrants to boycott the US Census until immigration reform was enacted. Other Latino organizations and leaders fought back against the boycott, arguing that because the census count affects funding for a range of public services as well as congressional districts, it was important for Latinos to be counted properly (El Nasser 2009).

3. See Kingdon (1984) for a discussion of "focusing events."

4. My thanks to Ezra Zuckerman for suggesting this body of literature.

5. Nothing in the methodological descriptions provided by Geoscape, or in follow-up communications, accounts for these differences.

6. The quasi-experimental research design undertaken throughout this book is similar to other analyses that use the LNS to study the effects of the 2006 protests on Latino attitudes (Branton, Carey, Martinez-Ebers et al. 2015; Carey, Branton, and Martinez-Ebers 2014; Silber Mohamed 2013; Wallace, Zepeda-Millán, and Jones-Correa 2014; Zepeda-Millán and Wallace 2013), although the precise treatment of the protests and the cutoff date varies. Because my treatment variable refers not just to the protests, but the protests with a pro-American frame, and I am interested in understanding intragroup variation within the Latino population, dividing the data into two groups and using the April 1 cutoff date represents the best approach to capture my core variables of interest, particularly in light of data limitations. Another potential strategy for gauging the effects of the protests would be a regression discontinuity design (RDD) that would compare individuals interviewed immediately before a certain date with those interviewed immediately after. Unfortunately, given the significant variation in the rate of weekly or monthly interviewing, as well as the difficulty in establishing an appropriate cutoff date, an RDD approach would be challenging to undertake with this particular dataset. For instance, compared with most other months of surveying, a relatively small number of respondents were interviewed in April; within this month, 45 percent (N=197) of respondents were interviewed before the major wave of April 10 protests, whereas 55 percent were interviewed after. Limiting the data to a small number of interviewees would also make it impossible to study differences within the Latino population.

7. Fixed effects are calculated in Stata, using dummy variables for each state, with Florida as the omitted state.

Chapter 3. From Assimilation to Nationalism to "We Are America"

1. In 1928, Congress debated placing restrictions on immigrants from the Western Hemisphere, but ultimately defeated the proposal; opponents of these limits argued that these efforts specifically targeted Mexicans (Balderrama and Rodriguez 2006). Despite the absence of formal federal restrictions, however, many Mexicans seeking to come to the United States faced other obstacles in admissions, with the number of immigrants from Mexico declining substantially during this time (Ngai 2004).

2. The 1965 law established an overall immigration ceiling of 270,000 annual immigrants, with a 20,000 cap per country. Additionally, ceilings were established for the Eastern Hemisphere (170,000) and the Western Hemisphere (120,000). Although several revisions to these ceilings have been enacted since 1965, the basic guiding principles of family reunification and professional skills continue to define contemporary immigration policy (McCabe and Meissner 2010).

3. Indeed, during debate over the 1965 law, numerous experts and politicians asserted that the legislation would not have a significant impact on the demographics of newcomers in the United States. For instance, at the signing ceremony, President Lyndon Johnson asserted, "This bill that we will sign today is not a revolutionary bill. It does not affect the lives of millions. It will not reshape the structure of our daily lives, or really add importantly to either our wealth or our power" (Ludden 2006).

4. This provision allowed undocumented aliens employed in agriculture for at least ninety days the opportunity to apply for permanent residence after two years as "temporary residents" (Zolberg 2006).

5. In the Senate, the vote on final passage was 63–24, with 34 Democrats and 29 Republicans voting for the bill and 16 Republicans and 8 Democrats in opposition. The final passage vote in the House was 238–173, with 161 Democrats and 77 Republicans voting in support and 80 Democrats and 93 Republicans opposing the legislation (Pear 1986b).

6. In an attempt to alleviate these concerns, the legislation included civil rights protections and the creation of a new office within the Justice Department to investigate allegations of discrimination.

7. Although California voters approved Proposition 187, it was subsequently declared unconstitutional by the courts, based on the precedent of the *Plyer v. Doe* ruling.

8. The initiative later became a key issue in Governor Wilson's 1994 reelection campaign (Martin 1995), and the polarizing debate was instrumental in solidifying California's Latinos as Democratic partisans (Abrajano and Alvarez 2010). Despite the fact that immigration falls under the federal government's purview, California's Proposition 187 helped to spark a series of state-level immigration initiatives, which increased exponentially at the start of the twenty-first century in the absence of federal action on the immigration issue.

9. Significantly, the 1996 act replaced the historic categories of aliens excludable from the United States (and considered not physically present) and aliens deportable from the United States following entry with new categories of aliens inadmissible to the United States—those not lawfully admitted irrespective of physical presence—and those deportable from the United States (IIRIRA, PL 104–208).

10. Additionally, laws designed to fight terrorism often affected all foreign-born noncitizens living in the United States. For instance, the controversial Patriot Act, signed into law a month after the 9/11 attacks, included provisions allowing for the search, monitoring, detention, and deportation of suspected terrorists and gave the government the right to detain foreign nationals for up to seven days while deciding whether to file charges against them (McCabe and Meissner 2010). That act and subsequent legislation also further tightened controls at international borders. For additional discussion of the Patriot Act, controversy over the legislation, and the law's impact on US immigration policy, see Zolberg (2006).

11. The Immigration Reform Act of 2004: Strengthening America's National Security, Economy, and Families (S. 2010) was introduced in the Senate while

the Safe, Orderly, Legal Visa, and Enforcement (SOLVE) Act (H.R. 4262/S. 2381) was introduced in the House.

12. Although their provision was not included in the final version of the bill, Republicans in the House of Representatives, led by Tom Tancredo (R-CO), also sought to include a provision that would have ended the right of "birth-right citizenship" to the children of undocumented immigrants.

13. Although the Congressional Hispanic Caucus was founded as a bipartisan organization, following a dispute over Cuba policy, Republican members left the caucus in the late 1990s. Since that time, membership has been limited to Democratic members. In 2003, the Congressional Hispanic Conference was founded as a Republican counterpoint.

14. The exception in the Hispanic Caucus was Rep. Napolitano (D-CA), who did not vote on the legislation. In the Hispanic Conference, Cuban representatives Ileana Ros-Lehtinen (R-FL) and Lincoln Diaz-Balart (R-FL) opposed the legislation, whereas Mario Diaz-Balart (R-FL) did not vote and Henry Banilla (R-TX) supported H.R. 4437.

15. At the beginning of the twenty-first century, these trends began to change. With Puerto Rico affected disproportionately by the economic recession, since 2006, the island has experienced a "brain drain" driven primarily by educated professionals coming to the mainland in pursuit of career opportunities (El Nasser 2012).

16. Those arriving prior to the 1980s were primarily white and middle or upper class, though recent Cuban immigrants are more diverse (Rieff 1995). This latter group, and subsequent immigrants who came after the boatlift, tend to be more working class; like most other contemporary immigrants from Latin America, the majority emigrated in search of improved economic opportunities (Eckstein and Barberia 2002).

17. Under the original CAA, Cubans were required to be in the United States for two years before qualifying as legal permanent residents. The act was updated in 1976, with the residential requirement reduced to 366 days. In 1996, as part of IIRIRA, Congress included language that would repeal the CAA if Cuba adopts a democratic system of government (Wasem 2009). Over time, hundreds of thousands of Cubans have also been admitted to the United States through the US attorney general's "parole" authority, which provides temporary authorization to stay in the country (Wasem 2009).

18. This political leaning is particularly strong among earlier immigrants, and evidence suggests that partisanship may be changing among younger Cubans (Bishin and Klofstad 2011). García Bedolla (2014) also argues that local politics has contributed to Cuban partisanship, with Miami's Democrats historically limiting opportunities for Cubans who sought elective office. In response, the local Republican Party created openings for ethnic leadership.

19. An International Truth Commission report determined that the US-backed Salvadoran government was responsible for 85 percent of the deaths in that conflict, whereas just 15 percent was attributed to insurgent activity (Wood 2008).

20. The judicial process to reevaluate Salvadoran asylum claims began in 1985, when the American Baptist Church (ABC) and other activists sued the US government for discrimination against asylum applicants from El Salvador and Guatemala. The settlement of this case overturned previous asylum decisions for an estimated 150,000 asylees present in the United States before 1990 (García Bedolla 2014).

21. Salvadorans were designated as the first recipients of Temporary Protected Status (TPS), which effectively stopped the deportation of eligible individuals during the covered period (Wasem and Ester 2011). In 1992, the Bush administration granted Deferred Enforced Departure (DED) to nearly 200,000 of those protected under the initial TPS statute through 1994. Following a major earthquake in El Salvador in 2001, the nation received TPS designation again that year.

22. More recently, the number of undocumented immigrants from Mexico has declined, whereas growing numbers of individuals from El Salvador and neighboring countries in Central America have fled to the United States, often in response to violence in their home countries (Gonzalez-Barrera, Krogstad, and Lopez 2014; Preston 2013).

23. A main part of Operation Wetback was the deportation of Mexicans within the United States. In total 1.3 million Mexicans were removed, ironically as the *bracero* program continued to bring migrant laborers from Mexico (García Bedolla 2014).

24. Working with LULAC, the American GI Foundation secured a major legal victory in the case of *Hernández v. Texas* (1954), in which the Supreme Court ruled that under the Fourteenth Amendment all-white juries violated the civil rights of Mexican Americans by denying them a jury of their peers. The court's decision extended these civil rights protections beyond black and white to include nationality. For details, see Ramos 2014.

25. For instance, in the 1947 case *Mendez v. Westminster,* LULAC successfully fought Latino school desegregation in Orange County, California. This groundbreaking victory set the stage for the more widely known *Brown v. Board of Education* case, which ruled that separate schools for black and white students were unconstitutional.

26. For instance, in Colorado, Rodolfo "Corky" Gonzáles helped unite the youth movement and define the meaning of Chicano through his poetry as well as efforts to organize the 1969 Chicano Youth Liberation Conference. In New Mexico, Reies López Tijerina led the Federal Alliance of Land Grants, which fought for the land rights of Mexican individuals and small communities based on ownership patterns prior to the Mexican-American War (1846–1848).

27. See Beltrán (2010) for a discussion of divisions within these movements, differences between the movements, and a comprehensive treatment of efforts to construct unity among a diverse population.

28. For an extensive discussion of the transformation of the NCLR into a pan-ethnic group, see Mora (2014).

29. S. 2611, the Comprehensive Immigration and Reform Act, was advanced

by Senator John McCain (R-AZ) and the late senator Edward M. Kennedy (D-MA). Following the wave of national protests, S. 2611 passed by a vote of 62–36 on May 25, 2006.

30. There were nearly 700 Spanish-language radio stations across the country as of 2006 (Félix, González, and Ramirez 2008). By comparison, nationwide, there were three major Spanish-language television networks, more than 160 local Spanish television stations, and 60 cable stations as of 2004. Additionally, there were more than 700 daily and weekly newspapers in Spanish (Ayón 2006).

31. In Mexico, *el Cucuy* refers to a mythical creature that is part human, part animal and draws children out of dark, scary places (Casillas 2008).

32. Even after the protests, key figures in Spanish radio continued to promote the goal of immigrant incorporation in the United States. For instance, Coello initiated the *Votos por America* (Votes for America) campaign, which reported registering more than 1 million Latino voters.

Chapter 4. The Immigration Paradox

1. In contrast to research drawing on national survey data, Farris focuses specifically on elite-level attitudes in her study of local Latino elected officials.

2. For instance, Branton, Cary, Martinez-Ebers et al. (2015) find that not only did first generation respondents hold more liberal views on immigration policy, but they were most influenced by the 2006 protests.

3. Historically, members of different Latino origin groups have settled in distinct geographical regions of the country, so the generalizability of these findings across the United States might be limited. Nevertheless, the overwhelming number of Mexicans at this event lends support for arguments that the movement was Mexican-led.

4. Although ordinary least squares regression is more straightforward and easier to interpret, having a dependent variable with ordinal outcomes can violate the assumptions underlying linear regression and may result in inaccurate conclusions. As an alternative, ordered logistic regression is used to estimate these nonlinear models.

5. Although clear limitations exist to using a self-reported skin-color measure, given that the LNS was conducted by phone, this variable is the best indicator available for gauging an individual's phenotype. See Chapter 5 for a discussion of the drawbacks of this type of measure.

6. Existing literature also suggests a conflicting role for local context in influencing individual-level attitudes toward immigration policy. Some scholars find that Latinos residing in a community with a high concentration of Latinos have more conservative attitudes toward immigration (Hood, Morris, and Shirkey 1997; Rouse, Wilkinson, and Garand 2010), whereas others conclude that Latinos in these environments have more liberal views (Rocha, Longoria, Wrinkle et al. 2011). This variation might be based on whether the local population is composed of Latinos born in the United States or newer arrivals.

7. For instance, Congressman Luis Gutierrez (D-IL), whose parents are from Puerto Rico, has been a vocal supporter of immigration reform (Campo-Flores 2010).

Chapter 5. Defining American

1. Paradoxically, even as the immigration debate in the 1920s emphasized this ascriptive approach, Mexican immigrants were excluded from this debate, instead entering through a "backdoor" of immigration policy (Ngai 2004; Zolberg 2006).

2. Principal investigators of the Twenty-First Century Americanism Survey are Deborah Schildkraut and Ashley Grosse (ICPSR 27601).

3. Race and ethnicity were treated as separate categories in the GSS. Consequently, respondents could identify as both white/black/other and Latino. Reported race of Latino respondents in the survey is as follows: 61 percent white, 4 percent black, and 35 percent other. Although LNS respondents did not report race, they were asked questions about both ethnicity and skin color.

4. Unfortunately, the series of questions about what it means to be American was not repeated on the 2006 GSS, which specifically targeted the Spanish-speaking population for the first time.

5. After the first phase of the LNS, 1,200 additional respondents were interviewed the following summer to make the survey's findings more geographically representative. Principal investigators for Phase 2 of the LNS include Evelyn Hu-Dehart, Matthew Garcia, Cynthia Garcia Coll, Jose Itzigsohn, Marion Orr, Tony Affigne, and Jorge Elorza (Hu-Dehart, Garcia, Garcia Coll et al. 2006). In order to capture the broadest possible account of Latino views, the comparison to GSS uses data from both rounds of interviews (total n = 9,834). Following initial data collection, each respondent was assigned three weights: national, state, and urban/rural. These weights were subsequently revised in March 2010 and apply only to Phase 1 of the LNS. In multivariate analysis, the sample is limited to Phase 1 of data collection and employs the revised, nationally weighted figures.

6. The GSS question on birthplace is dichotomous, asking respondents whether they were born in this country, whereas the LNS includes Puerto Rico as a separate, third category. Because those born in Puerto Rico also have birthright citizenship, the above statistic includes those born in Puerto Rico as born in the United States.

7. Political context might also contribute to the differences between the surveys, with the immigration debate highly politicized during the interviews for the LNS and relatively less so when the GSS was conducted. It is also possible that the unclear language in the LNS question contributed to this discrepancy. However, the consistency of responses across the other two ascriptive categories, phrased in the same way, suggest that question wording is not the driving force behind this disparity. Subsequent findings that later-generation immigrants are

more likely to emphasize birthplace than their first-generation counterparts reiterate that differences in the sample are more likely to be the source of this discrepancy.

8. Because the results of ordered logistic regression are more difficult to interpret, predicted probabilities are calculated for "prototype" respondents using SPost postestimation analysis (Long and Freese 2006). The use of predicted probabilities allows us to measure the effects of a change in one independent variable, holding all other independent variables constant at some predefined level. Tables with confidence intervals for the predicted probabilities can be found in Appendix D.

9. Income is divided into three categories: respondents earning under $25,000, respondents earning between $25,000 and $44,999, and respondents earning $45,000 and above. Following Lavariega Monforti and Michelson (2014), in cases where respondents' income is missing, an imputed value is used.

10. All independent variables that are not dummy variables are scaled to range from 0–1 to facilitate comparisons across variables.

11. Predicted probabilities were calculated with continuous independent variables moving from their minimum to maximum values, holding all other continuous independent variables constant at their means. For dummy variables, a prototypical respondent is used with the following characteristics: male, Mexican, from the Southwest, born outside the United States but arriving more than five years ago, with survey responses in English.

Chapter 6. American Identities

1. In contrast to early European immigrants, today's Latino immigrants live in a context of "replenishment" primarily as a result of changing immigration laws. In particular, the strict national origin quotas that defined immigration policy in the 1920s cut off most new arrivals during that period. In contrast, the current immigration system, with its emphasis on skills and family reunification, allows for a continual influx of a capped number of immigrants annually (see Chapter 3 for more details).

2. Given the relatively small variation in the percentage of respondents identifying pan-ethnically, with 90.9 percent indicating that they strongly or very strongly identify as Latino/Hispanic, the variable regarding the importance of maintaining a distinct culture is especially useful. I thank Michael Jones-Correa for suggesting these variables.

3. All models use robust standard errors, and all continuous variables are scaled to range from 0 to 1.

4. In separate specifications, a variable was also included for marital status, but that variable did not reach significance across any model.

5. The prototype possesses the following characteristics: respondent is male, Mexican, prefers Spanish, is born outside the United States, lives in California, is a US citizen, has mixed friends and primarily Latino coworkers, has no kids in school, and works outside the home.

Chapter 7. Can Protests Make Latinos "American"?

1. As Chapter 3 describes, the protests' frame changed dramatically over time. Whereas early events prominently featured foreign flags, by April 1, 2006, leaders consistently encouraged Latinos to demonstrate how *similar* they were to other Americans. Because I am interested in not only the protests themselves but also their patriotic frame, this date choice best captures both of these elements. If anything, this date choice is likely to underestimate the effects of the protests (see Chapter 2 for more details about the research design).

2. Although a month-by-month analysis of identity choices would have been ideal, over the course of data collection, significant variation exists in both the number of people surveyed each month and the characteristics of these respondents. As a robustness check, however, I also ran the models using dummy variables for each month (see Appendix F, Table F.1). The models presented in this chapter were also conducted without state-level fixed effects (see Appendix F, Table F.2). The main findings with respect to pre- and post-protest groups retain statistical significance across models. In two cases, control variables that fail to obtain statistical significance when fixed effects are included become statistically significant when fixed effects are omitted. In no case does a variable that has obtained significance in the fixed effects models lose significance in the models without the fixed effects.

3. Predicted probabilities are calculated with all continuous variables held at their mean and dummy variables held at their modal value (post-protest = 1, female = 1, Spanish speaker = 1, respondent was born outside the United States but arrived more than five years ago). All predicted probabilities reported above use the same prototype respondent; full list available upon request.

4. Among the respondents included here, an estimated 91 percent "very strongly" or "somewhat strongly" identified with a pan-ethnic identifier, and an estimated 88 percent did so with a national origin identifier.

5. In particular, the question about maintaining a distinct culture is informative, as there is more variation in responses to this question compared with the question on pan-ethnic identity.

6. Specifically, Dunaway, Branton, and Abrajano (2010) find that on average, newspapers published nearly sixty immigration-related articles in April 2006, compared with less than twenty in most other months that year.

Chapter 8. Epilogue

1. For instance, in contrast to H.R. 4437, the bipartisan Senate bill would have provided a pathway to citizenship for undocumented immigrants, a provision strongly opposed by Republicans in the House of Representatives.

2. In President Obama's first years in office, the number of undocumented immigrants deported from the United States increased to unprecedented levels; from the start of the Obama presidency to July 2012, for instance, total deportations surged to 1.4 million (Khimm 2012). Obama also expanded the

controversial 287(g) program, through which local law enforcement agencies could enter into agreements with the Department of Homeland Security (see Wallace 2012). Latino advocates widely criticized this program for increasing racial profiling and decreasing trust between community members and the local police force (Hesson 2012). With respect to decreased Latino support for Obama, Gallup polls conducted prior to the midterm elections showed Latino approval for the president decreasing from 69 percent at the start of 2010 to 57 percent by May of that year. In a June 2010 Univision/AP poll of Latinos, just 43 percent of respondents indicated that Obama was adequately responding to their concerns (Brown 2010).

3. Qualifying individuals were required to meet a number of eligibility requirements, including arrival in the United States before turning sixteen; at least five years of continuous residence in the United States; possession of a high school degree, general equivalency diploma (GED) or honorable discharge from the military; and two years of college or military service.

4. Although DACA did not provide a path to citizenship for these individuals, most eligible applicants would be granted temporary employment authorization.

5. S. 744, the Border Security, Economic Opportunity, and Immigration Modernization Act, was advanced by four Democratic and four Republican senators referred to as the "Gang of Eight." Membership in the Gang of Eight included Senators Michael Bennet (D-CO), Richard Durbin (R-IL), Jeff Flake (R-AZ), Lindsey Graham (R-SC), John McCain (R-AZ), Bob Menendez (D-NJ), Marco Rubio (R-FL), and Chuck Schumer (D-NY).

Works Cited

Abdelal, Rawi, Yoshiko M. Herrera, Alastair Iain Johnston, and Rose McDermott. 2006. "Identity as a Variable." *Perspectives on Politics* 4, no. 4: 695–711.

———. 2009. "Identity as a Variable." In *Measuring Identity: A Guide for Social Scientists,* edited by Rawi Abdelal, Yoshiko M. Herrera, Alastair Iain Johnston, and Rose McDermott, 17–32. New York: Cambridge University Press.

Abrajano, Marisa A. 2010. *Campaigning to the New American Electorate: Advertising to Latino Voters.* Palo Alto, CA: Stanford University Press.

Abrajano, Marisa A., and R. Michael Alvarez. 2010. *New Faces, New Voices: The Hispanic Electorate in America.* Princeton, NJ: Princeton University Press.

Abrajano, Marisa A., and Zoltan L. Hajnal. 2015. *White Backlash: Immigration, Race, and American Politics.* Princeton, NJ: Princeton University Press.

Alba, Richard D., and Victor Nee. 1997. "Rethinking Assimilation Theory for a New Era of Immigration." *International Migration Review* 31, no. 4: 826–874.

———. 2003. *Remaking the American Mainstream: Assimilation and Contemporary Immigration.* Cambridge, MA: Harvard University Press.

Aleinikoff, T. Alexander, and Rubén G. Rumbaut. 1998. "Terms of Belonging: Are Models of Membership Self-Fulfilling Prophecies?" *Georgetown Immigration Law Journal* 13, no. 1: 1–24.

Andersen, Kristi. 1997. "Gender and Public Opinion." In *Understanding Public Opinion,* edited by Barbara Norrander and Clyde Wilcox, 19–36. Washington, DC: Congressional Quarterly Press.

Anderson, Benedict. 1983. *Imagined Communities: Reflections on the Origin and Spread of Nationalism.* London: Verso.

Ansolabehere, Stephen, and Shanto Iyengar. 1995. *Going Negative: How Political Advertisements Shrink and Polarize the Electorate.* New York: Free Press.

Archibold, Randal C. 2014. "Trying to Slow the Illegal Flow of Young Migrants." *New York Times,* July 20. http://www.nytimes.com/2014/07/21/world/amer icas/trying-to-slow-the-illegal-flow-of-young-migrants-at-the-border-reports -show-decline-in-texas.html?partner=rss&emc=rss&module=Search&mab Reward=relbias%3Aw%2C%7B%221%22%3A%22RI%3A5%22%7D&_r=0. Accessed July 21, 2014.

Ayón, David R. 2006. *Spanish-Language Media and Mexican Migrant Civic Participation.* Santa Cruz, CA: Center for Global, International, and Regional Studies.

Bada, Xochitl, Jonathan Fox, Elvia Zazueta, and Ingrid García. 2006. *Database, Immigrant Rights Marches, Spring 2006.* Santa Cruz, CA: Mexico Institute of the Woodrow Wilson International Center for Scholars.

Baerg, Nicole Rae, Julie L. Hotchkiss, and Myriam Quispe-Agnoli. "Documenting the Unauthorized: Political Responses to Unauthorized Immigration."

Unpublished paper. http://www.nicolebaerg.com/sites/default/files/re search/BHQ_2015.pdf. Accessed August 16, 2016.

Baerg, Nicole Rae, and Erik Voeten. 2016. "Why Republicans Should Love Undocumented Immigrants." *Washington Post,* March 17. https://www.washingtonpost.com/news/monkey-cage/wp/2016/03/17/why-republicans-should-cherish-undocumented-immigrants/. Accessed August 16, 2016.

Baker-Cristales, Beth. 2009. "Mediated Resistance: The Construction of Neoliberal Citizenship in the Immigrant Rights Movement." *Latino Studies* (Spring): 60–82.

Balderrama, Francisco E., and Raymond Rodriguez. 2006. *Decade of Betrayal: Mexican Repatriation in the 1930s.* Albequerque: University of New Mexico Press.

Barreto, Matt A., and Loren Collingwood. 2015. "Group-Based Appeals and the Latino Vote in 2012: How Immigration Became a Mobilizing Issue." *Electoral Studies* 40: 490–499.

Barreto, Matt A., Sylvia Manzano, Ricardo Ramirez, and Kathy Rim. 2009. "Mobilization, Participation, and Solidaridad: Latino Participation in the 2006 Immigration Protest Rallies." *Urban Affairs Review* 44, no. 5: 736–764.

Barreto, Matt A., and Gary M. Segura. 2014. *Latino America: How America's Most Dynamic Popuation Is Poised to Transform the Politics of the Nation.* New York: Public Affairs.

Barreto, Matt A., Gary M. Segura, and Nathan Woods. 2004. "The Mobilizing Effect of Majority-Minority Districts on Latino Turnout." *American Journal of Political Science* 98, no. 1: 65–75.

Bates, Karen Grigsby. 2012. "How Koreatown Rose from the Ashes of L.A. Riots." National Public Radio, April 27. http://www.npr.org/2012/04/27/151524921/how-koreatown-rose-from-the-ashes-of-1-a-riots. Accessed April 27, 2012.

Bates, Robert. 1981. *Markets and States in Tropical Africa.* Berkeley: University of California Press.

Baumgartner, Frank, Suzanna L. De Boef, and Amber E. Boydstun. 2008. *The Decline of the Death Penalty and the Discovery of Innocence.* New York: Cambridge University Press.

Bean, Frank D., Gillian Stevens, and Susan Wierzbicki. 2003. "The New Immigrants and Theories of Incorporation." In *America's Newcomers and the Dynamics of Diversity,* edited by Frank D. Bean and Gillian Stevens, 94–113. New York: Russell Sage Foundation.

Bejarano, Christina. 2013. *The Latina Advantage: Gender, Race, and Political Success.* Austin: University of Texas Press.

———. 2014. *The Latino Gender Gap in U.S. Politics.* New York: Routledge.

Beltrán, Christina. 2010. *The Trouble with Unity: Latino Politics and the Creation of Identity.* New York: Oxford University Press.

Benford, Robert D., and David A. Snow. 2000. "Framing Processes and Social Movements: An Overview and Assessment." *Annual Review of Sociology* 26: 611–639.

Benjamin-Alvarado, Jonathan, Louis DeSipio, and Celeste Montoya. 2009.

"Latino Mobilization in New Immigrant Destinations: The Anti H.R. 4437 Protest in Nebraska's Cities." *Urban Affairs Review* 44, no. 5: 718–735.

Berelson, Bernard R., Paul F. Lazarsfeld, and William N. McPhee. 1956. *Voting: A Study of Opinion Formation in a Presidential Campaign.* Chicago: University of Chicago Press.

Bergman, Elizabeth, Gary Segura, and Matt Barreto. 2014. "Immigration Politics and Electoral Consequences: Anticipating the Dynamics of the Latino Vote in the 2014 Election." *California Journal of Politics and Policy* 6, no. 3: 339–359.

Berinsky, Adam J., and Donald R. Kinder. 2006. "Making Sense of Issues through Media Frames: Understanding the Kosovo Crisis." *Journal of Politics* 68, no. 3: 640–656.

Binder, Norman, J. L. Polinard, and Robert Wrinkle. 1997. "Mexican American and Anglo Attitudes toward Immigration Reform: A View from the Border." *Social Science Quarterly* 78, no. 2: 324–337.

Bishin, Benjamin, and Casey Klofstad. 2011. "The Political Incorporation of Cuban Americans: Why Won't Little Havana Turn Blue?" *Political Research Quarterly* 65, no. 3: 586–599.

Bloemraad, Irene. 2006. "Becoming a Citizen in the United States and Canada: Structured Mobilization and Immigrant Political Incorporation." *Social Forces* 85, no. 2: 667–695.

Bloemraad, Irene, and Christine Trost. 2008. "It's a Family Affair: Intergenerational Mobilization in the Spring 2006 Protests." *American Behavioral Scientist* 52, no. 4: 507–532.

Bloemraad, Irene, Kim Voss, and Taeku Lee. 2011. "The Protests of 2006: What Were They, How Do We Understand Them, Where Do We Go?" In *Rallying for Immigrant Rights: The Fight for Inclusion in 21st Century America,* edited by Kim Voss and Irene Bloemraad, 3–43. Berkeley: University of California Press.

Bowler, Shaun, Stephen P. Nicholson, and Gary M. Segura. 2006. "Earthquakes and Aftershocks: Direct Democracy and Partisan Change." *American Journal of Political Science* 50, no. 1: 146–159.

Brader, Ted, Nicholas A. Valentino, and Elizabeth Suhay. 2008. "What Triggers Public Opposition to Immigration? Anxiety, Group Cues, and Immigration Threat." *American Journal of Political Science* 52, no. 4: 959–978.

Branton, Regina P. 2007. "Latino Attitudes toward Various Areas of Public Policy: The Importance of Assimilation." *Political Research Quarterly* 60, no. 2: 293–303.

Branton, Regina P., Tony E. Carey Jr., Valerie Martinez-Ebers, and Tetsuya Matsubayashi. 2015. "Social Protest and Policy Attitudes: The Case of the 2006 Immigrant Rallies." *American Journal of Political Science* 59, no. 2: 390–402.

Branton, Regina P., and Johanna Dunaway. 2008. "English and Spanish-Language Media Coverage of Immigration: A Comparative Analysis." *Social Science Quarterly* 89, no. 4: 1006–1022.

Breton, Charles. 2015. "Making National Identity Salient: Impact on Attitudes toward Immigration and Multiculturalism." *Canadian Journal of Political Science* 48, no. 2: 1–25.

Brewer, Marilyn B. 2003. *Intergroup Relations*. Buckingham, UK: Open University Press.

Brown, Carrie Budoff. 2010. "Hispanic Media Take on Obama." *Politico,* August 11. http://www.politico.com/news/stories/0810/40927.html. Accessed April 1, 2014.

Brown, Susan K., and Frank D. Bean. 2006. "Assimilation Models, Old and New: Explaining a Long-Term Process." *Migration Information Source*, 3–41.

Browning, Rufus P., Dale Rogers Marshall, and David H. Tabb. 1984. *Protest Is Not Enough: The Struggle of Blacks and Hispanics for Equality in Urban Politics*. Berkeley: University of California Press.

Brubaker, Rogers. 1999. "The Manichean Myth: Rethinking the Distinction between 'Civic' and 'Ethnic' Nationalism." In *Nation and National Identity*, edited by Kriesti Hanspeter, Klaus Armingeon, Hannes Siegrist, and Andreas Wimmer, 55–71. Zurich: Ruegger.

Buergenthal, Thomas. 1994. "The United Nations Truth Commission for El Salvador." *Vanderbilt Journal of Transnational Law* 27, no. 3: 497–941.

Burns, Nancy, Kay Lehman Schlozman, and Sidney Verba. 2001. *The Private Roots of Public Action*. Cambridge, MA: Harvard University Press.

Bush, Jeb, and Clint Bolick. 2013. "A Republican Case for Immigration Reform." *Wall Street Journal,* June 30. http://online.wsj.com/news/articles/SB100014 24127887324328204578571641599272504. Accessed April 1, 2014.

Cable News Network. 2006. "Rallies across U.S. Call for Illegal Immigrant Rights." CNN.com, April 10. http://www.cnn.com/2006/POLITICS/04/10/immigration/. Accessed June 20, 2015.

———. 2010. "CNN Poll: Quarter of Hispanics Support Arizona Law." July 27. http://politicalticker.blogs.cnn.com/2010/07/27/cnn-poll-quarter-of-hispanics-support-arizona-law/?fbid=3ggJSZYgG9s. Accessed June 13, 2013.

Cain, Bruce E., and D. Roderick Kiewiet. 1985. "Ethnicity and Electoral Choice: Mexican American Voting Behavior in the 30th Congressional District." In *The Mexican-American Experience: An Interdisciplinary Anthology*, edited by Rodolfo O. de la Garza, Frank D. Bean, Charles Bonjean, Ricardo Romo, and Ramiro Alvarez, 213–227. Austin: University of Texas Press.

Calavita, Kitty. 1992. *Inside the State: The Bracero Program, Immigration, and the I.N.S.* New York: Routledge.

Campbell, Andrea Louise. 2002. "Self-Interest, Social Security, and the Distinctive Participation Patterns of Senior Citizens." *American Political Science Review* 96, no. 3: 565–574.

———. 2003. "Participatory Reactions to Policy Threats: Senior Citizens and the Defense of Social Security and Medicare." *Political Behavior* 25, no. 1: 29–49.

———. 2012. "Policy Makes Mass Politics." *Annual Review of Political Science* 15: 333–351.

Campbell, Donald T., and Julian C. Stanley. 1963. *Experimental and Quasi-Experimental Designs for Research*. Chicago: Rand McNally.

Campo-Flores, Arian. 2010. "Pushing Obama on Immigration Reform." *Newsweek*, November 29. http://www.newsweek.com/pushing-obama-immigration-reform-70093. Accessed April 1, 2016.

Canaday, Margot. 2009. *The Straight State: Sexuality and Citizenship in Twentieth-Century America*. Princeton, NJ: Princeton University Press.

Carey, Tony E. Jr., Regina P. Branton, and Valerie Martinez-Ebers. 2014. "The Influence of Social Protests on Issue Salience among Latinos." *Political Research Quarterly* 67, no. 3: 615–627.

Carrigan, William D., and Clive Webb. 2013. *Forgotten Dead: Mob Violence against Mexicans in the United States, 1848–1928*. New York: Oxford University Press.

Carroll, Susan J. 1989. "Gender Politics and the Socializing Impact of the Women's Movement." In *Political Learning in Adulthood*, edited by Roberta S. Sigel, 306–339. Chicago: University of Chicago Press.

Carter, Prudence L., Sherrill L. Sellers, and Catherine Squires. 2002. "Reflections on Race/Ethnicity, Class, and Gender Inclusive Research." *African American Research Perspectives* 8, no. 1: 111–124.

Casillas, Dolores Inés. 2008. "A Morning Dose of Latino Masculinity: U.S. Spanish-Language Radio and the Politics of Gender." In *Latina/o Communication Studies Today*, edited by Angharad N. Valdivia, 161–186. New York: Peter Lan

Chander, Anupam. 2007. "Flying the Mexican Flag in Los Angeles." *Fordham Law Review* 75, no. 5: 2455–2467.

Chandra, Kanchan. 2004. *Why Ethnic Parties Succeed*. New York: Cambridge University Press.

———. 2009. "Making Causal Claims about the Effect of 'Ethnicity.'" In *Comparative Politics: Rationality, Culture, and Structure*, edited by Marc I. Lichbach and Alan Zuckerman, 376–412. New York: Cambridge University Press.

Chavez, Leo R. 2008. *The Latino Threat: Constructing Immigrants, Citizens, and the Nation*. Palo Alto, CA: Stanford University Press.

Chavez, Linda. 2006. "American Dreams, Foreign Flags." *New York Times*, March 30, A-25.

Chavez, Lydia. 1986. "Fears Prompted Hispanic Votes in Bill's Support." *New York Times*, November 11, A-12.

Cheek, Jonathan M., and Stephen R. Briggs. 1982. "Self-Consciousness and Aspects of Identity." *Journal of Research in Personality* 16, no. 4: 401–408.

Chin, Gabriel J., and Rose Cuison Villazor, eds. 2015. *The Immigration and Nationality Act of 1965: Legislating a New America*. New York: Cambridge University Press.

Chong, Dennis, and James N. Druckman. 2007. "A Theory of Framing and Opinion Formation in Competitive Elite Environments." *Journal of Communication* 57: 99–118.

Citrin, Jack, Donald P. Green, Christopher Muste, and Cara Wong. 1997. "Public Opinion toward Immigration Reform: The Role of Economic Motivations." *Journal of Politics* 59, no. 3: 858–881.

Citrin, Jack, Amy Lerman, Michael Murakami, and Kathryn Pearson. 2007. "Testing Huntington: Is Hispanic Immigration a Threat to American Identity?" *Perspectives on Politics* 5, no. 1: 31–48.

Citrin, Jack, Beth Reingold, and Donald P. Green. 1990. "American Identity and the Politics of Ethnic Change." *Journal of Politics* 52, no. 4: 1124–1154.

Citrin, Jack, and David O. Sears. 2014. *American Identity and the Politics of Multiculturalism.* New York: Cambridge University Press.

Citrin, Jack, Cara Wong, and Brian Duff. 2001. "The Meaning of American National Identity: Patterns of Ethnic Conflict and Consensus." In *Social Identity, Intergroup Conflict, and Conflict Reduction,* edited by Richard D. Ashmore, Lee Jussim, and David Wilder, 71–100. New York: Oxford University Press.

Cohen, Cathy. 1999. *The Boundaries of Blackness.* Chicago: University of Chicago Press.

Cohn, D'Vera. 2015. "Census Considers New Approach to Asking about Race—by not Using the Term at All." Pew Research Center, June 18. http://www.pewresearch.org/fact-tank/2015/06/18/census-considers-new-approach-to-asking-about-race-by-not-using-the-term-at-all/. Accessed August 9, 2016.

Confessore, Nicholas, and Julia Preston. 2016. "Soros and Other Liberal Donors to Fund Bid to Spur Latino Voters." *New York Times,* March 10. http://www.nytimes.com/2016/03/10/us/politics/george-soros-and-other-liberal-donors-to-fund-bid-to-spur-latino-voters.html. Accessed March 10, 2016.

Connolly, James J. 1998. *The Triumph of Ethnic Progressivism: Urban Political Culture in Boston, 1900–1925.* Cambridge, MA: Harvard University Press.

Conover, Pamela Johnston. 1984. "The Influence of Group Identifications on Political Perception and Evaluation." *Journal of Politics* 46, no. 3: 760–785.

Constable, Pamela. 1996. "Latinos Demand Rights, Respect at D.C. March; Diverse Gathering Denounces Anti-Immigration Movement." *Washington Post,* October 13, A1.

Cook, Thomas D., and Donald T. Campbell. 1986. "The Causal Assumptions of Quasi-Experimental Practice." *Syntheses* 68: 141–180.

Corasaniti, Nick. 2016. "Univision Aims to Make Hispanic Voting Bloc Even More Formidable." *New York Times,* February 22. http://www.nytimes.com/2016/02/23/us/politics/univision-hispanic-voting.html. Accessed March 10, 2016.

Cordero-Guzman, Hector, Nina Martin, Victoria Quiroz-Becerra, and Nik Theodore. 2008. "Voting with Their Feet: Nonprofit Organizations and Immigrant Mobilization." *American Behavioral Scientist* 52, no. 4: 598–617.

Cornell, Stephen. 2000. "That's the Story of Our Life." In *We Are a People: Narrative and Multiplicity in Constructing Ethnic Identity,* edited by Paul Spickard and W. Jeffrey Burroughs, 41–56. Philadelphia: Temple University Press.

Coutin, Susan Bibler. 2000. *Legalizing Moves: Salvadoran Immigrants' Struggle for U.S. Residency.* Ann Arbor: University of Michigan Press.

Crenshaw, Kimberlé. 1989. "Demarginalizing the Intersection of Race and Sex." *University of Chicago Legal Forum* 39: 139–167.

———. 1994. "Mapping the Margins: Intersectionality, Identity Politics, and Violence against Women of Color." In *The Public Nature of Private Violence,* edited by Martha Albertson Fineman and Rixanne Mykitiuk, 93–118. New York: Routledge.

CSPAN. 1996. *Latino and Immigrant Rights Rally—October 12.*

Dade, Corey. 2012. "Census Bureau Rethinks the Best Way to Measure Race." December 26. http://www.npr.org/2012/12/26/168077473/census-bureau -rethinks-the-best-way-to-measure-race. Accessed December 28, 2012.

Dade, Corey, and Liz Halloran. 2012. "President Obama's Immigration Shift Could Bolster Latino Support in November." June 15. http://www.npr.org /blogs/itsallpolitics/2012/06/15/155126911/president-obamas-immigra tion-shift-could-bolster-latino-support-in-november. Accessed June 13, 2013.

Dahl, Robert. 1998. *On Democracy*. New Haven, CT: Yale University Press.

Davies, Paul G., Claude M. Steele, and Hazel Rose Markus. 2008. "A Nation Challenged: The Impact of Foreign Threat on America's Tolerance for Diversity." *Journal of Personality and Social Psychology* 95, no. 2: 308.

Davila, Arlene. 2001. *Latinos, Inc.: The Marketing and Making of a People*. Berkeley: University of California Press.

Davis, James Allan, and Tom W. Smith. 2004. General Social Survey (machine-readable data file). Principal Investigator, James A. Davis; Director and Co-Principal Investigator, Tom W. Smith; Co-Principal Investigator, Peter V. Marsden, NORC ed. Chicago: National Opinion Research Center, producer, 2002; Storrs, CT: The Roper Center for Public Opinion Research, University of Connecticut, distributor.

Davis, Julie Hirschfield, and Julia Preston. 2014. "Obama Says He'll Order Action to Aid Immigrants." *New York Times*, June 30. http://www.nytimes .com/2014/07/01/us/obama-to-use-executive-action-to-bolster-border-en forcement.html?_r=0. Accessed April 30, 2015.

Davos, Thierry, and Mahzarin R. Banaji. 2005. "American = White?" *Journal of Personality and Social Psychology* 88, no. 3: 447–466.

Dawson, Michael C. 1994. *Behind the Mule: Race and Class in African-American Politics*. Princeton, NJ: Princeton University Press.

De Genova, Nicholas P. 2002. "Migrant 'Illegality' and Deportability in Everyday Life." *Annual Review of Anthropology* 31: 419–447.

de la Cruz, Patricia G., and Roberto R. Ramirez. 2003. "The Hispanic Population in the United States: March 2002." U.S. Department of Commerce, Economic and Statistics Administration, June. http://www.census.gov /prod/2003pubs/p20-545.pdf. Accessed April 20, 2010.

de la Garza, Rodolfo O., Louis DeSipio, F. Chris Garcia, John García, and Angelo Falcón. 1992. *Latino Voices: Mexican, Puerto Rican, and Cuban Perspectives on American Politics*. Boulder, CO: Westview Press.

de la Garza, Rodolfo O., Angelo Falcón, and F. Chris Garcia. 1996. "Will the Real Americans Please Stand Up? Anglo and Mexican-American Support of Core American Political Values." *American Journal of Political Science* 40: 335–351.

de los Angeles Torres, María. 1999. *In the Land of Mirrors: Cuban Exile Politics in the United States*. Ann Arbor: University of Michigan Press.

DeSipio, Louis. *Counting on the Latino Vote*. 1996a. Charlottesville: University of Virginia Press.

———. 1996b. "More Than the Sum of Its Parts: The Building Blocks of a Pan-Ethnic Latino Identity." In *The Politics of Minority Coalitions: Race, Ethnicity, and Shared Uncertainties,* edited by Wilbur C. Rich, 177–189. Westport, CT: Praeger.

————. 2006. "Latino Civic and Political Participation." In *Hispanics and the Future of America,* edited by Marta Tienda and Faith Michell, 447–479. Washington, DC: National Academies Press.

Dion, Karen K., and Kenneth L. Dion. 2001. "Gender and Cultural Adaptation in Immigrant Families." *Journal of Social Issues* 57, no. 3: 511–521.

Dionne, Kim Yi, Darin DeWitt, Michael Stone, and Michael Suk-Young Chwe. 2015. "The May 1 Marchers in Los Angeles: Overcoming Conflicting Frames, Bilingual Women Connectors, English Language Radio, and Newly Politicized Spanish Speakers." *Urban Affairs Review* 51, no. 4: 533–562.

Dolan, Kathleen. 2014. *When Does Gender Matter? Women Candidates and Gender Stereotypes in American Elections.* New York: Oxford University Press.

Druckman, James N. 2001. "On the Limits of Framing Effects: Who Can Frame?" *Journal of Politics* 63, no. 4: 1041–1066.

Dunaway, Johanna, Regina P. Branton, and Marisa A. Abrajano. 2010. "Agenda Setting, Public Opinion, and the Issue of Immigration Reform." *Social Science Quarterly* 91, no. 2: 359–378.

Dunning, Thad. 2008. "Improving Causal Inference: Strengths and Limitations of Natural Experiments." *Political Research Quarterly* 61, no. 1: 282–293.

————. 2012. *Natural Experiments in the Social Sciences: A Design-Based Approach.* New York: Cambridge University Press.

Eckstein, Susan, and Lorena Barberia. 2002. "Grounding Immigrant Generations in History: Cuban Americans and Their Transnational Ties." *International Migration Review* 36, no. 3: 799–837.

Edsall, Thomas B. 2013. "The Republican Autopsy Report." *New York Times,* March 20. http://opinionator.blogs.nytimes.com/2013/03/20/the-republican-autopsy-report/. Accessed March 11, 2016.

Eifert, Benn, Edward Miguel, and Daniel N. Posner. 2010. "Political Competition and Ethnic Identification in Africa." *American Journal of Political Science* 54, no. 2: 494–510.

Eisenstadt, David. 1996. "Latinos March on DC." *New York Daily News,* October 13.

Ellison, Christopher G., Samuel Echevarría, and Brad Smith. 2005. "Religion and Abortion Attitudes among U.S. Hispanics: Findings from the 1990 Latino National Political Survey." *Social Science Quarterly* 86, no. 1: 192–208.

El Nasser, Haya. 2009. "Hispanic Groups Call for Census Boycott." *USA Today,* April 15. http://usatoday30.usatoday.com/news/nation/census/2009-04-15-census_N.htm. Accessed August 12, 2016.

————. 2012. "Puerto Rico's Population Exodus Is All about Jobs." *USA Today,* March 11. http://usatoday30.usatoday.com/news/nation/story/2012-03-11/puerto-rico-economy-brain-drain-exodus/53490820/1. Accessed June 21, 2013.

Ennis, Sharon R., Merarys Rios-Vargas, and Nora G. Albert. 2011. "The Hispanic Population: 2010." *2010 Census Briefs,* May. http://www.census.gov/prod/cen2010/briefs/c2010br-04.pdf. Accessed January 24, 2012.

Entman, Robert M. 1993. "Framing: Toward Clarification of a Fractured Paradigm." *Journal of Communication* 43, no. 4: 51–58.

Epstein, Edward, and James Sterngold. 2006. "Huge Crowds March for Immigration Reform: Up to 2 Million Nationwide Vow to Use Ballot-Box Power; Protesters Are Careful to Wave U.S. Flags This Time." *San Francisco Chronicle,* April 11, A1.

Erie, Steven P. 1988. *Rainbow's End: Irish-Americans and the Dilemmas of Urban Machine Politics, 1840–1985.* Berkeley: University of California Press.

Espiritu, Yen Le. 1992. *Asian American Panethnicity: Bridging Institutions and Identities.* Philadelphia: Temple University Press.

Falomir-Pichastor, Juan M., Fabrice Gabarrot, and Gabriel Mugny. 2009. "Group Motives in Threatening Contexts: When a Loyalty Conflict Paradoxically Reduces the Influence of an Anti-discrimination Ingroup Norm." *European Journal of Social Psychology* 39, no. 2: 196–206.

Farris, Emily. 2013. *Latino Leadership in City Hall.* Unpublished diss., Brown University.

Fears, Darryl. 2006. "An Immigrant DJ's Morning in America." *Washington Post,* April 30. http://www.washingtonpost.com/wp-dyn/content/article /2006/04/29/AR2006042901532.html. Accessed June 5, 2010.

Félix, Adrián, Carmen González, and Ricardo Ramirez. 2008. "Political Protest, Ethnic Media, and Latino Naturalization." *American Behavioral Scientist* 52, no. 4: 618–634.

Ferriss, Susan, and Ricardo Sandoval. 1998. *The Fight in the Fields: Cesar Chávez and the Farmworkers Movement.* New York: Mariner Books.

Flores-González, Nilda, Amalia Pallares, Cedric Herring, and Maria Krysan. 2006. UIC Immigrant Mobilization Project: General Survey Findings. http://texasedequity.blogspot.com/2006/07/uic-immigrant-mobilization. html.

Fraga, Luis R., John A. Garcia, Rodney Hero, Michael Jones-Correa, Valerie Martinez-Ebers, and Gary M. Segura. 2006a. Latino National Survey (LNS). ICPSR20862-v6. Ann Arbor, MI: Inter-university Consortium for Political and Social Research [distributor], 2013-06-05. http://doi.org/10.3886 /ICPSR20862.v6.

———. 2006b. "*Su Casa Es Nuestra Casa:* Latino Politics Research and the Development of American Political Science." *American Political Science Review* 100, no. 4: 515–521.

———. 2010. *Latino Lives in America: Making It Home.* Philadelphia: Temple University Press.

———. 2012. *Latinos in the New Millennium: An Almanac of Opinion, Behavior, and Policy Preferences.* New York: Cambridge University Press.

Fuchs, Lawrence H. 1990. *The American Kaleidoscope: Race, Ethnicity, and the Civic Culture.* Hanover, NH: Wesleyan University Press.

"Full Text: Donald Trump Announces a Presidential Bid." 2015. *Washington Post,* June 16. http://www.washingtonpost.com/news/post-politics/wp /2015/06/16/full-text-donald-trump-announces-a-presidential-bid/#. Accessed September 21, 2015.

Gammage, Sarah. 2007. "El Salvador: Despite End to Civil War, Emigration Continues—Country Profiles." Migration Policy Institute, July 27. http://www.migrationinformation.org/Profiles/display.cfm?ID=636. Accessed March 10, 2010.

Gamson, William A., and Andre Modigliani. 1987. "The Changing Culture of Affirmative Action." In *Research in Political Sociology*, edited by Richard D. Braungart, 137–177. Greenwich, CT: JAI Press.

———. 1989. "Media Discourse and Public Opinion on Nuclear Power: A Constructionist Approach." *American Journal of Sociology* 95, no. 1: 1–37.

Gans, Herbert J. 1973. "Introduction." In *Ethnic Identity and Assimilation: The Polish-American Community*, edited by Neil C. Sandberg, 1–7. New York: Praeger.

———. 1979. "Symbolic Ethnicity: The Future of Ethnic Groups and Cultures in America." *Ethnic and Racial Studies* 2, no. 1: 1–20.

———. 1992. "Comment: Ethnic Invention and Acculturation: A Bumpy-Line Approach." *Journal of American Ethnic History* 12, no. 1: 42–52.

Ganz, Marshall. 2009. *Why David Sometimes Wins: Leadership, Organization, and Strategy in the California Farm Worker Movement.* New York: Oxford University Press.

Garcia, Alma M., ed. 1989. "The Development of Chicana Feminist Discourse, 1970–1980." *Gender and Society* 3, no. 2: 217–238.

———. 1997. *Chicana Feminist Thought: The Basic Historical Writings.* New York: Routledge.

García, Ignacio M. 1997. *Chicanismo: The Forging of a Militant Ethos among Mexican Americans.* Tucson: University of Arizona Press.

García, John A. 1981. "Political Integration of Mexican Immigrants: Explorations into the Naturalization Process." *International Migration Review* 15, no. 4: 608–625.

———. 2003. *Latino Politics in America: Community, Culture, and Interests.* Lanham, MD: Rowman and Littlefield.

García, Sonia R., and Marisela Márquez. 2001. "Motivational and Attitudinal Factors amongst Latinas in US Electoral Politics." *National Women's Studies Association Journal* 13, no. 2: 112–122.

García, Sonia R., Valerie Martinez-Ebers, Irasema Coronado, Sharon A. Navarro, Patricia A. Jaramillo, and Patricia Madrid. 2008. *Politicas: Latina Public Officials in Texas.* Austin: University of Texas Press.

García Bedolla, Lisa. 2003. "The Identity Paradox: Latino Language, Politics, and Selective Dissociation." *Latino Studies* 1, no. 2: 264–283.

———. 2005. *Fluid Borders: Latino Power, Identity, and Politics in Los Angeles.* Berkeley: University of California Press.

———. 2007. "Intersections of Inequality: Understanding Marginalization and Privilege in the Post–Civil Rights Era." *Politics and Gender* 3, no. 2: 232–248.

———. 2014. *Latino Politics,* 2nd ed. Malden, MA: Polity.

García Bedolla, Lisa, Jessica L. Lavariega Monforti, and Adrian D. Pantoja. 2007. "A Second Look: Is There a Latina/o Gender Gap?" *Journal of Women, Politics, and Policy* 28, no. 3: 147–174.

García Bedolla, Lisa, and Melissa R. Michelson. 2012. *Mobilizing Inclusion: Transforming the Electorate through Get-Out-the-Vote Campaigns.* New Haven, CT: Yale University Press.

Geertz, Clifford. 1973. "Thick Description: Toward an Interpretive Theory of Culture." In *The Interpretation of Cultures,* edited by Clifford Geertz, 3–32. New York: Basic Books.

Gerstein, Josh. 2016. "Supreme Court to Rule on Obama Immigration Orders." *Politico,* June 19. http://www.politico.com/story/2016/01/supreme-court-to-rule-on-obama-immigration-orders-217860. Accessed March 20, 2016.

Gerstle, Gary, and John Mollenkopf, eds. 2001. *E Pluribus Unum? Contemporary and Historical Perspectives on Immigrant Political Incorporation.* New York: Russell Sage Foundation.

Gimpel, James G., and J. R. Edwards Jr. 1999. *The Congressional Politics of Immigration Reform.* Boston: Allyn and Bacon.

Glass, Andrew. 2009. "Castro Launches Mariel Boatlift, April 20, 1980." *Politico,* April 20. http://www.politico.com/news/stories/0409/21421.html. Accessed March 10, 2012.

Glazer, Nathan. 1993. "Is Assimilation Dead?" *Annals of the American Academy of Political and Social Science* 530: 122–136.

———. 1997. *We Are All Multiculturalists Now.* Cambridge, MA: Harvard University Press.

Glazer, Nathan, and Daniel P. Moynihan. 1963. *Beyond the Melting Pot: The Negroes, Puerto Ricans, Jews, Italians, and Irish of New York City.* Cambridge: Massachusetts Institute of Technology Press.

Goffman, Erving. 1974. *Frame Analysis: An Essay on the Organization of Experience.* Cambridge, MA: Harvard University Press.

Golash-Boza, Tanya. 2006. "Dropping the Hyphen? Becoming Latino(a)-American through Racialized Assimilation." *Social Forces* 85, no. 1: 27–55.

González, Andrea G., Adriana J. Umaña-Taylor, and Mayra Y. Bámaca. 2006. "Familial Ethnic Socialization among Adolescents of Latino and European Descent: Do Latina Mothers Exert the Most Influence?" *Journal of Family Issues* 27, no. 2: 184–207.

Gonzalez, Juan. 1996. "In Washington, Latino Chorus Lifts Its Voice." *New York Daily News,* October 15.

Gonzalez-Barrera, Ana, Jens Manuel Krogstad, and Mark Hugo Lopez. 2014. "DHS: Violence, Poverty, Are Driving Children to Flee Central America to U.S." Pew Research Center, July 1. http://www.pewresearch.org/fact-tank/2014/07/01/dhs-violence-poverty-is-driving-children-to-flee-central-america-to-u-s/. Accessed August 22, 2016.

Gordon, Milton M. 1964. *Asssimilation in American Life: The Role of Race, Religion, and National Origins.* New York: Oxford University Press.

Gorman, Anna. 2006. "Flag's Meaning Is in the Eye of the Beholder." *Los Angeles Times,* March 29.

Goss, Kristin. 2013. *The Paradox of Gender Equality: How American Women's Groups Gained and Lost Their Public Voice.* Ann Arbor: University of Michigan Press.

Gould, Roger V. 1995. *Insurgent Identities: Class, Community, and Protest in Paris from 1848 to the Commune.* Chicago: University of Chicago Press.

Grasmuck, Sherri, and Patricia R. Pessar. 1991. *Between Two Islands: Dominican International Migration.* Berkeley: University of California Press.

Grieco, Elizabeth. 2004. "The Dominican Population in the United States: Growth and Distribution." Migration Policy Institute, September. http:// www.migrationpolicy.org/pubs/MPI_Report_Dominican_Pop_US.pdf. Accessed April 20, 2010.

Gutiérrez, David G. 1995. *Walls and Mirrors: Mexican Americans, Mexican Immigrants, and the Politics of Ethnicity*. Berkeley: University of California Press.

———. 1999. "Migration, Emergent Ethnicity, and the 'Third Space': The Shifting Politics of Nationalism in Greater Mexico." *Journal of American History* 86, no. 2: 481–517.

Gutmann, Amy. 2003. *Identity in Democracy*. Princeton, NJ: Princeton University Press.

Hackney, Sheldon. 1997. *One America Indivisible: A National Conversation on American Pluralism and Identity*. Washington, DC: National Endowment for the Humanities.

Hagan, Jacqueline, Brianna Castro, and Nestor Rodriguez. 2009. "The Effects of U.S. Deportations and Policies on Immigrant Families and Communities: Cross-Border Perspectives." *North Carolina Law Review* 99: 1799–1823.

Hainmueller, Jens, and Michael Hiscox. 2010. "Attitudes towards Highly Skilled and Low-Skilled Immigration: Evidence from a Survey Experiment." *American Political Science Review* 104, no. 1: 61–84.

Hainmueller, Jens, and Daniel J. Hopkins. 2014. "Public Attitudes toward Immigration." *Annual Reviews of Political Science* 17: 225–249.

Hajnal, Zoltan J., Elisabeth R. Gerber, and Hugh Louch. 2002. "Minorities and Direct Legislation: Evidence from California Ballot Proposition Elections." *Journal of Politics* 64, no. 1: 154–177.

Hajnal, Zoltan J., and Michael U. Rivera. 2014. "Immigration, Latinos, and White Partisan Politics: The New Democratic Defection." *American Journal of Political Science* 58, no. 4: 773–789.

Hancock, Ange-Marie. 2007a. *The Politics of Disgust: The Public Identity of the Welfare Queen*. New York: New York University Press.

———. 2007b. "When Multiplication Doesn't Equal Quick Addition: Examining Intersectionality as a Research Paradigm." *Perspectives on Politics* 5, no. 1: 63–79.

Hardy-Fanta, Carol, ed. 1993. *Latina Politics, Latino Politics: Gender, Culture, and Political Participation in Boston*. Philadelphia: Temple University Press.

———. 2006. *Intersectionality and Politics: Recent Research on Gender, Race, and Political Representation in the United States*. London: Haworth.

Hartz, Louis. 1950. *The Liberal Tradition in America*. New York: Harcourt, Brace, Jovanovich.

Heclo, Hugh. 1974. *Modern Social Politics in Britain and Sweden*. New Haven, CT: Yale University Press.

Heiskanen, Benita. 2009. "A Day without Immigrants." *European Journal of American Studies*. Special Issue: Immigration 4, no. 3. http://ejas.revues.org /7717. Accessed August 22, 2016.

Hendricks, Tyche, and Joe Garofoli. 2006. "Spanish-Language Radio DJs Tone Down Call for Action on May 1." *San Francisco Chronicle*, April 26, A4.

Hero, Rodney E. 1992. *Latinos and the U.S. Political System: Two-Tiered Pluralism.* Philadelphia: Temple University Press.

Hero, Rodney E., and Robert R. Preuhs. 2007. "Immigration and the Evolving American Welfare State: Examining Policies in the US States." *American Journal of Political Science* 51, no. 3: 498–517.

Hesson, Ted. 2012. "As One Immigration Enforcement Program Fades Away, Another Rises." *ABC News/Univision,* December 27. http://abcnews.go.com /ABC_Univision/News/immigration-enforcement-program-287g-scaled-back /story?id=18077757#.UbTGbrXVDrc. Accessed May 28, 2013.

Higham, John. 1955. *Strangers in the Land: Patterns of American Nativism, 1860– 1925.* New Brunswick, NJ: Rutgers University Press.

Hochschild, Jennifer L. 1995. *Facing Up to the American Dream: Race, Class, and the Soul of the Nation.* Princeton, NJ: Princeton University Press.

Hochschild, Jennifer L., and John H. Mollenkopf. 2009. "Modeling Immigrant Political Incorporation." In *Bringing Outsiders In: Transatlantic Perspectives,* edited by Jennifer L. Hochschild and John H. Mollenkopf, 15–29. Ithaca, NY: Cornell University Press.

Hoefer, Michael, Nancy Rytina, and Bryan C. Baker. 2010. "Estimates of the Unauthorized Immigrant Population Residing in the United States: January 2009." *Population Estimates,* January. Department of Homeland Security, Office of Immigration Statistics. http://www.dhs.gov/xlibrary/assets/statis tics/publications/ois_ill_pe_2009.pdf. Accessed April 19, 2010.

———. 2012. "Estimates of the Unauthorized Immigrant Population Residing in the United States: January 2011." Office of Immigration Statistics, March. http://www.dhs.gov/xlibrary/assets/statistics/publications/ois_ill _pe_2011.pdf. Accessed June 18, 2013.

Hollinger, David. 1995. *Postethnic America.* New York: Basic Books.

Holman, Mirya R., Monica C. Schneider, and Kristin Pondel. 2015. "Gender Targeting in Political Advertisements." *Political Research Quarterly* 68, no. 4: 816–829.

Holmes, Steven A. 1996. "Hispanic March Draws Crowd to Capital." *New York Times,* October 13, 26.

Holzner, Claudio. 2012. "The Political and Civic Engagement of Undocumented Immigrants." Paper presented at the Annual Conference of the American Political Science Association, New Orleans, LA, August 29–September 2.

Hondagneu-Sotelo, Pierrette. 1992. "Overcoming Patriarchal Constraints: The Reconstruction of Gender Relations among Mexican Immigrant Women and Men." *Gender and Society* 6: 393–415.

Hood, M. V. III, Irwin L. Morris, and Kurt A. Shirkey. 1997. "'¡Quedate o Vente!': Uncovering the Determinants of Hispanic Public Opinion toward Immigration." *Political Research Quarterly* 50, no. 3: 627–647.

hooks, bell. 1984. *Feminist Theory from Margin to Center.* Boston: South End.

Horowitz, Donald. 1985. *Ethnic Groups in Conflict.* Berkeley: University of California Press.

Huckfeldt, Robert, and John Sprague. 1987. "Networks in Context: The Social

Flow of Political Information." *American Political Science Review* 81, no. 4: 1197–1216.

Huddy, Leonie. 2001. "From Social to Political Identity: A Critical Examination of Social Identity Theory." *Political Psychology* 22, no. 1: 127–156.

———. 2016. "Unifying National Identity Research: Interdisciplinary Perspectives." In *Dynamics of National Identity: Media and Societal Factors of What We Are,* edited by Jürgen Grimm, Leonie Huddy, Peter Schmidt, and Josef Seethaler, 9–21. New York: Routledge.

Huddy, Leonie, and Nadia Khatib. 2007. "American Patriotism, National Identity, and Political Involvement." *American Journal of Political Science* 51, no. 1: 63–77.

Hu-Dehart, Evelyn, Matthew Garcia, Cynthia Garcia Coll, Jose Itzigsohn, Marion Orr, Tony Affigne, and Jorge Elorza. 2006. Latino National Survey (LNS)—New England. ICPSR24502-v2. Ann Arbor, MI: Inter-university Consortium for Political and Social Research [distributor], 2015-07-17. http://doi.org/10.3886/ICPSR24502.v2.

Huntington, Samuel P. 1981. *American Politics: The Promise of Disharmony.* Cambridge, MA: Belknap Press of Harvard University Press.

———. 2004a. "The Hispanic Challenge." *Foreign Policy* (March/April): 30–45.

———. 2004b. *Who Are We? The Challenges to America's National Identity.* New York: Simon and Schuster.

Itzigsohn, Jose. 2009. *Encountering American Faultlines: Race, Class, and the Dominican Experience in Providence.* New York: Russell Sage Foundation.

Itzigsohn, Jose, and Carlos Dore-Cabral. 2000. "Competing Identities? Race, Ethnicity, and Panethnicity among Dominicans in the United States." *Sociological Forum* 15, no. 2: 225–247.

Itzigsohn, Jose, and Silvia Giorguli. 2005. "Incorporation, Transnationalism, and Gender: Immigrant Incorporation and Transnational Participation as Gendered Processes." *International Migration Review* 39, no. 4: 895–920.

Iyengar, Shanto. 1991. *Is Anyone Responsible? How Television Frames Political Issues.* Chicago: University of Chicago Press.

Iyengar, Shanto, and Donald R. Kinder. 1987. *News That Matters: Television and American Opinion.* Chicago: University of Chicago Press.

Jachimowicz, Maia. 2004. "Bush Proposes New Temporary Worker Program." Migration Policy Institute, February 1. http://www.migrationinformation.org/Feature/display.cfm?ID=202. Accessed March 6, 2012.

Janiot, Patricia. 2006. *Impacto de los medios de comunicación hispanos en Estados Unidos.* CNN en Español.

Jaramillo, Patricia A. 2010. "Building a Theory, Measuring a Concept: Exploring Intersectionality and Latina Activism at the Individual Level." *Journal of Women, Politics, and Policy* 31, no. 3: 193–216.

Jenkins, Krista. 2013. *Mothers, Daughters, and Political Socialization.* Philadelphia: Temple University Press.

Jiménez, Tomás. 2009. *Replenished Ethnicity: Mexican Americans, Immigration, and Identity.* Berkeley: University of California Press.

Jones-Correa, Michael. 1998a. *Between Two Nations.* Ithaca, NY: Cornell University Press.

————. 1998b. "Different Paths: Gender, Immigration, and Political Participation." *International Migration Review* 32, no. 2: 326–349.

Jones-Correa, Michael, and David Leal. 1996. "Becoming 'Hispanic': Secondary Panethnic Identification among Latin-American-Origin Populations in the United States." *Hispanic Journal of Behavioral Sciences* 18, no. 2: 214–254.

Kahneman, Daniel, and Amos Tversky. 1984. "Choice, Values, and Frames." *American Psychologist* 39: 341–350.

Kam, Cindy D., and Jennifer M. Ramos. 2008. "Joining and Leaving the Rally: Understanding the Surge and Decline in Presidential Approval Following 9/11." *Public Opinion Quarterly* 72, no. 4: 619–650.

Kastoryano, Riva. 2002. *Negotiating Identities*. Princeton, NJ: Princeton University Press.

Khimm, Suzy. 2012. "Obama Is Deporting Immigrants Faster Than Bush. Republicans Don't Think That's Enough." *Washington Post,* August 27. http://www.washingtonpost.com/blogs/wonkblog/wp/2012/08/27/obama-is-deporting-more-luumigrants-than-bush-republicans-dont-think-thats-enough/. Accessed June 3, 2013.

Kibria, Nazli. 2002. *Becoming Asian American: Second Generation Chinese and Korean American Identities*. Baltimore, MD: Johns Hopkins University Press.

Kinder, Donald R. 2003. "Communication and Politics in the Age of Information." In *Oxford Handbook of Political Psychology,* edited by David O. Sears, Leonie Huddy, and Robert Jervis, 357–393. New York: Oxford University Press.

Kinder, Donald, and Wendy Kam. 2012. *Us Against Them: Ethnocentric Foundations of American Opinion*. Chicago: University of Chicago Press.

King, Desmond. 2001. "Making Americans: Immigration Meets Race." In *E Pluribus Unum? Contemporary and Historical Perspectives on Immigrant Political Incorporation,* edited by G. Gerstle and J. Mollenkopf, 143–172. New York: Russell Sage Foundation.

Kingdon, John. 1984. *Agendas, Alternatives, and Public Policies*. Boston: Little, Brown.

Klar, Samara, Joshua Robison, and James N. Druckman. 2013. "Political Dynamics of Framing." In *New Directions in Media and Politics,* edited by Travis Ridout, 173–192. New York: Routledge.

Knoll, Benjamin R. 2012. "¿Compañero o Extranjero? Anti-Immigrant Nativism among Latino-Americans." *Social Science Quarterly* 93, no. 4: 911–931.

Kurtz, Judy. 2015. "Pitbull: Trump Had No Idea 'What He Was Saying' about Latinos." *The Hill,* October 21. http://thehill.com/blogs/in-the-know/257676-pitbull-trump-had-no-idea-what-he-was-saying-about-latinos. Accessed April 1, 2016.

Kymlicka, Will. 1995. *Multicultural Citizenship: A Liberal Theory of Minority Rights*. New York: Oxford University Press.

Lakoff, George. 1987. *Women, Fire, and Dangerous Things: What Categories Reveal about the Mind*. Chicago: University of Chicago Press.

Lapidos, Juliet. 2013. "Steve King Still Stands by 'Cantaloupe' Comments." *New York Times,* August 12. http://takingnote.blogs.nytimes.com/2013/08/12/steve-king-still-stands-by-cantaloupe-comments/?_r=0. Accessed March 25, 2016.

Latino Decisions. 2012a. "2012 Election Eve Poll." November. http://www.lati-nodecisions.com/2012-election-eve-polls/. Accessed June 14, 2013.

———. 2012b. "New Poll: Obama Leads Romney among Latinos in Key 2012 Battleground States." June 22. http://www.latinodecisions.com/blog /2012/06/22/new-poll-obama-leads-romney-among-latinos-in-key-2012-bat tleground-states/. Accessed June 14, 2013.

———. 2014. "Election Eve Poll—National Toplines." November. http://www .latinodecisions.com/2014-election-eve-poll/. Accessed March 3, 2015.

———. 2015. "New Poll: Hostile Talk Hurts GOP with Latino Voters." November 16. http://www.latinodecisions.com/blog/2015/11/16/new-poll-hostile-talk -hurts-gop-with-latino-voters/. Accessed March 15, 2016.

Latino National Survey. 2006. *Latino National Survey: Executive Summary.* Washington, DC: Woodrow Wilson Center, December, 7. https://depts.washing ton.edu/uwiser/documents/LNS-Executive_Summary_LNS.pdf. Accessed August 21, 2016.

Lavariega Monforti, Jessica. 2007. "Rhetoric or Meaningful Identifiers? Latinos(as) and Panethnicity." *Latino(a) Research Review* 6, no. 1–2: 7–32.

Lavariega Monforti, Jessica, and Melissa R. Michelson. 2014. "Multiple Paths to Cynicism: Social Networks, Identity, and Linked Fate among Latinos." In *Latino Politics en Ciencia Política: The Search for Latino Identity and Racial Consciousness,* edited by Tony Affigne, Evelyn Hu-DeHart, and Marion Orr, 92–112. New York: New York University Press.

Leal, David L. 2007. "Latino Public Opinion: Does It Exist?" In *Latino Politics: Identity, Mobilization, and Representation,* edited by R. Espino, David L. Leal, and Kenneth J. Meier, 27–42. Charlottesville: University of Virginia Press.

———. 2014. "Immigration Policy versus Immigration Politics: Latinos and the Reform Debate." In *Undecided Nation: Political Gridlock and the Immigration Crisis,* edited by Tony Payan and Erika de la Garza, 79–95. New York: Springer.

Leal, David L., Stephen A. Nuño, Jongho Lee, and Rodolfo O. de la Garza. 2008. "Latinos, Immigration, and the 2006 Midterm Elections." *PS: Political Science and Politics* 42, no. 1: 309–317.

Leary, Mark R., David S. Wheeler, and T. Brant Jenkins. 1986. "Aspects of Identity and Behavioral Preference: Studies of Occupational and Recreational Choice." *Social Psychology Quarterly* 49, no. 1: 11–18.

Lee, Jennifer, and Frank D. Bean. 2004. "America's Changing Color Lines: Immigration, Race/Ethnicity, and Multiracial Identification." *Annual Review of Sociology* 30: 221–242.

Lee, Taeku. 2008. "Race, Immigration, and the Identity-to-Politics Link." *Annual Review of Political Science* 11: 457–478.

Leighley, Jan E. 2001. *Strength in Numbers? The Political Mobilization of Racial and Ethnic Minorities.* Princeton, NJ: Princeton University Press.

Lien, Pei-te, Margaret Conway, and Janelle Wong. 2004. *The Politics of Asian Americans: Diversity and Community.* New York: Routledge.

Liptak, Adam, and Michael D. Shear. 2016. "Supreme Court Tie Blocks Obama Immigration Plan." *New York Times,* June 23. http://www.nytimes

.com/2016/06/24/us/supreme-court-immigration-obama-dapa.html?_
r=0. Accessed August 1, 2016.

Long, J. Scott, and Jeremy Freese. 2006. *Regression Models for Categorical Dependent Variables Using Stata.* College Station, TX: Stata Press.

Lopez, Mark Hugo, and Ana Gonzalez-Barrera. 2013. "Salvadorans May Soon Replace Cubans as Third-Largest U.S. Hispanic Group." Pew Hispanic Center, June 19. http://www.pewresearch.org/fact-tank/2013/06/19/salvador ans-may-soon-replace-cubans-as-third-largest-u-s-hispanic-group/. Accessed July 3, 2013.

Lopez, Mark Hugo, Ana Gonzalez-Barrera, and Jens Manuel Krogstad. 2014. "Chapter 4: Top Issues in This Year's Election for Hispanic Voters." Pew Research Center Hispanic Trends, October 29. http://www.pewhispanic .org/2014/10/29/chapter-4-top-issues-in-this-years-election-for-hispanic -voters/. Accessed April 17, 2015.

Lopez, Mark Hugo, and Paul Taylor. 2010. "Latinos and the 2010 Census: The Foreign Born Are More Positive." Pew Research Center Hispanic Trends, April 1. http://www.pewhispanic.org/2010/04/01/latinos-and-the-2010-census -the-foreign-born-are-more-positive/. Accessed February 8, 2012.

Lowi, Theodore. 1965. "American Business, Public Policy, Case-Studies, and Political Theory." *World Politics* 16, no. 4: 677–715.

———. 2012. "Latino Voters in the 2012 Election." Pew Hispanic Center, November 7. http://www.pewhispanic.org/2012/11/07/latino-voters-in-the -2012-election/. Accessed November 11, 2012.

Ludden, Jennifer. 2006. "1965 Immigration Law Changed Face of America." National Public Radio, May 9. http://www.npr.org/templates/story/story .php?storyId=5391395. Accessed March 12, 2012.

Manzano, Sylvia. 2016. "Latino Voters in Battleground States Survey Results." Latino Decisions. June 27. http://www.latinodecisions.com/files /8414/6984/0573/LVP_Battleground_Deck.pdf. Accessed August 14, 2016.

Marquez, Benjamin. 1989. "The Politics of Race and Assimilation: The League of United Latin American Citizens 1929–1940." *Western Political Quarterly* 42, no. 2: 355–375.

———. 1993. *LULAC: The Evolution of a Mexican American Political Organization.* Austin: University of Texas Press.

———. 2001. "Choosing Issues, Choosing Sides: Constructing Identities in Mexican-American Social Movement Organizations." *Racial and Ethnic Studies* 24, no. 2: 218–235.

Marrow, Helen B. 2006. "New Destinations and Immigrant Incorporation." *Perspectives on Politics* 3, no. 4: 781–799.

Martin, Philip. 1995. "Proposition 187 in California." *International Migration Review* 29, no. 1: 255–263.

Martinez, Lisa M. 2011. "Mobilizing Marchers in the Mile-High City: The Role of Community-Based Organizations." In *Rallying for Immigrant Rights: The Fight for Inclusion in 21st Century America,* edited by Kim Voss and Irene Bloemraad, 123–124. Berkeley: University of California Press.

Massey, Donald S., ed. 2008. *New Faces in New Places: The Changing Geography of American Immigration*. New York: Russell Sage Foundation

Massey, Donald S., Jorge Durand, and Nolan J. Malone. 2002. *Beyond Smoke and Mirrors: Mexican Immigration in an Era of Economic Integration*. New York: Russell Sage Foundation.

Massey, Douglas S., and Magaly Sánchez R. 2010. *Brokered Boundaries: Creating Immigrant Identity in Anti-Immigrant Times*. New York: Russell Sage Foundation.

Masuoka, Natalie. 2006. "Together They Become One: Examining the Predictors of Panethnic Group Consciousness among Asian Americans and Latinos." *Social Science Quarterly* 87, no. 5: 993–1011.

———. 2008. "Defining the Group: Latino Identity and Political Participation." *American Politics Research* 36, no. 1: 33–61.

Masuoka, Natalie, and Jane Junn. 2013. *The Politics of Belonging: Race, Public Opinion, and Immigration*. Chicago: University of Chicago Press.

Mayda, Anna Maria, Giovanni Peri, and Walter Steingress. 2016. "Immigration to the U.S.: A Problem for the Republicans or the Democrats?" NBER Working Paper No. 21941, January. Cambridge, MA: National Bureau of Economic Research.

McAdam, Doug. 1982. *Political Process and the Development of Black Insurgency, 1930–1970*. Chicago: University of Chicago Press.

McAdam, Doug, Sidney Tarrow, and Charles Tilly. 2001. *The Dynamics of Contention*. New York: Cambridge University Press.

McCabe, Kristen, and Doris Meissner. 2010. "Immigration and the United States: Recession Affects Flows, Prospects for Reform." Migration Policy Institute, January 10. http://www.migrationinformation.org/Profiles/display.cfm?ID=766#3. Accessed March 6, 2012.

McClain, Paula D., Jessica D. Johnson Carew Jr., Eugene Walton, and Candis S. Watts. 2009. "Group Membership, Group Identity, and Group Consciousness: Measures of Racial Identity in American Politics?" *Annual Review of Political Science* 12: 471–485.

McDonnell, Patrick J., and Robert J. Lopez. 1994. "L.A. March against Prop. 187 Draws 70,000; Immigration: Protesters Condemn Wilson for Backing Initiative That They Say Promotes 'Racism, Scapegoating.'" *Los Angeles Times*, October 17.

Melendez, Miguel "Mickey." 2003. *We Took the Streets: Fighting for Latino Rights with the Young Lords*. New York: St. Martin's.

Menjívar, Cecilia. 2000. *Fragmented Ties: Salvadoran Immigrant Networks in America*. Berkeley: University of California Press.

Mettler, Suzanne. 2005. *Soldiers to Citizens: The G.I. Bill and the Making of the Greatest Generation*. New York: Oxford University Press.

Mettler, Suzanne, and Mallory Sorelle. 2014. "Policy Feedback Theory." In *Theories of the Policy Process*, edited by Paul A. Sabatier and Christopher Veible, 151–182. Boulder, CO: Westview Press.

Mettler, Suzanne, and Joe Soss. 2004. "The Consequences of Public Policy for Democratic Citizenship: Bridging Policy Studies and Mass Politics." *Perspectives on Politics* 2, no. 1: 55–73.

Meyer, Bruce D. 1995. "Natural and Quasi-Experiments in Economics." *Journal of Business and Economic Statistics* 13, no. 2: 151–161.

Miller, John J. 1998. *The Unmaking of Americans: How Multiculturalism Has Undermined the Assimilation Ethic.* New York: Free Press.

Milloy, Courtland. 1996. "No Banners from the Brothers." *Washington Post,* October 20, B1.

Minnite, Lorraine C. 2009. "Lost in Translation? A Critical Reappraisal of the Concept of Immigrant Political Incorporation." In *Bringing Outsiders In: Transatlantic Perspectives on Immigrant Political Incorporation,* edited by Jennifer L. Hochschild and John H. Mollenkopf, 48–60. Ithaca, NY: Cornell University Press.

Montoya, Lisa J., Carol Hardy-Fanta, and Sonia Garcia. 2000. "Latina Politics: Gender, Participation, and Leadership." *PS: Political Science and Politics* 33, no. 3: 555–561.

Mora, G Christina. 2014. *Making Hispanics: How Activists, Bureaucrats, and Media Constructed a New American.* Chicago: University of Chicago Press.

Morone, James. 1990. *The Democratic Wish.* New York: Basic Books.

Nagel, Joane. 1986. "The Political Construction of Ethnicity." In *Competitive Ethnic Relations,* edited by Susan Olzak and Joane Nagel, 93–112. Orlando, FL: Harcourt, Brace, Jovanovich.

Navarrette, Ruben Jr. 2006. "Forget the Mexican Flags." *San Francisco Chronicle,* March 31. http://articles.sfgate.com/2006-03-31/opinion/17288124_1_israeli-flag-mexican-american-latinos. Accessed April 10, 2010.

Navarro, Mireya. 2006. "Between Gags, a D.J. Rallies Immigrants." *New York Times,* April 30, H12.

Neckerman, Kathryn M., Prudence Carter, and Jennifer Lee. 1999. "Segmented Assimilation and Minority Cultures of Mobility." *Ethnic and Racial Studies* 22, no. 6: 945–965.

Nelson, Thomas E., Rosalee A. Clawson, and Zoe M. Oxley. 1997. "Media Framing of a Civil Liberties Conflict and Its Effect on Tolerance." *American Political Science Review* 91, no. 3: 567–583.

Newport, Frank. 2016. "Trump Has a Major Image Problem with Hispanics." Gallup, March 11. http://www.gallup.com/poll/189887/trump-major-image-problem-hispanics.aspx. Accessed March 15, 2016.

Newton, Lina Y. 2008. *Illegal, Alien, or Immigrant: The Politics of Immigration Reform.* New York: New York University Press.

Ngai, Mae M. 2004. *Impossible Subjects: Illegal Aliens and the Making of Modern America.* Princeton, NJ: Princeton University Press.

NietoGomez, Anna. 1997. "*Chicana* Feminism." In *Chicana Feminist Thought: The Basic Historical Writings,* edited by Alma M. Garcia, 52–57. Reprinted from *Caracol* 2, no. 5 (1976): 3–5. New York: Routledge.

Northern Manhattan Coalition for Immigrant Rights. 2009. "Deportado, Dominicano, y Humano: The Realities of Dominican Deportations and Related Policy Recommendations." New York University School of Law. http://www.law.nyu.edu/sites/default/files/upload_documents/Deportado%20Dominicano%20y%20Humano.pdf. Accessed March 22, 2016.

Oberlander, Jonathan. 2003. *The Political Life of Medicare*. Chicago: University of Chicago Press.

Oboler, Suzanne. 1995. *Ethnic Labels, Latino Lives: Identity and the Politics of (Re) Presentation in the United States*. Minneapolis: University of Minnesota Press.

———. 2014. "Foreword." In *Transforming Citizenship: Democracy, Membership, and Belonging in Latino Communities*, edited by Raymond A. Rocco, xi–xviii. East Lansing: Michigan State University Press.

Omi, Michael, and Howard Winant. 1994. *Racial Formation in the United States: From the 1960s to the 1990s*. New York: Routledge.

Orey, Byron D'Andrá, Wendy Smooth, Kimberly S. Adams, and Kisha Harris-Clark. 2006. "Race *and* Gender Matter: Refining Models of Legislative Policy Making in State Legislatures." In *Intersectionality and Politics: Recent Research on Gender, Race, and Political Representation in the United States*, edited by Carol Hardy-Fanta, 97–120. New York: Haworth.

Orozco, Cynthia E. 2010. "Order of Sons of America." *Handbook of Texas Online*, June 15. http://www.tshaonline.org/handbook/online/articles/veotu. Accessed July 18, 2013.

Orr, Marion, Kenneth Wong, Emily Farris, and Domingo Morel. 2016. "Latino Political Engagement and Public School Quality." In *Urban Citizenship and American Democracy*, edited by Amy Bridges and Michael Javen Fortner, 93–124. Albany: State University of New York Press.

Oz, Luis. 2006. "El Poder Latino." *El Mundo*, July 5, 68, col. 1.

Padilla, Felix M. 1985. *Latino Ethnic Consciousness: The Case of Mexican Americans and Puerto Ricans*. Notre Dame, IN: Notre Dame University Press.

Pallares, Amalia, and Nilda Flores-González. 2010. *Marcha: Latino Chicago and the Immigrant Rights Movement*. Champaign: University of Illinois Press.

Pantoja, Adrian D., Cecilia Menjívar, and Lisa Magaña. 2008. "The Spring Marches of 2006: Latinos, Immigration, and Political Mobilization in the 21st Century." *American Behavioral Scientist* 52, no. 4: 499–506.

Pardo, Mary. 1997. "Mexican American Women Grassroots Community Activists: 'Mothers of East Los Angeles.'" In *Pursuing Power: Latinos and the Political System*, edited by F. Chris Garcia, 151–168. Notre Dame, IN: University of Notre Dame Press.

Park, Robert E. 1928. "Human Migration and the Marginal Man." *American Journal of Sociology* 33: 881–893.

———. 1950. *Race and Culture*. Glencoe, IL: Free Press.

Parker, Ashley, Nick Corasaniti, and Erica Berenstein. 2016. "Voices from Donald Trump's Rallies, Uncensored." *New York Times*, August 3. http://www.nytimes.com/2016/08/04/us/politics/donald-trump-supporters.html. Accessed August 14, 2016.

Passel, Jeffrey S., and D'Vera Cohn. 2015. "Unauthorized Immigrant Population Stable for Half a Decade." Pew Research Center. July 22. http://www.pewresearch.org/fact-tank/2015/07/22/unauthorized-population-stable-for-half-a-decade/. Accessed August 14, 2016.

Patashnik, Eric M., and Julian E. Zelizer. 2013. "The Struggle to Remake Politics: Liberal Reform and the Limits of Policy Feedback in the Contemporary American State." *Perspectives on Politics* 11, no. 4: 1071–1087.

Patterson, Crystal. 2005. "Quick Guide to Kennedy-McCain Immigration Bill." *Daily Kos,* May 13. http://www.dailykos.com/story/2005/05/13/113818 /-Quick-Guide-to-Kennedy-McCain-Immigration-Bill. Accessed March 6, 2012.

Pear, Robert. 1986a. "House Approves Compromise Bill on Illegal Aliens." *New York Times,* October 16, B15.

———. 1986b. "Congress, Winding Up Work, Votes Sweeping Aliens Bill; Reagan Expected to Sign It." *New York Times,* October 18, A1.

———. 1996. "Citizenship Proposal Faces Obstacle in the Constitution." *New York Times,* August 7, A13.

Pear, Robert, and Carl Hulse. 2007. "Immigration Bill Fails to Survive Senate Vote." *New York Times,* June 28. http://www.nytimes.com/2007/06/28 /washington/28cnd-immig.html. Accessed March 12, 2016.

Pew Hispanic Center. 2009. "Demographic Profile of Hispanics in Alabama, 2009." http://www.pewhispanic.org/states/state/al/. Accessed March 12, 2012.

———. 2012. "2012 National Survey of Latinos." October 4. http://www.pewhis panic.org/files/2012/10/Politics_Topline_NSL_2012_FINAL.pdf. Accessed May 13, 2013.

Phinney, Jean S. 1990. "Ethnic Identity in Adolescents and Adults: Review of Research." *Psychological Bulletin* 108: 499–514.

Phinney, Jean S., Gabriel Horenczyk, Karmela Liebkind, and Paul Vedder. 2001. "Ethnic Identity, Immigration, and Well-Being: An Interactional Perspective." *Journal of Social Issues* 57, no. 3: 493–510.

Pickett, Cynthia L., and Marilynn B. Brewer. 2005. "The Role of Exclusion in Maintaining In-group Inclusion." In *The Social Psychology of Inclusion and Exclusion,* edited by Dominic Abrams, Michael A. Hogg, and Jose Marqués, 89–112. New York: Psychology Press.

Pierson, Paul. 1993. "When Effect Becomes Cause: Policy Feedback and Political Change." *World Politics* 45, no. 4: 595–618.

———. 1994. *Dismantling the Welfare State? Reagan, Thatcher, and the Politics of Retrenchment.* New York: Cambridge University Press.

Pineda, Richard D., and Stacey K. Sowards. 2007. "Flag Waving as Visual Argument: 2006 Immigration Demonstrations and Cultural Citizenship." *Argumentation and Advocacy* 43, (Winter/Spring): 164–174.

Plumer, Brad. 2013. "Congress Tried to Fix Immigration Back in 1986. Why Did It Fail?" *Washington Post,* June 13. http://www.washingtonpost.com/blogs /wonkblog/wp/2013/01/30/in-1986-congress-tried-to-solve-immigration -why-didnt-it-work/. Accessed January 30, 2014.

Popkin, Samuel. 1994. *The Reasoning Voter.* Chicago: University of Chicago Press.

Porter, Eduardo. 2016. "Racial Identity, and Its Hostilities, Are on the Rise in American Politics." *New York Times,* January 5. http://www.nytimes .com/2016/01/06/business/economy/racial-identity-and-its-hostilities -return-to-american-politics.html. Accessed March 26, 2016.

Portes, Alejandro, and Ramón Grosfoguel. 1994. "Caribbean Diasporas: Migration and Ethnic Communities." *Annals of the American Academy of Political and Social Science* 533: 48–69.

Portes, Alejandro, and Rubén G. Rumbaut. 2001. *Legacies: The Story of the Immigrant Second Generation.* Berkeley: University of California Press.

————. 2006. *Immigrant America: A Portrait.* Berkeley: University of California Press.

Portes, Alejandro, and Min Zhou. 1993. "The New Second Generation: Segmented Assimilation and Its Variants." *Annals of the American Academy of Political and Social Science* 530: 74–96.

Posner, Daniel N. 2004. "The Political Salience of Cultural Difference: Why Chewas and Tumbukas Are Allies in Zambia and Adverseries in Malawi." *American Political Science Review* 98, no. 4: 529–545.

"The Power of Symbols: Flags Have Ability to Trigger Profound Reactions, as Recent Events Have Shown." 2006. *Omaha World-Herald,* April 1.

Preston, Julia. 2013. "Number of Illegal Immigrants in U.S. May Be on Rise Again, Estimates Say." *New York Times,* September 23. http://www.nytimes.com/2013/09/24/US/immigrant-population-shows-signs-of-growth-estimates-show.html. Accessed August 14, 2016.

Rappeport, Alan. 2016. "Donald Trump Says His Remarks on Judge Were 'Misconstrued.'" *New York Times,* June 7. http://www.nytimes.com/2016/06/08/US/politics/trump-university-judge.html?_r-0. Accessed August 14, 2016.

Ramakrishnan, S. Karthick, and Thomas J. Espenshade. 2001. "Immigrant Incorporation and Political Participation in the United States." *International Migration Review* 35, no. 3: 870–909.

Ramírez, Ricardo. 2013. *Mobilizing Opportunities: The Evolving Latino Electorate and the Future of American Politics.* Charlottesville: University of Virginia Press.

Ramos, Henry A. 2014. *The American GI Forum: In Pursuit of the Dream, 1948–1983.* Houston, TX: Arte Público.

Rieff, David. 1995. "From Exiles to Immigrants." *Foreign Affairs* 74, no. 4: 76–89.

Rieser-Murphy, Elizabeth M., and Kathryn D. DeMarco. 2012. "The Unintended Consequences of Alabama's Immigration Law on Domestic Violence Victims." *University of Miami Law Review* 66: 1059–1088.

Rim, Kathy H. 2009. "Latino and Asian American Mobilization in the 2006 Immigration Protests." *Social Science Quarterly* 90, no. 3: 703–721.

Rocco, Raymond A. 2014. *Transforming Citizenship: Democracy, Membership, and Belonging in Latino Communities.* East Lansing: Michigan State University Press.

Rocha, Rene R., Benjamin R. Knoll, and Robert D. Wrinkle. 2015. "Immigration Enforcement and the Redistribution of Political Trust." *Journal of Politics* 77, no. 4: 901–913.

Rocha, Rene R., Thomas Longoria, Robert D. Wrinkle, and Benjamin R. Knoll et al. 2011. "Ethnic Context and Immigration Policy Preferences among Latinos and Anglos." *Social Science Quarterly* 92, no. 1: 1–19.

Rodriguez, America. 1999. *Making Latino News: Race, Language, Class.* Thousand Oaks, CA: Sage.

Rodriguez, Cindy Y. 2012. "Latino Vote Key to Obama's Re-election." CNN, November 9. http://www.cnn.com/2012/11/09/politics/latino-vote-key-election. Accessed May 14, 2013.

Rodríguez, Clara E. 2000. *Changing Race: Latinos, the Census, and the History of Ethnicity in the United States.* New York: New York University Press.

Roediger, David. 2005. *Working toward Whiteness: How America's Immigrants Became White.* New York: Basic Books.

Rosales, F. Arturo. 2006. *Dictionary of Latino Civil Rights History.* Houston, TX: Arte Público.

Rosman, John. 2013. "If Vote Was Today, Immigration Reform Would Fail House." ABC News, May 27. http://abcnews.go.com/ABC_Univision/vote -today-immigration-reform-fail-house/story?id=19252777#.UaYdALXVDre. Accessed May 28, 2013.

Rouse, Stella M. 2013. *Latinos in the Legislative Process: Interests and Influence.* New York: Cambridge University Press.

Rouse, Stella M., Betina Cutaia Wilkinson, and James C. Garand. 2010. "Divided Loyalties? Understanding Variation in Latinos' Attitudes toward Immigration." *Social Science Quarterly* 91, no. 3: 856–882.

Roybal-Allard, Lucille. 2005. Border Protection, Antiterrorism, and Illegal Immigration Control Act of 2005, H11820. House of Representatives, December 15. *Congressional Record.* thomas.loc.gov. Accessed February 11, 2012.

Rumbaut, Rubén. 1994. "The Crucible Within: Ethnic Identity, Self-Esteem, and Segmented Assimilation among Children of Immigrants." *International Migration Review* 28, no. 4: 748–795.

Rumbaut, Rubén G., and Alejandro Portes, eds. 2001. *Ethnicities: Children of Immigrants in America.* Berkeley: University of California Press.

Sanchez, Gabriel. 2006a. "The Role of Group Consciousness in Latino Public Opinion." *Political Research Quarterly* 59, no. 3: 435–446.

———. 2006b. "The Role of Group Consciousness in Political Participation among Latinos in the United States." *American Politics Research* 34, no. 4: 427–450.

———. 2011. "Immigration Policy Is Personal for Latinos." July 18. http://www .latinodecisions.com/blog/2011/07/18/immigration-policy-is-personal-for -latinos/. Accessed June 4, 2013.

San Miguel, Guadalupe Jr. 1983. "The Struggle against Separate and Unequal Schools: Middle-Class Mexican Americans and the Desegregation Campaign in Texas, 1929–1957." *History of Education Quarterly* 23, no. 3: 343–359.

Schattscheider, E. E. 1935. *Politics, Pressure, and the Tariff.* New York: Prentice-Hall.

Scheve, Kenneth F., and Matthew J. Slaughter. 2001. "Labor Market Competition and Individual Preferences over Immigration Policy." *Review of Economics and Statistics* 83, no. 1: 133–145.

Schildkraut, Deborah J. 2005a. *Press One for English: Language Policy, Public Opinion, and American Identity.* Princeton, NJ: Princeton University Press.

———. 2005b. "The Rise and Fall of Political Engagement among Latinos: The Role of Identity and Perceptions of Discrimination." *Political Behavior* 27, no. 3: 285–312.

———. 2007. "Defining American Identity in the Twenty-First Century: How Much 'There' Is There?" *Journal of Politics* 69, no. 3: 597–615.

———. 2011. *Americanism in the Twenty-First Century: Public Opinion in the Age of Immigration.* New York: Cambridge University Press.

————. 2014. "Boundaries of American Identity: Evolving Understandings of 'Us.'" *Annual Review of Poitical Science* 17: 441–460.

————. 2015. "Latino Attitudes about Spheres of Political Representation." *Hispanic Journal of Behavioral Sciences* 37, no. 3: 398–419.

Schildkraut, Deborah, and Ashley Grosse. 2004. 21st Century Americanism: Nationally Representative Survey of the United States Population. ICPSR27601-v3. Ann Arbor, MI: Inter-university Consortium for Political and Social Research [distributor], 2015-04-02. http://doi.org/10.3886/ICPSR27601.v3.

Schmidt, Ronald Sr. 2000. *Language Policy and Identity Politics in the United States.* Philadelphia: Temple University Press.

————. 2002. "Racialization and Language Policy: The Case of the U.S.A." *Multilingua* 21: 141–161.

Schneider, Anne, and Helen Ingram. 1993. "Social Construction of Target Populations." *American Political Science Review* 87, no. 2: 334–347.

————. 1997. *Policy Design for Democracy.* Lawrence: University Press of Kansas.

Segura, Gary M., and Helena Alves Rodrigues. 2006. "Comparative Ethnic Politics in the United States: Beyond Black and White." *Annual Review of Political Science* 9: 375–395.

Shadish, William R., Thomas D. Cook, and Donald T. Campbell. 2001. *Experimental and Quasi-Experimental Designs for Generalized Causal Inference.* Boston: Houghton Mifflin.

Shah, Dhavan V., Mark D. Watts, David Domke, and David P. Fan. 2002. "News Framing and Cueing of Issue Regimes: Explaining Clinton's Public Approval in Spite of Scandal." *Public Opinion Quarterly* 66, no. 3: 339–370.

Shapiro, Robert, and Harpeet Mahajan. 1986. "Gender Differences in Policy Preferences: A Summary of Trends from the 1960s to 1980s." *Public Opinion Quarterly* 48: 384–396.

Shaw, Randy. 2008. *Beyond the Fields: Cesar Chávez, the UFW, and the Struggle for Justice in the 21st Century.* Berkeley: University of California Press.

Shefter, Martin. 1986. "Political Incorporation and the Extrusion of the Left: Party Politics and Social Forces in New York City." *Studies in American Political Development* 1: 50–90.

Sidanius, Jim, Seymour Feshbach, Shana Levin, and Felicia Pratto. 1997. "The Interface between Ethnic and National Attachment: Ethnic Pluralism or Ethnic Dominance." *Public Opinion Quarterly* 61, no. 1: 102–133.

Silber Mohamed, Heather. 2013. "Can Protests Make Latinos 'American'? Identity, Immigration Politics, and the 2006 Marches." *American Politics Research* 41, no. 2: 298–326.

————. 2014. "The Boundaries of American-ness: Perceived Barriers among Latino Subgroups." In *Latino Politics en Ciencia Política: The Search for Latino Identity and Racial Consciousness,* edited by Tony Affigne, Marion Orr, and Evelyn Hu-DeHart, 132–157. New York: New York University Press.

————. 2015. "*Americana* or *Latina*? Gender and Identity Acquisition among Hispanics in the United States." *Politics, Groups, and Identities* 3, no. 1: 40–58.

————. Forthcoming. "Immigration Reform and the 2014 Midterms: The

Politics of Executive Action." In *Beyond the Midterms: Implications of the 2014 Election*, edited by Chris Galdieri, Tauna Sisco, and Jennifer Lucas. Akron, OH: University of Akron Press.

Simon, Bernd, and Bert Klandermans. 2001. "Politicized Collective Identity: A Social Psychological Analysis." *American Psychologist* 56, no. 4: 319–331.

Skerry, Peter. 1993. *Mexican Americans: The Ambivalent Minority*. Cambridge, MA: Harvard University Press.

———. 2000. *Counting on the Census? Race, Group Identity, and the Evasion of Politics*. Washington, DC: Brookings Institution.

Skocpol, Theda. 1992. *Protecting Soldiers and Mothers*. Cambridge, MA: Harvard University Press.

Slothuus, Rune. 2010. "When Can Political Parties Lead Public Opinion? Evidence from a Natural Experiment." *Political Communication* 27, no. 2: 158–177.

Smith, Jason P., and Barry Edmonston, eds. 1998. *The Immigration Debate: Studies on the Economic, Demographic, and Fiscal Effects of Immigration*. Washington, DC: National Academy.

Smith, Rogers M. 2011. "Living in a Promiseland? Mexican Immigration and American Obligations." *Perspectives on Politics* 9, no. 3: 545–557.

Snow, David A., and Robert D. Benford. 1992. "Master Frames and Cycles of Protest." In *Frontiers in Social Movement Theory*, edited by Aldon D. Morris and Carol McClurg Mueller, 133–155. New Haven, CT: Yale University Press.

Snow, David A., and Doug McAdam. 2000. "Identity Work Processes in the Context of Social Movements: Clarifying the Identity/Movement Nexus." In *Self, Identity, and Social Movements*, vol. 13: *Social Movements, Protests, and Contention*, edited by Sheldon Stryker, Timothy J. Owens, and Robert W. White, 41–67. Minneapolis: University of Minnesota Press.

Soss, Joe. 1999. "Lessons of Welfare: Policy Design, Political Learning, and Political Action." *American Political Science Review* 93, no. 2: 363–380.

———. 2000. *Unwanted Claims: The Politics of Participation in the U.S. Welfare System*. Ann Arbor: University of Michigan Press.

Soss, Joe, Richard C. Fording, and Sanford Schram. 2011. *Disciplining the Poor: Neoliberal Paternalism and the Persistent Power of Race*. Chicago: University of Chicago Press.

Soss, Joe, and Sanford F. Schram. 2007. "A Public Transformed? Welfare Reform as Policy Feedback." *American Political Science Review* 101, no. 1: 111–127.

Spinner-Halev, Jeff, and Elizabeth Theiss-Morse. 2003. "National Identity and Self-Esteem." *Perspectives on Politics* 1, no. 3: 515–532.

Starr, Alexandra. 2006. "Voice of América: The Spanish-language DJs behind the New Wave of Latino Activism." *Slate*, May 3. http://www.slate.com/articles/news_and_politics/politics/2006/05/voice_of_america.html. Accessed January 20, 2012.

Sterne, Evelyn Savidge. 2001. "Beyond the Boss: Immigration and American Political Culture from 1880 to 1940." In *E Pluribus Unum? Contemporary and Historical Perspectives on Immigrant Political Incorporation*, edited by Gary Gerstle and John Mollenkopf, 33–66. New York: Russell Sage Foundation.

Sterngold, James, and Tyche Hendricks. 2006. "Spanish-Language Radio Spread

Word of LA Protest." *San Francisco Chronicle*, March 30. http://www.sfgate
.com/news/article/Spanish-language-radio-spread-word-of-L-A-2500911
.php#page-1. Accessed June 5, 2010.

Stokes, Atiya Kai. 2003. "Latino Group Consciousness and Political Participation." *American Politics Research* 31, no. 4: 361–678.

Strolovitch, Dara. 2007. *Affirmative Advocacy: Race, Class, and Gender in Interest
Group Politics*. Chicago: University of Chicago Press.

Stryker, Sheldon. 1968. "Identity Salience and Role Performance." *Journal of
Marriage and the Family* 30: 558–564.

Stryker, Sheldon, Timothy J. Owens, and Robert W. White, eds. 2000. *Self, Identity, and Social Movements*. Minneapolis: University of Minnesota Press.

Suro, Roberto, and Gabriel Escobar. 2006. "2006 National Survey of Latinos:
The Immigration Debate." Pew Research Center Hispanic Trends, July 13.
http://www.pewhispanic.org/2006/07/13/2006-national-survey-of-lati
nos/. Accessed August 14, 2016.

Swers, Michelle. 2002. *The Difference Women Make: The Policy Impact of Women in
Congress*. Chicago: University of Chicago Press.

Tafoya, Sonya. 2004. "Shades of Belonging." Pew Research Center, December 6.
http://www.pewhispanic.org/2004/12/06/shades-of-belonging/. Accessed
August 9, 2016.

Tajfel, Henri. 1970. "Experiments in Intergroup Discrimination." *Scientific American* 223: 96–102.

———. ed. 1982. *Social Identity and Intergroup Relations*. New York: Cambridge
University Press.

Tajfel, Henri, and John C. Turner. 1979. "An Integrative Theory of Group Conflict." In *The Social Psychology of Intergroup Relations*, edited by William G.
Austin and Stephen Worchel, 33–47. Monterey, CA: Brooks-Cole.

———. 1986. "The Social Identity Theory of Intergroup Behavior." In *Psychology
of Intergroup Relations*, edited by William G. Austin and Stephen Worchel,
7–24. Chicago: Nelson-Hall.

Tarrow, Sidney G. 1998. *Power in Movement: Social Movement and Cotentious Politics*. New York: Cambridge University Press.

Tatalovich, Raymond. 1995. *Nativism Reborn? The Official English Language Movement and the American States*. Lexington: University Press of Kentucky.

Tate, Katherine. 1993. *From Protest to Politics: The New Black Voters in American
Elections*. Cambridge, MA: Harvard University Press.

Taylor, J. Benjamin, Sarah Allen Gershon, and Adrian D. Pantoja. 2014. "Christian America? Understanding the Link between Churches, Attitudes, and
'Being American' among Latino Immigrants." *Politics and Religion* 7, no. 2:
339–365.

Telles, Edward M., and Vilma Ortiz. 2008. *Generations of Exclusion: Mexican Americans, Assimilation, and Race*. New York: Russell Sage Foundation.

Terrazas, Aaron. 2010a. "Mexican Immigrants in the United States." Migration
Policy Institute, February 22. http://www.migrationpolicy.org/article/mex
ican-immigrants-united-states-2. Accessed May 15, 2012.

———. 2010b. "Salvadoran Immigrants in the United States." Migration Policy

Institute, January 5. http://www.migrationpolicy.org/article/salvadoran-im migrants-united-states. Accessed May 15, 2012.

Tesler, Michael. 2016a. "A Newly Released Poll Shows the Populist Power of Donald Trump." *Washington Post,* "Monkey Cage," January 27. https://www.washingtonpost.com/news/monkey-cage/wp/2016/01/27/a-newly -released-poll-shows-the-populist-power-of-donald-trump/. Accessed March 16, 2016.

———. 2016b. "Trump Is the First Modern Republican to Win the Nomination Based on Racial Prejudice." *Washington Post,* "Monkey Cage," August 1. https://www.washingtonpost.com/news/monkey-cage/wp/2016/08/01 /trump-is-the-first-republican-in-modern-times-to-win-the-partys-nomina tion-on-anti-minority-sentiments/. Accessed August 14, 2016.

Theiss-Morse, Elizabeth. 2009. *Who Counts as an American? The Boundaries of National Identity.* New York: Cambridge University Press.

Tichenor, Daniel. 2002. *Dividing Lines: The Politics of Immigration Control in America.* Princeton, NJ: Princeton University Press.

Tocqueville, Alexis de. 1969 [1848]. *Democracy in America.* New York: Perennial Books.

Transue, John E. 2007. "Identity Salience, Identity Acceptance, and Racial Policy Attitudes: American National Identity as a Uniting Force." *American Journal of Political Science* 51, no. 1: 78–91.

Turner, J. C., M. A. Hogg, P. J. Oakes, and S. D. Reicher et al. 1987. *Rediscovering the Social Group: A Self-Categorization Theory.* Oxford, UK: Blackwell.

Uhlaner, Carole J., Bruce E. Cain, and D. Roderick Kiewiet. 1989. "Political Participation of Ethnic Minorities in the 1980s." *Political Behavior* 11, no. 3: 195–231.

Ullah, Philip. 1985. "Second-Generation Irish Youth: Identity and Ethnicity." *Journal of Ethnic and Migration Studies* 12, no. 2: 310–320.

U.S. Citizenship and Immigration Services (USCIS). 2014. "INS Records for 1930s Mexican Repatriations." March 3. https://www.uscis.gov/history -and-genealogy/our-history/historians-mailbox/ins-records-1930s-mexi can-repatriations. Accessed August 6, 2016.

U.S. Department of State Bureau of Consular Affairs. 2014. "Visa Bulletin for August 2014," August. http://travel.state.gov/content/visas/english/law -and-policy/bulletin/2014/visa-bulletin-for-august-2014.html. Accessed July 16, 2014.

U.S. House of Representatives. 2005. Border Protection, Antiterrorism, and Illegal Immigration Control Act of 2005, H.R. 4437. 109th Congress.

Valenzuela, Ali A., and Melissa R. Michelson. Forthcoming. "Turnout, Status, and Identity: Mobilizing Latinos to Vote with Group Appeals." *American Political Science Review.*

Vargas, Jose Antonio. 2011. "How Do You Define American? Share Your Story." *Huffington Post,* November 18. http://www.huffingtonpost.com/jose-anto nio-vargas/how-do-you-define-america_b_1099844.html. Accessed July 25, 2013.

Varshney, Ashutosh. 2007. "Ethnicity and Ethnic Conflict." In *The Oxford*

Handbook of Comparative Politics, edited by Carlos Boix and Susan Stokes, 274–296. New York: Oxford University Press.

Vasquez, Jessica M. 2011a. "The Bumpy Road of Assimilation: Gender, Phenotype, and Historical Era." *Sociological Spectrum* 31, no. 6: 718–748.

———. 2011b. *Mexican Americans across Generations: Immigrant Families, Racial Realities.* New York: New York University Press.

Verba, Sidney, Kay Lehman Schlozman, and Nancy Burns. 2005. "Family Ties: Understanding the Intergenerational Transmission of Political Participation." In *The Social Logic of Politics: Personal Networks as Contexts for Political Behavior,* edited by Alan S. Zuckerman, 95–114. Philadelphia: Temple University Press.

Waldinger, Roger D. 2007. "The Bounded Community: Turning Foreigners into Americans in Twenty-First Century L.A." *Ethnic and Racial Studies* 30, no. 3: 341–374.

Waldinger, Roger D., Thomas Soehl, and Nelson Lim. 2012. "Emigrants and the Body Politic Left Behind: Results from the Latino National Survey." *Journal of Ethnic and Migration Studies* 38, no. 5: 711–736.

Wallace, Sophia J. 2012. "It's Complicated: Latinos, President Obama, and the 2012 Election." *Social Science Quarterly* 93, no. 5: 1360–1383.

Wallace, Sophia J., Chris Zepeda-Millán, and Michael Jones-Correa. 2014. "Spatial and Temporal Proximity: Examining the Effects of Protests on Political Attitudes." *American Journal of Political Science* 58, no. 2: 433–448.

Wals, Sergio. 2011. "Does What Happens in Los Mochis Stay in Los Mochis? Explaining Postmigration Political Behavior." *Political Research Quarterly* 20, no. 10: 1–12.

Walzer, Michael. 1983. *Spheres of Justice: A Defense of Pluralism and Equality.* New York: Basic Books.

Warikoo, Natasha. 2006. "Gender and Ethnic Identity among Second-Generation Indo-Caribbeans." *Ethnic and Racial Studies* 28, no. 5: 803–831.

Warner, William Lloyd, and Leo Strole. 1945. *The Social Systems of American Ethnic Groups.* New Haven, CT: Yale University Press.

Wasem, Ruth Ellen. 2009. "Cuban Migration to the U.S.: Policy and Trends." Washington, DC: Congressional Research Service.

———. 2013a. "Brief History of Comprehensive Immigration Reform Efforts in the 109th and 110th Congresses to Inform Policy Discussions in the 113th Congress." Washington, DC: Congressional Research Service.

———. 2013b. "U.S. Immigration Policy: Chart Book of Key Trends." Washington, DC: Congressional Research Service.

Wasem, Ruth Ellen, and Karma Ester. 2011. "Temporary Protected Status: Current Immigration Policy and Issues." Washington, DC: Congressional Research Service.

Watanabe, Teresa, and Hector Becerra. 2006. "The Immigration Debate: How DJs Put 500,000 Marchers in Motion." *Los Angeles Times,* March 28, A1.

Waters, Mary C. 1990. *Ethnic Options: Choosing Identities in America.* Berkeley: University of California Press.

————. 1999. *Black Identities: West Indian Immigrant Dreams and American Realities*. New York: Russell Sage Foundation.

Waters, Mary C., and Tomás R. Jiménez. 2005. "Assessing Immigrant Assimilation: New Empirical and Theoretical Challenges." *Annual Review of Sociology* 31: 105–125.

Weaver, Vesla M., and Amy E. Lerman. 2010. "Political Consequences of the Carceral State." *American Political Science Review* 104, no. 4: 817–833.

Weiner, Rachel. 2013. "AP Drops 'Illegal Immigrant' from Stylebook." *Washington Post*, April 2. http://www.washingtonpost.com/blogs/post-politics /wp/2013/04/02/ap-drops-illegal-immigrant-from-stylebook/. Accessed April 2, 2013.

Welch, Susan. 1977. "Women as Political Animals? A Test of Some Explanations for Male-Female Political Participation Differences." *American Journal of Political Science* 21, no. 4: 711–730.

Welch, Susan, and Lee Sigelman. 1992. "A Gender Gap among Hispanics? A Comparison with Blacks and Anglos." *Western Political Quarterly* 45: 181–199.

Wilson, Kenneth L., and Alejandro Portes. 1980. "Immigrant Enclaves: An Analysis of the Labor Market Experience of Cubans in Miami." *American Journal of Sociology* 86, no. 2: 295–312.

Wong, Carolyn. 2006. *Lobbying for Inclusion: Rights Politics and the Making of Immigration Policy*. Palo Alto, CA: Stanford University Press.

Wong, Janelle S. 2006. *Democracy's Promise: Immigrants and American Civic Institutions*. Ann Arbor: University of Michigan Press.

Wood, Elisabeth Jean. 2003. *Insurgent Collective Action and Civil War in El Salvador*. New York: Cambridge University Press.

————. 2008. "The Social Processes of Civil War: The Wartime Transformation of Social Networks." *Annual Review of Political Science* 11: 539–561.

Wright, Matthew, and Jack Citrin. 2010. "Saved by the Stars and Stripes? Images of Protest, Salience of Threat, and Immigration Attitudes." *American Politics Research* 39, no. 2: 323–343.

Wrinkle, Robert D. 1991. "Understanding Intra-Ethnic Attitude Variations: Mexican Origin Population Views of Immigration." *Social Science Quarterly* 21: 343–359.

Zaller, John. 1992. *The Nature and Origin of Mass Public Opinion*. New York: Cambridge University Press.

Zepeda-Millán, Chris. 2014. "Perceptions of Threat, Demographic Diversity, and the Framing of Illegality: Explaining (Non)Participation in New York's 2006 Immigrant Protests." *Political Research Quarterly* 67, no. 4: 880–888.

Zepeda-Millán, Chris, and Sophia J. Wallace. 2013. "Racialization in Times of Contention: How Social Movements Influence Latino Racial Identity." *Politics, Groups, and Identities* 1, no. 4: 510–527.

Zhou, Min. 1997. "Segmented Assimilation: Issues, Controversies, and Recent Research on the New Second Generation." *International Migration Review* 31, no. 4: 975–1008.

Zhou, Min, and Jennifer Lee. 2007. "Becoming Ethnic or Becoming American?

Reflecting on the Divergent Pathways to Social Mobility and Assimilation among the New Second Generation." *Du Bois Review* 4, no. 1: 189–205.

Zolberg, Aristide R. 2006. *A Nation by Design: Immigration Policy in the Fashioning of America.* Cambridge, MA: Harvard University Press.

Zolberg, Aristide R., and Long Litt Woon. 1999. "Why Islam Is Like Spanish: Cultural Incorporation in Europe and the United States." *Politics and Society* 27, no. 1: 5–38.

Zuckerman, Alan, Josip Dasović, and Jennifer Fitzgerald. 2007. *Partisan Families: The Social Logic of Bounded Partisanship in Germany and Britain.* New York: Cambridge University Press.

Zuo, Jiping, and Robert D. Benford. 1995. "Mobilization Processes and the 1989 Chinese Democracy Movement." *Sociological Quarterly* 36, no. 1: 131–156.

Researcher Names Index

Subject Index

Note: page numbers in italics indicate figures or tables.